According to the Scriptures

According to the Scriptures

The Death of Christ
in the Old Testament and the New

David Allen

scm press

© David Allen 2018

Published in 2018 by SCM Press
Editorial office
3rd Floor, Invicta House,
108–114 Golden Lane,
London EC1Y 0TG, UK
www.scmpress.co.uk

SCM Press is an imprint of Hymns Ancient & Modern Ltd
(a registered charity)

Hymns Ancient & Modern® is a registered trademark of
Hymns Ancient & Modern Ltd
13A Hellesdon Park Road, Norwich,
Norfolk NR6 5DR, UK

British Library Cataloguing in Publication data

A catalogue record for this book is available from the British Library

978 0 334 05550 1

Typeset by Manila Typesetting Company
Printed and bound by
CPI Group (UK) Ltd

Contents

Acknowledgements   vii

1   Introduction   1
2   The Old Testament in Mark's Passion   26
3   The Old Testament in Matthew's Passion   52
4   The Old Testament in Luke–Acts' Passion   69
5   The Old Testament in John's Passion   95
6   The Old Testament in Paul's Depiction
    of Jesus' Death   119
7   The Old Testament in Hebrews' Passion   144
8   The Old Testament in the 'Passion' of the
    Other New Testament Epistles   160
9   Conclusion   172

Bibliography   185
Endnotes   202

Scriptural Index   227

Acknowledgements

This book arises out of a combination of areas of personal interest. I have been involved with the Annual Old Testament in the New Testament Seminar for a number of years now, and it remains a regular locus for stimulating and collegial engagement with a key area within biblical studies. I am grateful to all the members of the Seminar for their various contributions and engagement over that time, but I would particularly note the support of the Seminar's professorial convenors, Susan Docherty, Steve Moyise and the late Maarten Menken (whose encouraging, but nonetheless robust, scholarly insights we all miss).

The focus on Jesus' death and the Passion Narratives arises out of my teaching on such matters at the Queen's Foundation, Birmingham. I have welcomed the various ways in which I have been able to explore these matters with students, and this book is all the better for their contributions and feedback. And I remain particularly grateful to my colleagues at Queen's, and for their various ways in which they offered support (consciously or otherwise!) during the research and writing of the book. I am privileged to call them friends.

Particular thanks also go to the team at SCM, both for their patience with me in producing the book, and for their close attention to it as it went through the editing and production process.

1

Introduction

'If all you know is the New Testament, you do not know the New Testament.'

This catchy soundbite is apocryphally attributed to the renowned German biblical scholar Martin Hengel (1926–2009), the author of numerous volumes relating to New Testament (NT) and early Christian interpretation.[1] This book seeks to take Hengel at his word. Or at least it aspires to do so in relation to the importance of knowing the Old Testament (OT), in order that one might engage with how the NT writers go about formulating their particular discourse or narratives. That is, the imagery, vocabulary and culture of the OT permeate the NT writers' reflection on Jesus Christ and, with Hengel, one ventures that one cannot satisfactorily engage with the NT texts without paying attention to the way such OT imagery is shaping the account. Similarly, assessing the impact of the OT on the origins of the NT, Craig Evans concludes: 'Only the gospel itself makes a greater contribution in NT thought.'[2] Or to put it another way, when seeking to exegete or engage with a NT text, a valuable first question to ponder is: 'Where or how is the Old Testament operative in this?'

The other key dimension to the shape of this book derives similarly from the claim of another German biblical scholar, Martin Kähler (1835–1912), the renowned contributor to the so-called 'Quest for the Historical Jesus'.[3] Reflecting on the extended attention that the Gospel of Mark devotes to Jesus' final week (Mark 11 — 16), particularly when compared to the comparatively sweeping coverage of Jesus' prior life and ministry (Mark 1 — 10), Kähler famously opined that Mark was a 'passion narrative with an extended introduction'.[4] In so doing, Kähler underscored both the significance of Jesus' death for Mark (and, by extension, for the other canonical evangelists too), while also emphasizing the way the 'story' of Jesus' death derived from a self-standing, discrete narrative in its own right – a so-called Passion Narrative. While we might query the basic premise of his assertion (there is an inherent unity to Mark's account – notably through its consistent mode of structuring material in A-B-A triads – and Mark 1–10 is surely far more than just an 'introduction'), Kahler's articulation of a focused Passion recounting still holds, and it would seem to have been a discrete 'source' available to Mark, probably found originally in oral form.

This book seeks to proverbially juxtapose Hengel and Kahler, and thereby generate a conversation as to the way the NT is shaped by OT motifs and ideas, but specifically within the scope of the putative Passion Narrative(s). Put specifically, this book is a study of the way the NT writers utilized the Jewish Scriptures in order to describe, articulate and evaluate the death of Jesus.[5] The notion that Jesus Christ died and was raised according to the Scriptures (1 Cor. 15.3–4) seems to have become an established datum at a very early stage within christological formulation, and thus may well reflect the existence of some form of Passion Narrative that both contributed to, and was shaped by, such formulation. The fact that Paul can speak of Jesus dying *kata tas graphas* ('according to the Scriptures') as being effectively a creedal formula that he is 'handing on' to the Corinthians (1 Cor. 15.3) would also indicate that it is *pre-existing* material, rather than that which he is creating *de novo*. The structure of the creedal formula seems to testify to this, the three repeated '*hoti*' clauses (i.e. 'that . . .') suggestive of a form that enabled easy remembrance and recitation.

We assume, therefore, that the formulation of understanding Jesus' death through the lens of scriptural testimony was an early feature of church practice, and one that predated the Pauline correspondence. The fact that Paul can also speak of this tradition being 'of first importance' (1 Cor. 15.3) likewise adds further weight to the mooted relationship between Jesus' death and its scriptural warrant and attestation. The appeal to *kata tas*

• suggested

graphas might also be said to incorporate two dimensions, or be doing 'dual diligence'. On the one hand, the Scriptures provide an answer to the 'Why did it happen?' question – why or what occasioned the crucifixion of Jesus the Messiah? On the other, it could be seen as still answering the same 'why' question, but in respect of what Jesus' death achieved – that is, it was for our sins (cf. Gal. 1.4).[6] As Douglas Moo surmises in respect of Jesus' death: 'it was not only the necessity, but the significance as well, that was derived from the will of God revealed in the OT'.[7] As a rule of thumb therefore, Chapters 2 — 5 of our book, in engaging with the gospel Passion Narratives, will consider the first question, in respect of what OT texts the evangelists appeal to in terms of narrating Jesus' death, and the interpretative contexts they so adopt. Chapters 6 — 8, where we turn to the epistolary correspondence, will consider more the second aspect, and seek to evaluate their reflection on the achievements of Jesus' death. This is only a rule of thumb, however, as the gospel writers themselves are also theologians in their own right, and therefore trying to offer some explication of why Jesus died; Mark 10.45 (Matt. 20.28), the so-called 'ransom logion',[8] would be one such example. Equally, both Paul and Hebrews are seemingly aware of Passion Narrative material, and such tradition crops up at various places within their respective correspondence.

Of course, in terms of 1 Corinthians 15.3–4, Paul neither specifies the particular texts that he had in mind, nor indicates whether or not he was alluding to a wider scriptural perspective/narrative. Had he done so, far fewer books or theses would have been written attempting to identify those particular passages! Instead Paul's very *silence* on these matters is surely an interpretative datum in its own right, and thus enables the space for further exploration, encouraging the consideration of the different ways the Passion may have been understood or conceived of in scriptural terms. As well as exploring what specific texts might have generated the tradition espoused in 1 Corinthians 15.3, we will want to explore what it might mean for such texts to be functioning as 'Scripture', and thus how the early Church arrived at such fundamental, creedal formulations.

The Old Testament and the Passion

The foundation for Hengel's claim – and likewise the evidential backdrop to Kahler's Passion Narrative speculation – is manifest from even a cursory examination of the Passion Narratives in the Synoptic Gospels. Mark's use of Psalm 22, for example, would seem a significant example in this area – is this really a psalm of christological abandonment, or is it rather one espousing divine vindication (Ps. 22.1; cf. Mark 15.34)? Is God present with Jesus on the cross, or is the scene actually the ultimate, climactic moment of desertion? And to which of these perspectives is Mark appealing through the use of the psalm? Or what are we to make of Jesus' (apparently) strange quotation of Zechariah 13.7 (cf. Mark 14.27; Matt. 26.31), namely that the sheep will be scattered in the aftermath of his death? Is such an appeal to Zechariah an obscure reference, or might Mark and Matthew rather be engaging with a wider interpretative process? And why do Luke and John not include the same 'shepherd' claim at the equivalent point in their Passion retellings? Comparable questions likewise arise in terms of the non-gospel material, where similar associations are made with the OT in respect of Jesus' death, and like 1 Corinthians 15.3, they may evidence the early framing of a Passion Narrative. For example, why does Hebrews cite Psalm 40 in terms of Jesus' high-priestly self-offering (Heb. 10.4–10), and how does it relate to Hebrews' wider exposition of the New Covenant, with such exposition drawing foundationally on Jeremiah 31 (Heb. 10.15–18; cf. Heb. 8.7–13)? Or what value might 1 Peter glean from patterning Jesus' suffering and death against the imagery of Isaiah 53 (1 Pet. 2.21–25; cf. Isa. 52.13 – 53.12)? And are there other NT texts that might be doing likewise?

Furthermore, there are a number of other instances across the NT corpus in which the 'unspecified', broad scriptural attestation of Jesus' death – akin to that found in 1 Corinthians 15.3 – is similarly evidenced. Elsewhere in his letters, for example, Paul can speak of a messiah – and, by extension, the messiah's death – being promised by the prophets and in the Scriptures (Rom. 1.2; cf. also Rom. 16.26), suggestive of a very broad or expansive scriptural attestation. Similarly, Acts 3.18 has Peter confirming that the suffering messiah was the fulfilment of scriptural testimony – indeed that it was spoken in advance through all the prophets. As with the creedal formula of 1 Corinthians 15.3–4 (and, as we shall see, as is the case for a number of OT citations), there is no particular OT text specified, but rather the implication that the tenor of Scripture points towards the death of the Messiah in this regard. Later on in Acts, and in more narrative fashion perhaps, the text depicts Paul, reasoning from the Scriptures, the necessity that the Messiah should suffer and be raised from the dead (Acts 17.2–3). Such activity is not queried or unpacked further – rather, it is presented as an assumed practice and does not require any justification or explanation on Luke's part. Likewise, within the Lucan resurrection narrative, in two separate incidences, Luke's Jesus can explain how his suffering and death – and, of course, likewise his resurrection – are attested to and promised within the Scriptures (Luke 24.25–27, 44–46). In both incidences, Luke offers a broad scriptural tapestry for Jesus' exegetical discourse, without specifying any particular passages in support. (He cites Moses/Torah and the prophets in the first instance, and Moses/Torah, the prophets and the psalms in the second; the extent of these references may have something to say about the emerging status of the Hebrew canon, as we note below.) Indeed, the very *lack* of interest in citing specific scriptural texts, and instead the appeal to the wider, fuller arc of scriptural narrative, warrants further comment and explanation, both for understanding the perception of the Scriptures in the first-century context and for the way they were being used.

We will therefore have cause throughout the book to consider how/when the NT writers identify particular passages in respect of Jesus' death, and to what extent that matters, or alternatively whether the important element is that Scripture qua Scripture is being fulfilled. The 'resigned' claim of Jesus in Mark 14.49 that the Scriptures must be fulfilled would seem to be a primary testimony to this, as would 1 Peter's declaration that the OT prophets testified in advance to the sufferings destined for Christ (1 Pet. 1.10–11). To this end, Simon Gathercole's evocative turn of phrase would seem apposite: 1 Corinthians 15.3–4 'is thus not the peculiar eccentricity of an apostolic lone ranger but the proclamation of the whole apostolic college'.[9] Or to put it another way, Paul's Corinthian claim would seem to be standard, early Christian fare.

We recognize, of course, that the Gospels 'narrate' the death of Jesus in a different way from that of the rest of the NT, and therefore, by implication, there are generic differences in this regard. The Gospels use some form of Passion *Narrative* (pre-existent, or otherwise), and embed that into a wider narrative or biographical discourse in a way that epistolary literature lacks the generic capacity to do. At the same time, however, one should not overestimate the distinction between the different types of discourse. The gospel writers are simultaneously theologians, interpreting the Passion through their own particular lenses, and potentially use different OT texts to do this. As we will see, each gospel writer reads or understands Jesus' death in different ways, and their respective choice of OT citations is a significant factor in this regard. Likewise the epistolary – and apocalyptic – material will/can still 'narrate' the death of Jesus, but with a particular slant, again shaped by a particular lens or focus. For example, scholars have recently argued that Paul works with a narrative of Jesus Christ, and that his theology is narratively shaped in this regard.[10] This story of Christ, which is perhaps most succinctly summarized in the Christ hymn of Philippians 2.6–11, clearly incorporates Jesus' death (indeed, it is surely the integral part), and we will observe how Paul might use the OT to unpack its significance and effect.

In sum, then, it is difficult to dissent from Joel Marcus' summary declaration regarding the presence of a primitive Passion Narrative and the core, contributory role of the OT within it:

> The Gospel accounts of Jesus' suffering and death, probably in dependence upon this pre-Gospel passion narrative, are more strongly marked with OT references than any other sections of the Synoptics, with the possible exception of the birth narratives in Matthew and Luke.[11]

Indeed, we might suggest that it is particularly Jesus' birth and death that have excited distinctive scrutiny in terms of use of the OT. It is these especially *significant* events – the incarnation and the Passion – that, by their very nature, necessarily evoked and occasioned focused consideration of the relevant OT testimony. Steve Moyise's recent volume, *Was Jesus' Birth According to Scripture?*, seeks to ponder such matters in terms of the birth narratives;[12] our volume might be seen as asking similar questions, but from the perspective of Jesus' crucifixion and death.

Why so? An early Passion Narrative

Alongside the idea that the early Church tradition rooted their understanding of Jesus' death within scriptural testimony came the associated notion that a narrative or recounting of the death of Jesus had emerged to accompany such tradition and thereby narrate the story of Jesus' death.[13] It is this conceptual Passion Narrative to which Kahler refers above, and scholars generally concur that some form of broad tradition – or traditions? – was in place and acted as a source or foundation, both for the Passion accounts we find in the canonical Gospels and similarly for the reflection we find in the other NT texts.[14] Different explanations arise as to how it might have originated, but some pre-Pauline form would seem to be warranted, Paul's letter testifying to an existing body of material relating to Jesus' death.[15] Some have ventured, for example, that the origins of the Passion Narrative and its narration lie in early Christian liturgical practice.[16] The 'proto-eucharistic' tradition associated with 1 Corinthians 11.23–26, and the implications therein of a recounting of Jesus' death, may be significant in this regard; for example, both formulae effectively carry the vicarious '*for you*' designation (11.24; 15.3). The words of institution are also the other established tradition Paul specifies that he is handing over to the Corinthians (just like 1 Cor. 15.3–4), and within such recounting, there is the implication of some narration of the events surrounding Jesus' death, and the instructions he left for its ongoing remembrance.[17] One may equally see the impact of a primitive

Passion Narrative account within early Christian preaching and proclamation; Paul, for example, can speak of presenting Christ crucified as part of his mission to the Galatians (Gal. 3.1), or can encapsulate his mission to Corinth summarily as (their) knowing nothing except Christ crucified (1 Cor. 2.2).

Debates as to the origins of the Passion Narrative have invariably generated historical-critical approaches to the gospel accounts, notably in terms of source and form criticism, and these have similarly impacted on historical-Jesus concerns. The precise scope and content of any such Passion Narrative therefore remain contested, however, and there may actually be multiple sources or formats at work within the overall Passion tradition. Luke's narration of Jesus' death, for example, famously differs from that of its Synoptic counterparts, incorporating material and a flavour – particularly around Jesus' innocence or righteousness – that are not replicated in Matthew or Mark; it exhibits stronger parallels, perhaps, to the 'Passion' of characters in Acts, such as Stephen or Paul.[18] And, of course, while the concept of a Passion Narrative is a convenient one for our discussion of the Gospels' use of the OT in relation to Jesus' death, it is less appropriate perhaps for discussion of the epistolary material. Hence we might speak alternatively of a broader or more general 'Passion tradition', thereby offering an umbrella term for the way the NT writers engage with the implications of Jesus' death.

Therefore we are advisedly cautious about speaking of a generic or 'fixed' form of the Passion story, and remain generally agnostic as to its particular form(s) or shape. As such, the explicit content of the primitive (i.e. pre-Markan) Passion Narrative is outside our present scope. John Dominic Crossan's work is perhaps indicative in this regard.[19] Crossan proposed that the Passion Narrative took the form of what he terms a 'Cross Gospel', and this narrative provided the essential contours and content of the Passion – and Resurrection – narratives. He proposes that this filters into Mark (and the other Gospels), and eventually becomes the text we know of as the 'Gospel of Peter'.[20] It putatively contained four core elements (Jesus' Trial, the Abuse, the Crucifixion and the Burial), and one can see how it might have formed a discrete Passion Narrative in its own terms. With Crossan, there seems to be good evidence of pre-existing tradition around those four themes, but *pace* Crossan, we do not need to speculate on the Cross Gospel form and the putative relationship to the Gospel of Peter. Even so critical a scholar as Martin Dibelius can conclude: 'The Passion story is narrated by all four evangelists with a striking agreement never attained elsewhere';[21] the Lucan variations not withstanding, the pre-existence of a Passion tradition makes sense in view of such 'striking agreement'.

In general terms, one might aver that the four canonical Passion Narratives have five scenes in common: Jesus is arrested at night in a garden; he is questioned by the chief priests; he is interrogated by Pilate and condemned to death; he is executed by crucifixion; he is buried in a nearby stone tomb. There seems good reason, then, to think that these derive from a shared or common narratival source. We are not seeking to reconstruct the 'prehistory' of this Passion Narrative but merely to suggest that its existence seems to be plausible, probable even, and a contributory factor to making sense of what appears within the Passion accounts. Aspects of such a Passion Narrative – and their explication – are rooted in OT citation, as the testimony of 1 Corinthians 15.3 would seemingly confirm.

More specifically for our concerns, of course, the existence of a Passion account, and the emerging narrative traditions around Jesus' death, explicitly frame our presenting question. A primary difficulty for the early Church, arguably *the* primary one, was the essence of Jesus' (cruciform) death, and the necessity to justify why worship might be offered to one who had suffered such a cruciform demise. The 'foolishness' of the cross forms an explicit element of Paul's kerygmatic exposition to the Corinthians (cf. 1 Cor. 1.18–31), and he likewise recognizes how it is a stumbling block to Jews (1 Cor. 1.23), particularly as the crucified one is 'cursed' by such a death (Gal. 3.10–14; cf. Deut. 21.22–23).[22] The early Church may also have been faced with the question that one of the most prominent OT cruciform deaths (i.e. that of Haman – Esth. 7.9–10) was actually the very one that signalled Israel's triumph by the death of their *enemy* (rather than that of their messiah). That is, the immediate response to Christ's death is that it might be construed as *contra* – rather than *kata* – the

Scriptures, and that the scriptural testimony might be seen as depicting Christ's death as his *defeat* rather than his triumph. In terms of the need to justify Christ's death instead as victory, we might see a particular burden in this regard in respect of John's Gospel. On the one hand, John is absolutely clear that the cross is Jesus' moment of glory and triumph (12.32), but the gospel narrative needs explicit warrant of that fact. The preceding Johannine signs have manifested Jesus' significance, but in terms of the cross, it becomes incumbent on John to show that the crucifixion is the 'fulfilment' of Jesus' messianic credentials, not the critique or destruction of them (cf. John 19.24, 28, 36–37).[23] And for John, of course, it is not only the offence of the cross that requires OT warrant, but likewise, how does one explain the 'Jewish' rejection of the one crucified (cf. John 1.11; 12.37–41)? Does such rejection have similar scriptural warrant?

In short, a 'crucified Christ' is a problem – a contradiction in terms, one might say. How could it be that God's Messiah – God's Anointed One – would suffer such an ignominious, horrific death, one reserved for slaves or criminals? It is the 'problem' that occasions Cleopas and his fellow traveller's disappointment, as they journeyed to Emmaus and reflected on the cruciform death of one whom they had believed to be the one who would redeem Israel (Luke 24.18–21). Well in advance of Paul's letters – if the testimony of 1 Corinthians 15.3–4 is indeed pre-existing tradition – the early Church needed to find justification or support for what was so 'unexpected' or counter-intuitive. If the resurrection was always the divine goal or intention, why didn't God just prevent Jesus' death? Why was the death necessary?[24] Rather than seeking to water down the offence or scandal of the cross, as the early Church might have chosen to do, instead it seeks to embrace that offence and affront, and stipulate the reasons or justification for it.[25] Morna Hooker, for example, hence surmises that the early Church had to move from saying that the cross did *not* make sense to it being shown that it *did* make sense.[26] The 'making sense' appeal is geared – at least in part, if not primarily so – by the death being according to the Scriptures. As such, the appeal to the Old Testament became a core element in such an enterprise. For generally speaking, first-century Jews would conceive their Scriptures as 'the perfect will of God', and that which gave access to the mind of God; if it could be shown that the Scriptures testified to Christ's death, if, through them, the crucifixion could be seen to be part of the divinely instituted plan and testifying to God's will, then the horrific, problematic event could be vindicated and approved, however shockingly so.[27] One of the recent leading voices within OT/NT discourse, Richard Hays, opines: 'If we want to understand what the New Testament writers were doing theologically . . . we cannot avoid tracing and understanding their appropriation of Israel's Scriptures.'[28] In the light of the foundational significance of Jesus' death for theological and christological formulation, Hays' exhortation seems particularly appropriate in terms of the NT writers' exposition of that theme.

The Role of Isaiah 53

We might briefly consider a particular example as further justification for the matter we are seeking to explore. At the risk of generalization, the notion of scriptural attestation – or fulfilment – in respect of Jesus' death is commonly attributed to texts like Isaiah 52.13 – 53.12, the discourse of the Fourth Servant Song and its so-called 'Suffering Servant' figure. We find such connections made in early, extra-biblical writings, whereby Christ is painted in such Suffering Servant mode, and Isaianic association made accordingly. In his *Dialogue with Trypho*, for example, Justin Martyr outlines such connections, exegeting Christ's death explicitly in terms of the Isaianic servant. Interestingly, it is the concept of a 'crucified messiah' to which Trypho primarily objects, and Justin's response is to point to the Suffering Servant as OT testimony to this.[29] Earlier than Justin, at the end of the first century CE, Clement of Rome can cite Isaiah 53 in full in relation to Jesus, even if not explicitly correlating it with Jesus' death (*1 Clem.* 16.3–16). Whereas such connections have been found to be less persuasive in other scholarly circles, Moo, in his work on the use of the OT in the Passion Narratives, still opined that 'Isaiah 53, like no other OT text, portrays vicarious, redemptive suffering, and portrays it as the very will of God.'[30] Hence it gives a framework for making sense of Jesus' death in the light of the

Scriptures. Similarly, and more recently, Peter Stuhlmacher offers a robust defence of the Suffering Servant figure as a paradigm for interpreting Jesus' death, and particularly that the servant might have been a figure that Jesus himself employed in that regard.[31] The Isaianic servant also has something of a 'genetic closeness' to the lament psalms we will see extensively used in the gospel Passion Narratives, and may be seen as 'prophetic adaptation of the Righteous Sufferer motif' found within such psalms.[32] At first glance, then, one might surmise that Isaiah 53 offers an appropriate template for the idea that Christ died according to the Scriptures, and did so for our sins.

Such a proposal has its weaknesses, however. Significant ones include the fundamental distinction, namely that the Fourth Isaianic song speaks of a 'servant' figure (*pais* – Isa. 52.13 LXX) rather than a Messiah/Christ, and likewise that texts relating to a *suffering* Messiah – with perhaps the implicit exception of Daniel 9.26 – are generally absent from the OT record. The Targum on Isaiah 53.12 does qualify the servant in christological terms ('Behold, my servant, the Messiah, shall prosper'), and that such association may bridge the titular gap,[33] but the Targum is not easy to date, and one cannot guarantee the scope or extent of its usage. There is also the wider question – a prominent one within Old Testament studies – as to whether the Isaianic servant is a corporate (national) rather than individual role, and thus whether such an enigmatic figure can easily be transposed directly on to Jesus himself.[34] More specifically, perhaps, in the Greek text of Isaiah 53.12, the servant's action is on account of (*dia*) sins rather than on behalf of or for (*huper*) them, the prepositional difference hence cautioning against a simple appropriation of the servant's actions on to the atoning aspect of Jesus' death. Donald Juel, for example, comments how: 'The remarkable paucity of references to Isaiah in the passion narratives and in the passion tradition as a whole makes it difficult to support arguments that Isaiah 53 provided the foundation for Christian reflection on Jesus' death.'[35] Hooker, like Juel, has famously critiqued overzealous attempts to read Isaiah 53 imagery into NT texts[36] and, while we may not be persuaded by *every* aspect of her rebuttal, her caution is essentially valid, and it is fair to say that the contribution of the fourth servant song in NT articulation of Jesus' death has tended to be overstated.

Furthermore, in the Passion Narrative, or at least in the terms we are defining it, references to Isaiah 53 are far from prominent (and perhaps emerge only later in the development of the NT, notably in 1 Pet. 2.21–25). While it is certainly *plausible* that Isaiah 40–55 (Isaiah's so-called 'New Exodus') might have offered a wider tapestry for articulating Jesus' life and ministry (see the excellent work of Rikk Watts or David Pao in this regard),[37] it remains less clear that the Suffering Servant imagery can *fully* bear the load for explicating the use of the OT in Passion Narrative reflection. Indeed, Karen Jobes points out that there are only six direct appeals to Isaiah 53 in the NT, and only two of them are in direct relation to Jesus' death.[38] For example, Matthew's appeal to Isaiah 53.4 in Matthew 8.17 (one of Matthew's focused fulfilment quotations) is in the service of vindicating Jesus' healing ministry, and has no apparent connection to Jesus' death as a Suffering Servant.[39] Similarly, Jobes does not include Luke 22.37 (citing Isa. 53.12) within the two NT 'death' references. She avers that the citation extends merely to the purchase of swords (i.e. Luke 22.36–38), and rejects any 'Jesus as Suffering Servant' connotations accordingly. It is a peculiar citation and it is not immediately evident how the logic of Luke's argument flows, nor how the text of Isaiah 53.12 must be fulfilled, and thus how it relates to the discourse regarding swords. It could actually be evidence of a wider propitiatory or vicarious aspect to Jesus' anticipated suffering (e.g. the latter half of 53.12), but it remains an obscure reference, at least. We will come back to this passage in the Lucan chapter, but it raises some of the difficulties as to a simplistic 'Jesus as Suffering Servant' response as to what it means for Jesus' death to be *kata tas graphas*.

Hence one might say that Isaiah crops up enough to generate interest and potential christological significance, and does so at key moments (e.g. in Acts 8.32–33), but one might still expect to encounter it more frequently and/or explicitly. On a 'glass half-full' lens, there is enough Isaianic servant 'flavour' in the NT texts to create interest, and this needs to be accounted for and/or explained; on a 'glass half-empty' view, there is not enough explicit citation or

allusion to satiate such interest. Instead we will suggest that psalmic appeal, and particularly to righteous sufferer or lament psalms,
remains prominent in the Passion accounts (as it is elsewhere across
the NT), rather than the driving force being Isaiah's servant. We
will also note a perhaps surprising interest in the final chapters of
the book of Zechariah – not a text one commonly associates with
gospel writing but one that features at a number of instances across
the respective Passion accounts.

Of course, not every aspect of the Passion formulation was
necessarily rooted in the Old Testament, nor occasioned by apostolic reflection on the scriptural testimony. Other images or concepts from the first-century context are surely germane in this
regard (first-century honour/shame culture, for example, or the
experience of Roman rule), and one thereby sees their influence
in the Passion accounts.[40] The threefold linguistic titular reflects
the Jewish-Greek-Roman context for Jesus' death, for example,
while the Lucan interest in demonstrating Jesus' innocence of all
charges may have an apologetic or political dimension within the
Roman imperial context.[41] Paul's protestation to the Corinthians
that they were bought at a price (1 Cor. 6.20), presumably a reference to Jesus' death, would seem to draw on the language of slav-
ery purchase rather than explicit Old Testament motifs. Likewise,
while the concept of 'redemption' (cf. Rom. 3.24) could well refer
to the exodus narrative (and the 'sacrificial' context for Romans
3.21–26 might suggest that), it might equally derive from contemporary economic or mercantile practice. A variety of (non-OT)
reference points are potentially operative from within 'the cultural encyclopedia of early Judaism'.[42]

Moreover, there are other possible sources, beyond the Jewish
Scriptures, for the type of theological reflection we find in the New
Testament. The renowned German NT scholar Ernst Käsemann,
for example, famously opined that apocalyptic was 'the mother
of Christian theology', and such apocalypticism thereby shaped
Jesus' teaching and the subsequent kerygmatic formulation. And
there is the danger, of course, that the reader seeks for evidence of
the OT in every proverbial NT nook and cranny, and one would
be wise, therefore, to attend to Paul Foster's warning when assessing Paul's use of the OT:

This prior decision to limit Paul's cultural sphere solely to the Jewish Scriptures fails to take account of the multicultural world that Paul inhabited, and it ignores the variegated textual influences that may have shaped Paul's thought. Thus it constrains Paul's thought within one hermetically sealed set of textual references, and thereby entrenches scholarly research by forcing it to account for ideas within the Pauline writings solely through the lens of the scriptural writings of Judaism.[43]

But at the same time, it remains intriguing, indeed striking perhaps, that even when writing to predominantly Gentile churches, such as that in Corinth, Paul will still appeal to the Jewish Scriptures as the grounds or basis of his argument. He may utilize and exhibit knowledge of local culture or philosophy (cf. the quotation of Menander in 1 Cor. 15.33), but such appeals are far exceeded in number by apostolic appeal to the Jewish Scriptures. *Kata tas graphas* remains the NT writers' primary lens.

Establishing the Terminology

Before turning to our intertextual discussion, some form of definition of terms is apposite, necessary even. One must, for example, recognize the textual variation present at the time of the writing of the NT, and hence the various possibilities that exist when seeking to discern from where the NT writer has sourced a particular citation. At a high level, such textual fluidity is manifested by the two primary textual traditions. On the one hand, we have the so-called Masoretic text (MT), the Hebraic form of the Jewish Scriptures, and the text form that functions as the 'source text' for most English Bible translations. On the other hand, the Greek tradition, commonly known as the Septuagint or LXX, rather than being a 'translation' of the Hebrew text, becomes a discrete tradition in its own right, and attests the significant textual fluidity found within the first century. There was no one 'fixed' form, say, of the book of Genesis – indeed, it may have existed in a number of variant forms, but while still remaining recognizably 'Genesis'. A key part of the interpretative role, therefore, is to discern which text form the NT writer is utilizing – and why so. Furthermore, the different ordering of the Psalms corpus in the Masoretic and Greek traditions – and the associated contrasting versifications within English versions – can cause confusion as to which particular psalm one is referring to. Psalm 31.5, for example, cited by Luke 23.46 as Jesus' dying words (and arguably alluded to in Acts 7.59), is classified as Psalm 30.6 in the LXX and Psalm 31.6 in the Masoretic tradition. To limit such confusion, we will adopt the psalmic chapter–verse designation used in English translations, unless otherwise so specified. When citing the LXX, for convenience, we will use the *New English Translation of the Septuagint* (NETS), as this is a recognized critical translation of the various Septuagint texts.

Accompanying such interest has been the discussion of the particular text form that the New Testament writers use – and the availability of that text form. The findings that come from Qumran have helped in this regard, and have given wider exposure to text forms. While the majority of the NT authors primarily use the Septuagint form of the Scriptures, sometimes they utilize a form found in the Masoretic tradition instead. Alternatively, it may be a textual form to which we do not presently have access, perhaps a text form they themselves have created, or it may be simply not known to us. For example, Matthew's climactic claim, at the close of the birth narrative, that Jesus will be called a Nazorean (Matt. 2.23) is presented as a quotation thereby fulfilled, but the text of that 'quotation' is one not known in any of our ancient sources.

This also generates further terminological questions, namely as to what we might call the corpus of 'texts' on which the NT writers are drawing. Finding an appropriate nomenclature, however, is not straightforward:

- **'Old Testament'** is, of course, the commonly used designation, but its implications can be misleading. It can be problematic in terms of Jewish–Christian discussion (hence some would prefer to speak of 'First Testament').[44] Hebrews may speak of the old covenant (*diatheke*), and other NT writers speak of a new covenant or testament, but 'old testament' is not a term generally used within the NT confines. It remains the case, though, that the subdiscipline is still referred to as 'the use of the Old Testament in the New' (or OT/NT), and the scholarly literature tends to reflect that nomenclature.[45]

- **'Hebrew Bible'** may be a more appropriate or sensitive appellation, and it is the terminology generally used within scholarly circles. But it remains unhelpful for our mode of enquiry, as the NT writers tend to appeal to a Septuagint (LXX) form of the text, rather than the Masoretic one. In Acts' recounting of the so-called Council of Jerusalem (Acts 15.6–29), for example, James the Just, in Jerusalem, and the emerging leader of the 'church' there, and hence associated with the Hebrew custom, still cites the LXX form of Amos rather than the Masoretic one (Acts 15.16–17). 'Bible' can also assume a fixity or canonical standard that was not the case for Jesus' time, and thus the term 'Greek Bible'[46] similarly fails the appropriateness test. While a framework was emerging around the Law and the Prophets, the Writings corpus still remained fluid or undetermined (cf. the two contrasting 'canonical' groupings respectively in Luke 24.27 and Luke 27.44).[47]

- **'Jewish Scriptures'** (or 'Israel's Scriptures') is a more neutral term, and that will be our preferred designation, along with the related notion of 'scriptural interpretation'. However, even this title has its limitations – how/why does something become 'scriptural'?

We also recognize that the NT writers were among many other contemporary interpreters, all engaging with the Jewish Scriptures, and thereby seeking to make sense of them in their own context (whether at Qumran or in works like that of Philo of Alexandria). NT scriptural interpretation is therefore not an isolated affair, even if the focus we are interested in – that is, the death of Jesus – is of particular distinction.

Another area of terminological definition relates to the classification of the *way* the NT cites the OT text. The traditional tripartite categorization for this has been as follows:

- **Quotation:** this normally follows the precise form of the source text (or *Vorlage*), and would normally be 'signed' or preceded by an introductory formula that acts like quotation marks, setting off the text from the prior material. The nature of the introductory formula would vary according to the NT author, but might take the form of *'as it is written . . .'* or *'in order to fulfil'*. Sometimes the citation might be a composite one (e.g. Acts 1.20; John 12.38–40), thereby expanding the potential frame of reference.

- **Allusion:** this would be a phrase or sentence where there are several common words shared by the NT and OT source. The citation is embedded into the NT prose, though, without being signed or marked as a quotation would be, and thus requires some degree of scriptural literacy or competency on the part of the reader.
- **Echo:** this is a 'quieter' or more reduced allusion, perhaps manifested by just a couple of words. The association between OT and NT is therefore more subtle, but can equally by significant for generating a variety of possible intertextual connections. This does, of course, raise questions as to the intentionality of the putative echo/reference. When Paul alludes, say, to Christ dying for us (e.g. Rom. 5.8), is that a 'conscious' borrowing of Isaiah 53.11–12, or is the concept so embedded in the tradition, that one cannot separate it out?

This threefold categorization, and its ultimate efficacy, has not gone unchallenged,[48] and focusing on the differences between a quotation and allusion can often tend towards the pedantic. For example, when a citation is placed on a character's lips (as, say, Psalm 22.1 in Mark 15.34), it can seem awkward or inappropriate to include an introductory formula, and hence one could have a quotation masquerading as an allusion (and potentially vice versa). Likewise the methodological criteria for identifying the genuineness of a proposed echo remain queried, and the determination of echoes can remain an essentially subjective exercise, as it can be difficult to distinguish whether it is a genuine, intentional scriptural echo, or rather just received vocabulary for the author and no more than that. Hays proposed a set of seven criteria by which to identify the existence of such an echo,[49] but these have been extensively contested, and it remains difficult to discern how one can confidently demonstrate the presence of an echo. Perhaps one of the major criteria, though, must be whether the proposed echo 'makes sense' – Hays' 'satisfaction' measure; that is, does the mooted echo yield some explanatory power or significance? Recognizing the slipperiness associated with identifying echoes and the potential for recognizing innumerable 'faint' (and thus 'ineffective') ones across the Passion depictions, we will essentially focus on quotations and allusions as our primary investigative loci, at least unless there is good reason to think the echo has major interpretative significance.

The Use of the Old Testament in the New

The context for this book is the biblical studies discourse or subdiscipline that focuses on the use of the Old Testament in the New (OT/NT). There has, of course, been a long-standing interest in such inquiry,[50] but the subdiscipline has become more productive in the second half of the twentieth century, particularly in the light of C. H. Dodd's titular work on OT/NT, *According to the Scriptures* (1952). Dodd drew significant attention to the way the early Church went about demonstrating the scriptural basis for the emerging kerygma or gospel, such that the Old Testament effectively became the 'sub-structure' of New Testament Theology.[51] As such, he identified certain key OT texts as salient in this regard. In particular, Dodd surmised that the wider context of these OT passages, and wider narratives such as that of the Suffering Servant, were carried over when the NT writer cited one part of a source text; hence, for example, the whole of Psalm 22 could conceivably be in Mark's mind in 15.34 rather than just Psalm 22.1.

Barnabas Lindars (1961) built on Dodd's work, but he recognized a stronger *apologetic* perspective on the part of the NT authors in terms of their use of the Jewish Scriptures.[52] For Lindars, as with Dodd, the starting point was the kerygma/gospel, and the NT authors probed the OT (apologetically) for texts that might support or endorse kerygmatic formulation. The Scriptures were thus mined to show they were not inconsistent with Jesus' suffering, but rather that they demonstrated the scriptural witness to his cruciform, messianic death.[53] This may mean some 'discontinuity', though, in terms of the OT text and its (re-)location in the New Testament context.[54]

Juel offers a different view from that of Lindars and Dodd. Instead of the kerygma being the lens through which the Scriptures might be read/utilized, for Juel, Scripture was the starting point for discerning how Jesus might be the Christ, a process Juel terms 'messianic exegesis'.[55] In particular, Juel opined that Psalm 89 (especially vv. 50–51) was the starting point for such exegesis, in that it offered (uniquely so) a 'link between humiliation and messiahship',[56] and thus provided a paradigm or framework for finding scriptural testimony to a crucified Christ. The challenge with Juel's thesis, of course, is that the NT writers rarely, if at all, cite the psalm, and this is the primary scholarly critique of Juel's work;[57] Luke incorporates Psalm 89.20 into a mixed citation in Acts 13.22, but any christological or cruciform interpretation is difficult to detect. In short, for Juel, christological interpretation of Scripture (based on the premise that Jesus dies *as messiah*) served to understand or unpack the gospel (and that explained the texts so used – such as Psalm 22 or Psalm 110), whereas for Lindars, the gospel was shaped by apologetic appeal to Scripture (i.e. Scripture was used on behalf of the – pre-existent – gospel).[58] Each approach assumes a different direction of travel.

The scholarly literature on OT/NT matters has expanded significantly in recent years. For a comprehensive introduction to the topic, and to the salient questions it so raises, Moyise's various works on the subject warrant attention.[59] Other recent studies have sought to delve further into OT/NT matters, whether in exploring Paul's employment of echoes,[60] investigating questions of methodology[61] or seeking to 're-create' the source text of a NT writer.[62] A core text in OT/NT discourse has proved to be the Greg Beale and Donald Carson's recent one-volume commentary on the use of the OT in the NT, with comprehensive coverage of every OT citation in each constituent text of the NT. Its scope is detailed, and it is a mine of information for those engaging with this subject area. Alternatively, Maarten Menken and Steve Moyise have edited a series of volumes looking at the NT's use of a particular OT text or corpus of texts – with volumes thus far covering the use of Isaiah, Psalms, Deuteronomy, the Minor Prophets and, most recently, Genesis.[63] Our discussion of the NT writers' use of the Scriptures to unpack the significance of Jesus' death will draw on these critical and helpful volumes.

Perhaps our closest conversation partner, though, is Moo's volume on the use of the Old Testament in the gospel Passion Narratives.[64] Moo's analysis is at one level comprehensive, and offers an extended discussion of the matter in hand. We will not dissent significantly from his helpful discussion, even if the OT/NT world has moved on appreciably from when Moo wrote his work. However, as the title suggests, his attention remains purely on the *gospel* accounts, and it does not seek to extend the presentation of the Passion, or rather the way the Old Testament is used to frame or depict the understanding of Jesus' death, across the entire New Testament corpus. Another notable conversation partner is John Carroll and Joel Green's work on the NT writers' portrayal of Jesus' death, and particularly Marcus' chapter therein on the use of the OT in this regard. The same observation may be made, though, that Marcus does not substantially expand his analysis to the non-gospel material, to Paul or Hebrews or 1 Peter. Hooker observes:

> It is impossible to believe that the first Christians, faced by the dilemma of the cross, would *not* have turned to the Scriptures in attempting to explain it. In one way or another, we find each of our New Testament authors trying so to do so.[65]

We are seeking to put Hooker's summary to the test, particularly her claim that *each* NT author operates with this lens.

Shape/Structure of the Book

A further presenting question, of course, is to locate where one formally begins the recounting of the Passion Narrative. In one sense this is a very subjective question, and a case may be made for seeing it starting respectively at the triumphal entry, the trial, leaving the upper room or even the crucifixion itself. At the risk of subjectivity, but also in order to keep the length of the book reasonable (one thinks of the multi-volume work of Raymond Brown on this subject area, for example!),[66] we will adopt a fairly strict lens for interpreting the start and end of the Passion account, so as not to 'drown' in the extensive references it can generate. As a general rule of thumb, we will begin the Passion Narrative at the point of departure from the upper room, and the imminent Gethsemane arrest, and end the narrative at Jesus' burial. Most scholars adopt these contours (Brown's magisterial study classically so),[67] and it would seem appropriate to maintain that general consensus.

At the same time, we also recognize some intra-gospel tension in this regard. For example, a strong case can be made that Luke's Passion retelling begins at 22.1 (with the demarcating statements there – and also the declaration regarding Satan and Judas (22.3)), and likewise the prolonged upper-room Farewell Address sequence of John 13 – 17 is hard to divorce from what comes afterwards, once Jesus and the disciples leave the upper room (18.1). Hence we would be ill-advised to exclude discussion of those aspects of the gospel narrative that relate to Jesus' death (often significantly so), but do not fall within our prescribed Passion Narrative boundaries. For example, the entry into Jerusalem – which many, notably Kahler, might even consider genuine Passion Narrative material – would seem an appropriate area for consideration, partly for the way it heralds events ahead of Jesus' death and partly because of the way Psalm 118 in particular is used therein. All in all, this means letting the individual texts shape decisions on such matters, and thereby include material as seems pertinent and relevant.

Some further caveats need to be entered as to the parameters or scope of the exercise. First, generally speaking, *we will not comment on the use of the OT in terms of how the New Testament writers went about understanding and speaking of Jesus' resurrection.* Others have commented on this elsewhere[68] and have done so admirably. It is also common to think of the Passion Narrative and the resurrection narrative as different entities, or as comprising of different material (albeit brought together to have some form of unity within the gospel accounts). Therefore, for example, the perfectly pertinent questions of Jesus' resurrection after three days (1 Cor. 15.4), and the texts from which Paul might have sourced his material to make such a claim, are outside the scope of our enquiry. It is possible also that the dual claims of 1 Corinthians 15.3–4 (the death and resurrection both being *kata tas graphas*) reflect two discrete traditions, or one tradition came first (and thus it is legitimate to speak of them as separate entities in this regard).

Of course, omitting the resurrection may be construed as anachronistic, as the fulfilment aspect of an OT citation might pertain as much to the anticipated events of the resurrection as it does to Jesus' death; John 2.17 might be one such instance. Similarly, the so-called Passion predictions found in Mark's Gospel (8.31; 9.31; 10.33–34) technically include or anticipate resurrection/vindication, and hence it is not always easy to extrapolate one event from the other. It is even harder to extrapolate resurrection from death in Acts, and it would be inappropriate to obscure such resurrection references. As we shall see, Luke's citation of Psalm 16 in Acts 2.25–28 is explicitly located with the non-corruption of Jesus' flesh in the light of the resurrection, and thus death and resurrection are inextricably linked. Likewise the debate about whether all of Psalm 22 is at work in Mark's usage is, at least in part, contingent on the expectation that God will vindicate the sufferer – supremely with the resurrection.

Yet 'separating off' the resurrection remains justifiable overall. There does appear to be a discrete shape to the Passion Narrative within the gospel accounts that is distinct or separate from the resurrection accounts. This is what makes them different, for example, from Greco-Roman biographies, in that there is comparatively far more attention to the individual's death than to their life. The later NT writers are generally less interested in the life of the earthly Jesus.[69] It is his death on which they focus and thus OT usage will remain core to that. But perhaps most significantly, when compared to the Passion accounts, the resurrection narratives are surprisingly *limited* in terms of OT citation. There is the occasional reference to scriptural fulfilment in the resurrection narratives (cf. John 20.9), but far less so than in the Passion Narrative, and with few or no explicit texts cited in that regard.

One might surmise that, for the early Church, Jesus' death was more of a presenting 'problem' than the resurrection (however wonderfully mysterious that might be), and thus demanded more in terms of demonstrating divine purpose and scriptural vindication. Or to push the matter further, the resurrection – or at least the Church's 'belief' in the event – only makes theologizing on the crucifixion more problematic, emphasizing as it did that God's *Messiah* was the one who has died the cruciform death.

Second, we are not seeking to engage in discussion as to the historical actuality of the Passion accounts. Hence we will remain agnostic as to whether, particularly in the gospel accounts, an OT citation (on Jesus' lips) originates (or not) from the words of the historical Jesus, and thus how Jesus might have understood his death and his use of the OT in that regard.[70] Such questions are not unimportant ones, of course, and do yield insight on how a first-century Jew (i.e. Jesus) might have used Scripture to frame or articulate his ministry. It seems perfectly plausible, for example, that a crucified Jewish teacher might have grasped at the first line of Psalm 22 when experiencing such a criminal, painful death (cf. Mark 15.34). But to fully consider the implications of such matters remains beyond our scope.[71]

One cannot abandon historical questions completely, however. There are already points of departure between the respective Passion Narratives (e.g. over their respective chronologies), and thus, even without attention to the influence of the Old Testament, there are already points of tension between the respective Passion retellings. But this can be compounded when one considers the extent to which the Passion accounts have potentially been shaped by Scripture, and debates around this tend to fall into two distinct if still somewhat related aspects. Crossan is one of a number of scholars who have averred that the Passion Narrative is 'prophecy historicized'.[72] They suggest that the biblical accounts of Jesus' death have been given a 'historical' basis so as to confer veracity on them. History is accommodated to Scripture, in effect, and one might end up essentially with a mythical story shaped by scriptural citation. Alternatively, it might be argued that the historical 'core' to the events remains genuine, but they have been retold with a biblical slant or edge, what one might term 'prophesized history' or 'history remembered'. Scripture is the servant rather than the master of history. A variant form of the latter, proposed by Mark Goodacre, is the notion of 'scripturalization', namely the way the retelling of the Passion accounts has been done through the lens and focus of the Scriptures, as that was the primary mode of such telling within a liturgical context.[73] If we are interested in history at all, it would be to consider it through the scripturalization process that shapes the Passion Narrative into the form we encounter.[74]

But our interest remains predominantly intertextual rather than historical, the way the Old Testament and New Testament texts interrelate with each other and mutually shape interpretation and understanding. It is to such intertextual engagement that we now turn.

2

The Old Testament in Mark's Passion

We begin our discussion with Mark, primarily because scholars generally view it as being the first of the written canonical Gospels. As such, it was the one that probably provided a source for the other Synoptic accounts and on which they subsequently built their own evangelistic compositions (Matthew more so than Luke, as we shall see). From the very outset of his retelling, Mark's narration of the life of Jesus is impacted and shaped by its use of Old Testament imagery. This is signalled explicitly, of course, by the opening declaration of Mark 1.2–3, and its quasi-programmatic statement, attributed to Isaiah, and applied to the ministry of John the Baptist:

> *See, I am sending my messenger ahead of you,*
> *who will prepare your way;*
> *the voice of one crying out in the wilderness:*
> *'Prepare the way of the Lord,*
> *make his paths straight.'*

The ascription of the citation to Isaiah is incorrect, however, or at least the first clause is, and its precise 'source' or origin remains contested, as noted below. The fact, however, that such 'editorial' attribution is specifically given – however erroneously – warrants attention, as it is the only instance in Mark's account where the source of the scriptural citation is explicitly named.[1] It also makes it declarative that the Gospel is rooted in the Scriptures, and that it should therefore be read in conversation with them; from the very outset of Mark's evangelistic enterprise, the reader is invited to read the *euangelion* of Jesus against the backdrop, or through the lenses, of the Jewish Scriptures, and to interpret Mark's narration in that light. Bearing in mind the critical significance of the Christ event, and the theological import Mark is seeking to elucidate, such appeal to the OT is unsurprising. As Christopher Bryan opines: 'For one who has heard Scripture Sabbath by Sabbath, Scripture's language is the natural language of the divine event.'[2] Or as Eugene Boring more succinctly surmises: 'The better the readers know the Old Testament, the better they will understand Mark.'[3]

Detailed consideration of Mark 1.2 is also insightful in this regard. The citation seems to derive from an amalgam of two sources – Exodus 23.20 and Malachi 3.1 – but with the Malachi element being the more prominent. Malachi 3.1 continues with reference to the Lord coming to the Temple, perhaps in ominous fashion; the prophet ponders who might be able to endure the Lord's coming (Mal. 3.2). Bearing in mind Mark's narrative, which ultimately maps Jesus on a journey to – and ultimately to pronounce the end of – the Temple (Mark 11.15–20; 13.1–2), Malachi's wider narrative seems to be alluded to by Mark at this point. Mark 1.2 (and by extension Mal. 3.1–2) invites the reader to ponder how they will respond to the One in whose name the messenger comes. If so, this may suggest that when Mark elsewhere cites an OT text, the wider context of the citation is in view (as Dodd argued in his landmark study).[4]

Similarly, the fact that the whole discourse of Mark 1.2–3 is attributed to Isaiah – albeit incorrectly – might also suggest that Isaiah provides the primary tapestry on which Mark seeks to explicate and exegete the story of Jesus. This might be in terms of a so-called New Exodus journey, akin to that mapped in Isaiah 40–55.[5] Or it might function as a signpost to the declarative statement of Isaiah 6.9–10, which features regularly in the Markan account and most prominently in the programmatic announcement of Mark 4.11–12. Likewise the mooted associations between Mark 10.45 and Isaiah 53.11–12 (albeit contested, of course – cf. also Isa. 43.3–4) might offer further Isaiah–Mark 'collaboration' in this regard. Or to put in another way: 'the fact that Mark claimed that the beginning of that gospel was "as it is written in the prophet Isaiah" suggests that he was well aware that the Prophet had proclaimed "good news."'[6] In sum, the text of Isaiah is a core ingredient for Mark's evangelistic account, and its contribution demonstrates the way Mark might use Scripture both atomistically and also in more broad, narrative fashion; that is, it gives the possibility that, in appealing to one particular text, Mark might be understood as invoking the wider context of that text, rather than just the cited portion.

But of course, Isaiah is not the sole OT contributor to the Markan discourse. As we will see with other NT authors, and in common with other Second Temple texts, Mark also draws extensively on the Psalms corpus to explicate its gospel message. At key points in the Markan discourse, psalmic material is utilized (Jesus' baptism, for example, or the transfiguration, where in both instances Psalm 2.7 is so used).[7] Mark thereby utilizes OT citation to undergird and emphasize the significance of the 'divine' event. If this is true of the baptism and transfiguration in terms of their appeal to Psalm 2, it would seem likely to be so in the Passion, and especially in respect of Mark's use of Psalm 22.

Bearing in mind Mark's preference for threefold structuring (three Passion predictions, the threefold units of time for the crucifixion, three core divine 'events'),[8] Mark unsurprisingly similarly has three specific OT quotations that relate directly to Jesus' death (12.10–11; 14.27; 15.34). We will consider the latter two shortly, but the first of these also warrants consideration as, while it occurs prior to the Passion, it uses the OT to shed light on what will subsequently outwork within the recounting of Jesus' death. The quotation is found within Mark's parable of the vineyard (12.1–11), itself probably drawing on OT imagery, probably Isaiah 5.12, where a watchtower is similarly built in a vineyard, thereby adding to the Isaianic flavour of Mark, and presumably acting as a metaphor for Israel (the vineyard) and the Temple (the watchtower). The telling of the parable almost occasions Jesus' arrest (12.12), anticipating 14.43–49 perhaps, and the dispatch of the beloved son (cf. Mark 1.11; 9.7; Ps. 2.7), who is seized and killed, surely anticipates the seizure and death of Jesus 'the son'.[9] (Note how the Roman centurion, at point of Jesus' death, pronounces him to be 'God's *son*' – 15.39). The climax of the retelling (Mark 12.10–11) is a quotation of Psalm 118.22–23: '*The stone that the builders rejected has become the cornerstone; this was the Lord's doing, and it is amazing in our eyes.*' The vineyard owner, Mark says, destroys the tenants, and hands the vineyard over to other tenants (12.9), and thus the appeal to this part of the psalm – and the fact that such action is deemed to be 'amazing' (12.11) – seems somewhat contrary or counter-intuitive; what should have been a source of mourning (i.e. the death and rejection of the s/Son), Mark reads, through the psalm, actually as good news, or the vindication of the stone/son. As we shall see, the 'stone' metaphor also becomes a primary motif for interpreting Jesus' death in other NT texts (cf. Acts 4.11; Rom. 9.32–33; Eph. 2.20; 1 Pet. 2.3–8), and Mark's exploration of Psalm 118's stone imagery therefore seems of particular interest.

Mark has already recently used Psalm 118, a Hallel Psalm,[10] as part of the triumphal procession (11.9–10; cf. Ps. 118.25–26), and it will be likewise used by all four gospel writers, in variant forms, in this regard (Matt. 21.9; Luke 19.28; John 12.13). Its citation at this point probably underscores the Davidic or 'royal' nature of Jesus' entry, and the psalm's tenor is essentially positive in this regard. The targum on Psalm 118 associated the stone with David, one originally rejected but vindicated as king, and it would thus be an appropriate psalm to be uttered at such a triumphal entry. But as Watts notes: 'If the first citation is celebratory, the second has darker connotations',[11] or at least it has for the tenants, and in Mark's eyes would seem to be an indictment of the Temple authorities. A new stone – one might surmise a new 'Temple' – is anticipated and, while this might involve judgement for the existing Temple, it offers marvellous vindication for the new one, whose cornerstone will be the s/Son. Hence the citation is not just anticipating Jesus' death, it is also foreshadowing the Son's vindication and the associated implications of this for Israel. This overall appeal to Psalm 118 is therefore telling and enables the link to be made between the one who is welcomed as king being the same one who will subsequently be 'rejected' and die. As such, those with knowledge of the whole psalm might anticipate both the imminent suffering that will befall Jesus (Ps. 118.5, 18), but also the wider (divine? resurrection?) vindication to come (Ps. 118.6–7, 13–14). At the same time, they might raise a proverbial eyebrow at the psalmist's declaration that he would not be given over to death (Ps. 118.18), clearly an aspect of the psalm that

Mark does not fully embrace (cf. Mark 15.37). But that oddity aside, the usage of Psalm 118, and its dual manifestation of suffering and vindication, might also offer a window on to Mark's use of Psalm 22, and the capacity for both the suffering *and* vindicatory elements of that psalm to be similarly deployed.

The other core element, of course, in Mark's signposting of Jesus' impending death is three explicit passion predictions (8.31; 9.31; 10.33–34). These declarations, made prior to the Passion Narrative, have also generally been seen as invested with OT significance. This is particularly the case for Mark 10.33–34, and the subsequent declaration that the Son of Man would give his life as a ransom for many (10.45). The Son of Man imagery has possible connections to Daniel 7.13–14, but a potentially louder link is to the imagery of the Suffering Servant of Isaiah 53, and the sacrificial offering of that figure. There are problems, of course, with such a suggestion, most notably the lack of any unequivocal shared vocabulary in the respective passages, and we have noted in the previous chapter some of the scholarly hesitation in making the Suffering Servant connection. But if one takes seriously the Isaianic signalling that is found from the outset of the gospel account, it seems perfectly plausible to hear echoes of that discourse within Mark 10.45 and related texts,[12] and particularly in the ongoing reception of Mark 10.45, which is closely tied to the Suffering Servant narrative.[13] One might therefore surmise that Isaiah 53 is part of the matrix of imagery by which Mark understands Jesus' death, but without it necessarily being the major or driving one.

The Passion according to Mark

Mark's Passion is no exception to the preceding utilization of scriptural imagery. It is replete with Old Testament references, and unsurprisingly so bearing in mind what has been encountered thus far within its evangelistic recounting.[14] Admittedly extending the Passion Narrative to chapters 11–16, Howard Clark Kee counts 57 quotations, 160 allusions and 60 examples of influence within Mark's account of Jesus' death.[15] In terms of echoes within Mark's Passion, Kelli O'Brien identifies myriad potential points of connection between the Markan Passion, and in so doing, locates an 'underlying treasure [of OT echoes] in the outwardly simple story of the Gospel of Mark'.[16] Marcus' summation is perhaps the most explicit:

> Mark's account of Jesus' suffering, death, and resurrection in chapters 14—16 is suffused with Old Testament citations and allusions to an extent unparalleled in the rest of his narrative, a frequency that reflects the primitive Christian conviction that Christ died and was raised on the third day in accordance with the Scriptures (see 1 Corinthians 15.3–4).[17]

Consequently, attempting to attend to every nuance of OT citation, or every possible scriptural reference within Mark's Passion, becomes a challenging task and we will necessarily need to be selective.

In terms of our characterization of the shape of the Passion Narrative, and the debate as to when it 'begins', we suggest it commences at 14.26, and the departure from the upper room. This is a contested matter, however. Mary Ann Beavis, for example, locates its beginning at 14.1[18] and, as we have previously seen, Kahler effectively situates it at 11.1 and the entry into Jerusalem. But from wherever we locate its formal inception, we have been prepared for the Passion from very early on in the Markan retelling. As we have previously noted, Mark's Gospel could claim to be a Passion Narrative with a long introduction, such is the significance and length of the events narrated within it. But while that characterization has some heuristic merit to it, it fails to take account of earlier references to – or predictions of? – the Passion and to its associated implications. From early in the Gospel, opposition grows against Jesus, and a Herodian/Pharisaical plot emergences against him (3.6). When Jesus cleanses the Temple, further intrigue likewise emerges (11.18). Jesus himself has prepared the reader for a martyr death in the great threefold discourse at the centre of Mark's Gospel (8.22 — 10.52), and the three Passion predictions found therein (8.31; 9.31; 10.33–34). The reader is explicitly alerted to the inimical purposes of the chief priests and scribes (14.1, itself perhaps alluding to Hosea 6.2), and the subsequent anointing of Jesus' body for burial (14.3–9) demonstrably anticipates his impending death. Mark's Passion comes as no surprise.

What then of its shape or character? The Markan Jesus leaves the upper room realizing that he is due to die, yet wary and apprehensive of that fact. The disciples, however, remain *unaware* – they have yet to grasp the significance of Jesus' actions – and as such, they will be scattered like sheep (14.27). The Markan Passion begins on this tragic note and, frankly, only gets more tragic. For example:

- Jesus dies alone, abandoned by his disciples, abandoned by those closest to him, abandoned even to the extent that the unnamed young man leaves the Gethsemane scene, totally naked (Mark 14.51–52). Brown's summary of such desertion is suitably cutting: '(t)he first disciples to be called left nets and family (1.18, 20), indeed everything (10.28) to follow him; but this last disciple, who at first sought to follow Jesus, ultimately leaves everything to get away from him.'[19]
- At the Roman Trial, Jesus is similarly alone before Pilate, and offers no defence (15.1–5).
- Jesus' only words from the cross are, citing Psalm 22.1: 'My God, my God, why have you forsaken me?'
- Mary Magdalene, Mary (the mother of James) and Salome look on, but only from afar (15.40; cf. Ps. 38.11).[20] Are they still 'following' him in the way they *used* to (15.41)?

Hence overall, the Markan Jesus cuts something of a tragic, apprehensive figure. The earlier gospel material has presented several incidences of Jesus being abandoned or deserted – his family (3.31–35), his hometown (6.1–6)[21] – but the Passion account brings this aspect to its fore, with the Markan account 'resolute in testifying to the totality of the Christ's abandonment'.[22] Jesus responds neither to Judas' kiss (suggestive of reticence or wariness, perhaps?) nor to the cutting off of the ear of the high priest's slave (14.47–48). Instead his parting words are merely that the Scriptures should be fulfilled (14.49), timely words bearing in mind our focal topic. With the reference to 14.49, Mark emphasizes that scriptural fulfilment goes to the heart of his Passion depiction. He has previously alluded – implicitly, to be sure – to the expectation that the Son of Man would be scorned and endure suffering, and the fact that this had been 'written' of (cf. Mark 9.12–13),[23] but the Passion Narrative enhances this, its frequent explicit appeal to Scripture demonstrably showing how the Scriptures are so fulfilled. As such, Mark seems to reflect the essence of the 1 Corinthians 15.3 claim, and the invitation to read Jesus' death in the light of OT testimony.

One might thus bear two key points in mind in terms of Mark's passion OT usage here:

1 At a crucial dimension or aspect of the Passion scene, at the critical point of Jesus' arrest, he acknowledges that the Scriptures must be fulfilled (Mark 14.49), and hence implies that *the subsequent narrative enables or enacts such fulfilment*. Mark 14.49 is the only Markan use of *pleroo* in terms of scriptural fulfilment, so one might suggest that it thus bears a significant signposting or summative role in this regard. But importantly, this is not just a conceptual or principle statement without foundation or evidence. Rather, Mark avowedly uses scriptural citation to show Scripture being fulfilled, not in a slavish or awkward fashion but by applying a variety of scriptural allusions and imagery within the account. Scriptural 'fulfilment' thereby becomes thoroughly embedded into the Passion discourse and retelling. This is not as explicit as it is in the Matthean or Johannine accounts, where explicit 'fulfilment' notifications accompany the OT citation, but it is still signalled by the frequent quotation of, or allusion, to scriptural testimony.

2 Likewise *the essential shape or character of Mark's Passion is shaped by OT testimony*. As noted above, Mark depicts Jesus as abandoned or alone when going to his death; he is a tragic figure, portrayed in quasi-righteous sufferer terms. This characterization is shaped, at least in part, by the particular OT narratives and texts to which Mark appeals. The foundational contributor in this regard is undoubtedly Psalm 22 (cf. Mark 15.34), but there may be subtle allusions to other righteous sufferer psalms, often of a Davidic attribution, notably Psalm 69 or even Psalm 38.11 and the relatives standing afar.[24]

And much of the requisite scriptural citation is on Jesus' own lips (Mark 14.27, 34, 62; 15.34), giving further indication that Mark personifies or identifies Jesus as a righteous, suffering Davidic figure (perhaps even the true manifestation of such a figure). Furthermore, if the Passion Narrative is said to begin at 14.26, its first action or comment is a *scriptural* pronouncement of the anticipated desertion that Jesus will experience. In Mark 14.27, the words of Zechariah are placed on Jesus' lips (see below) and he 'prophesies' both his imminent 'striking' (death) and also the desertion that will soon come his way, as the sheep abandon their shepherd. The foregrounding of the 'desertion' citation sets the context for the narration of the 'desertion' theme.

Hence scriptural citation and fulfilment, or what Goodacre terms Mark's process of 'scripturalization', are not just 'extras' or by-products of Mark's portrayal of Jesus' death; rather they get to the very heart of the Passion account and determine its very shape and character. Indeed, if one were to remove the OT-related elements from Mark's Passion, one would be left with very little that was not in some way 'scripturalized'.[25] One surmises, then, that the Mark 14.49 reference point is central to the *alttestamentlich* character of the Markan Passion. As is the case of 1 Corinthians 15.3–4, no particular Scriptures are named in respect of fulfilment, and one senses, as with Paul, that it is the tenor of the Scriptures *as a whole* that Mark has in mind, rather than explicit or particular ones. Its pivotal role in the account suggests that the 'fulfilment' aspect embraces both the specific act of Jesus' arrest but also the portrayal of his death as a whole, perhaps with the implication of being 'handed over' for slaughter in the sense of the fourth Servant Song (cf. e.g. Isa. 53.7). At the same time, Mark 14.49 may have some 'specific' focus, and could be seen to be referring back to Mark 14.27 and the fulfilment of the Zechariah 13.7 citation therein – both the striking of the shepherd *and* the resultant desertion are fulfilled in Jesus' arrest. Jesus' seizure and abandonment effectively become two sides of the same coin for Mark, and both aspects of 14.27 are fulfilled within/by it. Immediately after Jesus' declaration that the Scriptures should be fulfilled (14.49), his followers – assuming they are the '*all of them*' – desert him (14.50), with the naked young man symbolic of such desertion, not even bothering to clothe himself before he abandons Jesus (14.51–52).

Moreover, the resigned appeal of 14.49 implies that Markan Jesus goes to his death *reluctantly* – and only in order that the Scriptures might be fulfilled. Jesus' death for Mark – and for most of the NT authors, we surmise – has a scriptural necessity that trumps any personal wish on Jesus' part.[26] This principle also connects with the claim of 14.36; Jesus' concession that God's will should prevail (14.36) correlates with the assertion that the Scriptures must be fulfilled, suggestive therefore that, for Mark, God's will is encountered within and through the Scriptures. The fulfilment of Scripture and the divine will are in concert.

Scriptural Citation in Mark's Passion Narrative

In terms of formal quotations in the Markan Passion, there is technically an OT quotation found within Mark 15.28, one that clearly refers to Isaiah 53.12. It reads: '*The scripture was fulfilled, which says, "He was numbered with transgressors."*' While this could offer further evidence of Markan usage of Isaiah material, and while there may be synergy in that regard, most scholars would now aver that 15.28 is a late addition to the Markan account, and not found in its earliest manuscripts (e.g. like the so-called longer ending of 16.9–20). Most contemporary English versions will therefore just omit the verse entirely and jump from 15.27 to 15.29. The verse is possibly an interpolation under the influence of Luke (who explicitly cites Isa. 53.12 in 22.37), but even if this (likely) scenario is the case, it nonetheless underscores the influence of the OT for interpreting Jesus' death – that is, what is deemed appropriate to borrow or 'add' is the very fact that Jesus' death fulfilled Scripture and that it did so in terms drawn from Isaiah 53. It is thus congruent with the wider Markan testimony (even if the introductory formula is not actually found elsewhere in Mark).

Upper-Room Discourse

Although uttered before the departure from the upper room, and thus technically outside our demarcation of the Markan Passion Narrative, Jesus' contribution to the upper-room discourse is riddled both with OT imagery and pertinence for his anticipated death. Hence Mark's narrative here warrants at least some comment when considering how it might shed light on Mark's portrayal of Jesus' death. First (14.18–21), Jesus predicts his betrayal, specifying that such betrayal will come from those with whom he is presently eating. The prediction confirms that which has already been mentioned in 3.19, but it is also shaped by an allusion to Psalm 41.9, and its suggestion that the betrayer is a 'friend' with whom the one betrayed has broken bread. This allusion is turned into a more formal 'fulfilment' quotation by John's Gospel (John 13.18), corroborating, one suggests, the anticipated psalmic allusion in Mark 14.18–20. The same psalm may also be being echoed or alluded to later on in the Markan Passion, the speaking of empty words (Ps. 41.6) equivalent perhaps to Judas' arrival and kiss of betrayal (14.45), though the lexical similarity remains somewhat limited in this instance.

More significant, perhaps, is Jesus' subsequent warning regarding his betrayer's fate (14.21), and its accompanying appeal to scriptural warrant that testified to the Son of Man being betrayed; such betrayal is given scriptural credence (the 'it is written' appeal), even if no actual scriptural 'writing' is specifically cited. The appeal perhaps refers back to the Passion predictions of 8.31 and 9.31, and the emerging discourse of rejection, perhaps alluding to the rejected stone figure of 12.10 (Ps. 118.22). It is also equivalent, one suggests, to the 'it is written' appeal made in respect of Elijah's suffering fate (9.12), and may therefore resonate in that regard. Indeed, Lindars averred that 9.12 and 14.21 formed key aspects of the apologetic aspect of scriptural usage, in finding scriptural precedent and warrant for the sufferings Jesus would endure, just as was the case for Elijah.[27] Such a notion has some resonance; from the outset of the Gospel, John the Baptist is patterned in terms of Elijah (1.6; cf. 2 Kings 1.7–8),[28] and John's execution seems thereby to anticipate and prepare the reader for Jesus' death. Mark claims that Elijah's

sufferings had some form of scribal warrant (Mark 9.13); the implication, then, is that those of the Son of Man are similarly inscribed
(14.21) and thus exhibit scriptural precedent. It is not obvious to
which scriptural citation 14.21 refers, but it could be reinforcing the
allusion to Psalm 41.9 in Mark 14.18 (in the way that we will see in
John's Gospel, though more formalized there). Similarly, Jesus' declaration at the moment of arrest that the Scriptures might be fulfilled
(14.49) may be referring back to the Psalm 41.9 allusion, Judas'
action thereby providing scriptural fulfilment. It may be, then, that
14.21, like 14.49, exhibits a wider *kata tas graphas* referent rather
than just one specific text or chapter/verse.

Second, Mark offers an account of Jesus' words of institution
(14.22–25), similar to but equally distinct from that found in the
Corinthian tradition. Evans describes Jesus' language here as 'prophetic Christology', with Jesus locating his death in terms of the
imagery of covenantal inauguration.[29] Jesus spoke of his covenant
blood being poured out for many (14.24), a claim that is often
thought to evoke Isaiah 53.10, 12 and the vicarious aspect of the
suffering found there, in such a way that initiates a new covenant moment, perhaps alluding to Jeremiah 31.31. As with Mark
10.45, it might also pick up wider covenantal imagery and draw
on OT motifs such as Israel's election, the Sinai/Exodus discourse
and the language of release and freedom. The Isaianic element
does, though, still remain significant, particularly when also set
alongside the potential Isaianic dimension to Mark 10.45. Otto
Betz even goes so far as to say that 'during the last supper *Jesus
enacted Isaiah 53.12*. He identified himself with the servant who
"poured out his soul to death" and "all the sins of the many."'[30]
Thus if one is looking for Isaiah 53 reference in Mark's recounting of Jesus' death, 14.24 would extend at least one possibility.

Mark 14.27 – Zechariah 13.7

After leaving the upper room, Jesus and his disciples depart
to the Mount of Olives, and Jesus utters what appears to be a
declarative prediction of the abandonment that is about to take

place (14.27). This prediction is a scriptural citation, effectively drawing on Zechariah 13.7. Previously, Mark's Jesus has spoken of the people as being like sheep without a shepherd (Mark 6.34), thus critical of the Jewish authorities and their responsibilities in this regard. Now within the Passion Narrative, the Markan Jesus, drawing on Zechariah, applies the shepherd motif to himself, and by extension to the 'sheep' who now desert him.[31] It is likewise a move from declaring one individual's betrayal (14.10–11, 18–21) to announcing that of the whole 'flock' (14.27). Peter subsequently denies the implications of the accusation (14.29), as do the other disciples (14.31), but the quotation holds aloft the ultimate fate of the group, and may act therefore as a programmatic statement for the whole of the Markan Passion, and for the respective fates of Jesus and the disciples within it. It is also the first reported 'incident' or 'discourse' after the departure for the Mount of Olives, and that may be significant for framing the subsequent recounting of the events leading to Jesus' death. If so, it is striking (no pun intended) that the OT is used in such a framing, paradigmatic fashion.

As we shall see, Zechariah 9—14 is one of the key OT textual units for unpacking the significance of Jesus' death,[32] and the citation of Zechariah 13.7 in Mark 14.27 is one such instance. Although clearly signalled as a quotation, and although the 'desertion' theme is subsequently articulated (cf. 14.50–52), Mark's process for arriving at the form/use of the citation is not straightforward. Jesus' words take the form of a quotation (the 'it is written' introductory formula surely signals this), and it is the only quotation signalled with that preceding formula in Mark's Passion. However, the text form cited in 14.27 is more of a paraphrase of Zechariah 13.7 than an explicit quotation, agreeing with neither the MT nor the LXX. Mark 14.27 itself reads '*I will strike the shepherd and the sheep will be scattered*', whereas the LXX form of Zechariah 13.7 reads somewhat differently: '*Smite the shepherds, and remove the sheep*' (NETS). As such, the source text is a command – implicitly from YHWH – addressed to a sword (13.7a), whereas Mark 14.27 renders a first-person declaration of intent to strike the shepherd. Hence Mark assumes that it is *God* – rather than the impersonal sword – who is the agent of the striking action; God voices the imperative/command himself ('*I will strike*') rather than issuing the command to the sword to do it on his behalf.[33] Mark also changes the plural shepherds to a singular figure being struck. And strictly speaking, the verb used in 14.27 is one of 'scandalization' rather than desertion (or at least it perceives the offence of the forthcoming betrayal and death as a source of scandal – cf. Mark 4.17, 6.3), and thus Mark uses a different form from that found in the Zechariah source.

Such paraphrased variance, though, is ultimately no reason to negate the existence of the quotation, and the paraphrase and its source remain recognizable. Hence there is no reason to query the Zechariah 13.7 origin; the switch from plural to singular is requisite for the impending crucifixion, and there would seem to be sufficient flexibility within the text for it to be 'reworked' or amended accordingly. R. T. France, for example, avers that Mark's emending of the Zechariah is 'a necessary grammatical adaptation to the New Testament context', as the sword reference is essentially meaningless.[34] More significant perhaps, then, is the *application* of the citation. Mark has read the (scriptural) words of Zechariah 13.7 as those voiced by God – Scripture is the divine word and by extension may be appropriated and placed on Jesus' lips. It is direct speech, and as we shall see, direct speech texts have a particular potential for transfer from the OT to the NT. There is something about first-person direct speech, and the capacity to 're-assign' its speaker:

> This exegetical method is paralleled in the works of rewritten bible, where a speech from one part of Scripture can be put into the mouth of a figure from a different period, illustrating an underlying axiom of scriptural coherence and inter-connectedness.[35]

One may also ponder why God is said to voice a declaration to strike the shepherd (Jesus) – that is, Jesus does not strike himself. At one level it would seem to offer further scriptural affirmation of the divine involvement in and 'endorsement' of the Passion account, and that 'for the evangelist, the death of Jesus is willed by God'.[36] There may, then, also be the influence here of Isaiah 53.4, 6, 10 – it is YHWH who both strikes the shepherd and 'bruises' the Servant figure.[37]

Mapping the context of the OT citation is not uncomplicated. Zechariah 13.7–9 may be a self-standing unit, and in view of its lack of direct association with its immediate context, some scholars associate it with Zechariah 11.4–17 and the worthless shepherd imagery found therein (cf. Zech. 11.17). This is plausible, and the singular figure is attractive in this regard, but 'worthless' fits ill with Mark's portrayal of Jesus, and thus it seems better to look to the immediate Zechariah 13 milieu.[38] In the LXX, the context for the divine imperative is the destruction of Israel's leaders – that is, 'my shepherds' (there is an assumed parallelism with 13.7a). It is implied, therefore, that the striking action is against those who seemingly *oppose* YHWH's purposes, and/or who have failed to exercise appropriate leadership. There may be some ultimately vindicatory or formative aspect later on (13.9), but generally speaking 13.7 bespeaks a divine critique of the present system. As such, it would seem the kind of text (in the plural form) Jesus (or another prophetic figure) might have prophetically uttered *against* the Jewish authorities, as a 'divine' utterance against them (and the 'sheep' who have followed their pastoral lead). On first view, it is not a text Jesus would seem to cite against *himself.*

The appeal to Zechariah 13.7 may also be part of a wider Markan engagement with the discourse of Zechariah 9 – 14. It is possible, for example, that Zechariah 9.11 has already been in Mark's mind in view of the 'blood of the covenant' imagery espoused therein (cf. Mark 14.24). Similarly, Mark may be picking up on other 'shepherding' imagery within Zechariah 9 – 14, for example the divine anger against the existing shepherds (Zech. 10.3 – appropriate bearing in mind Jesus' engagement with the Temple authorities), and the people's present suffering for the lack of a shepherd (Zech. 10.2), or the divine initiative to save the flock of his people (Zech. 9.16). If so, the irony, of course, is that a particular 'shepherd' (Jesus) is struck rather than the 'leader shepherds' (Zech. 10.3), in order for the flock to be reconfigured or restored. Hence one might also wonder whether Mark has in mind the continuing Zechariah narrative (cf. Zech. 13.9), when a refining process brings forth a new people (interestingly, bearing in mind Mark's interest in threes – a third! (cf. Zech. 13.8)), that will be declared *God*'s people. This may well, then, be in continuity with the positive exposition found in 14.28, and the implicit vindication therein; and thus rather than Mark's use of the Zechariah text being an imposition, it may actually be in continuity with the wider Zechariah portrayal. The shepherd may be struck, and the flock may desert him, but the 'end' of such striking is ultimately the vindication of the (struck) shepherd. The stark ending of the Gospel does not seem to signal that possibility, of course, and instead one surmises that the emphasis is here on the imminent isolation brought about by the action. But where 14.27 sounds the note of abandonment, Jesus immediately offers the hope of re-gathering (14.28) and the meeting afresh in Galilee. This assumes, one surmises, the vindication of Jesus, and assumes the resurrection and, like Psalm 118, gives the reader a (consistent?) steer as to how the Passion citations are to be read. It also requires a fair amount of Zechariah 'literacy' on the part of Mark's audience, but that is not impossible bearing in mind the familiarity of the text.[39] It might also correlate with the depiction of the 'royal shepherd' – David – who speaks the words from the cross as the righteous sufferer of Psalm 22 (Mark 15.34).

Gethsemane Allusions

After the citation of Zechariah 13.7, and the resultant discourse with Peter and his mooted desertion of Jesus (14.29–31), Mark moves the narrative to Gethsemane, and to a sequence of exchanges with the disciples involving a series of exhortations and prayers. The pericope of exchanges underscores Jesus' apprehension regarding his impending death and exemplifies the great anguish on his part (14.33–36). The discourse may well form the backdrop for the portrayal of Jesus' prayers and supplications as expressed in Hebrews 5.7–10, but it also probably borrows from a number of OT texts. In particular, Jesus' reference to his soul being troubled (14.34) seems to be an allusion to the recurring refrain found within Psalms 42 and 43 (Ps. 46.2, 11, 12; 43.5),[40] two more instances of righteous sufferer psalms thus being found within the Passion retelling. A similar refrain might also be found in Psalm 118.17–18, so giving a further instance of Markan use of that psalm,[41] but the lexical association is far stronger to the Psalms 42 and 43 instances. There may even be an echo of Jonah's protestations in Jonah 4.8–9,[42] but it would seem strange for Mark to pattern Jesus in the more 'negative' persona that Jonah portrays here. Whatever the source of the allusion, though, the rootedness of Jesus' sense of impending abandonment remains rooted in and shaped by OT citation.

Psalm 110.1; Daniel 7 in Mark 14.62

After his arrest, Jesus is taken to the high priest and to a trial before the council of the Temple authorities (14.53–64). Various testimony is offered against Jesus (14.56), particularly the accusation that he would destroy the Temple and rebuild it in three days (14.57–59), but no charge is found to 'stick'. Instead the high priest addresses Jesus with the direct question as to whether he is the Christ (14.62). Jesus' identity as the Messiah, the so-called 'messianic secret', has been kept undisclosed in Mark's retelling of the gospel, at least to the characters involved, but at this culmination of the evangelistic retelling, at the climactic trial scene, Jesus finally gives public affirmation of his messianic identity (14.62). His response, though, is somewhat telling, particularly for its use of Old Testament imagery. Indeed, at such a climactic moment it would seem entirely appropriate/consistent for Mark to find scriptural allusion or warrant to designate Jesus' status.

The declaration takes two forms or dimensions. First, Jesus' positive affirmation to the high priest's question is not a straight 'yes', rather an equally direct 'I am' (*ego eimi*). The inclusion of the personal pronoun 'I' gives the response the appearance of the form of the divine name – YHWH (cf. Exod. 3.14) – and bearing in mind Mark's prior patterning of Jesus in terms of YHWH, the divine/OT allusion seems hard to ignore (even if it not picked up as such by the high priest).[43] Second, and more extensively perhaps, Mark places a scriptural allusion on Jesus' lips, or at least a composite allusion drawing on Psalm 110.1 and Daniel 7.13: '*You will see the Son of Man* (Dan. 7.13) *seated at the right hand of Power* (Ps. 110.1) *and coming on the clouds of heaven*

(Dan. 7.13).' The construction of the allusion is notable for several reasons. Its A-B-A construction mimics Mark's wider A-B-A structural discourse. The allusion continues Jesus' prior appeal to Son of Man imagery in relation to his death (cf. 8.31; 9.12, 31; 10.33, 35; 14.21, 41), and continues, therefore, to juxtapose the Markan Passion with Danielic imagery. Notably, though, it reuses Psalm 110, offering a further instance of Mark's habitual duplication of psalmic testimony (cf. the similar dual citation of Psalms 2 and 118).[44] The Psalm 110-related question that was raised in the Temple (12.35–37) is answered in the trial scene, but in so doing, the psalm is used to underscore Jesus' vindication at the point at which his death is supposedly confirmed. Indeed, the appeal to Psalm 110.1 and Daniel 7.13 constitutes no 'defence' on Jesus' part, at least in terms of presenting him as innocent.[45] Instead the citations evidence Jesus' claim for exaltation and authority in judgement, with Mark ironically juxtaposing the Sanhedrin trial scene with the Danielic portrayal of the heavenly 'court' (Dan. 7.9–10). Hence the very 'confession' that may imminently lead to Jesus' death is actually the declaration of his triumph; Jesus is the one who can sit at YHWH's right hand, and his death – and subsequent vindication – will serve to confirm this status.

The wider discourse of Psalm 110 may also be in view here. It is possible that Mark has in mind the whole context of the psalm, and that the claim of Psalm 110.4 (relating to an eternal priesthood) is similarly invoked. Both parts of the psalm are picked up in Hebrews and, if that is the case here (though that is only tentative), then the psalmic allusion offers a condemnation of the high priest Jesus addresses; the priesthood of the one on trial is eternal and thus superior to the one who asks the question. Either way, the high priest's response is intriguing; the tearing of his clothes is indicative that blasphemy has been uttered, but the messianic claim is, in and of itself, not evidential of blasphemy. The 'I am' claim may have occasioned it, but Mark does not signal that explicitly, or it could be that the grounds for such blasphemy may reflect the Deuteronomic prohibition on false prophecy. The fact, though, that the priest's verdict follows the composite citation suggests that the issue here is the exalted position Jesus claims for himself; that is, the one who, seated at YHWH's right hand, will assume the Danielic judicial role. The one judged has become the judge.[46]

In sum, the composite allusion of Mark 14.62 shows the importance of paying attention to the OT backdrop; without due attention to it, the blasphemy verdict does not really make sense.[47] And once again, Mark has Jesus giving voice to Scripture so as both to articulate his authority and to evidence scriptural testimony to his vindication as Messiah. Not only does this serve as a further appeal to the fulfilment of Scriptures (14.49), it also acts as a Janus point in the Markan account; looking backwards, Jesus' declaration 'resolves' the messianic secret that has dominated the Gospel thus far, but also anticipates the vindication of the Son of God (15.39), the one who is seated at YHWH's right hand (Ps. 110.1).[48]

Psalm 22 in Mark 15.34

It remains the case, though, that Psalm 22 is the strongest contributor to Mark's Passion Narrative, in terms of both the potential number of intertextual connections found and the thematic resonance so generated. Attributed to David, as are a number of the other lament or sufferer psalms utilized by the Passion accounts (Pss. 35; 42; 43; 69), Jesus is found to give voice to or 'pray' the psalm, in such a way as to personify or characterize him as a suffering David figure.[49] The weight of citation is such that one might even suggest that the entire Markan Passion is structured around Psalm 22;[50] Vernon Robbins, likewise, proposed that Mark was offering a *backwards* reading of the psalm (Mark 15.24, cf. Ps. 22.18; Mark 15.29–31, cf. Ps. 22.7–8; Mark 15.32, cf. Ps. 22.6; Mark 15.34, cf. Ps. 22.1), reversing its direction of travel from abandonment to vindication.[51]

Psalm 22.18 is alluded to in Mark 15.24, and the recounting therein of the casting of lots for, and division of, Jesus' clothing. This image is picked up by all four canonical Gospels, suggesting that it had a core or consistent role within the earliest Passion Narrative, and John's Gospel formally presents Psalm 22.18 as being 'fulfilled' by the event (cf. John 19.24). The Markan example – and that of the Synoptic parallels – is more of an allusion than an explicit citation, but the consistent wording, and the appeal elsewhere to Psalm 22, leave little doubt that this is a genuine citation, and thus embedded into the Passion account. There is a potential further psalmic allusion in the previous verse (Mark 15.23), this time to Psalm 69.21 (Ps. 68.22 LXX), and the wine/myrrh offered to Jesus to drink. Again, this is picked up in the other gospel accounts, but is less explicit in the Markan example (the *oxos* drink of the psalm is absent in 15.23). Instead, for Mark at least, the second 'drink' offering (15.36) seems the stronger echo, for here the same psalmic *oxos* is proffered to Jesus. Like Psalm 22 (and Psalm 31, used by Luke), Psalm 69 might be characterized as a lament or righteous sufferer psalm and, also like Psalm 22, would seem to form a core feature of the Passion tradition, both texts manifesting the same sufferer-vindication framework.

A further, stronger Psalm 22 allusion occurs in Mark 15.29–30. It seemingly evokes Psalm 22.6–8, and the shared notion of mockery and derision (so perhaps also Mark 15.17–20), and the exhortation to Jesus to '*save yourself*' (15.30, 31; cf. Ps. 22.8). In both instances the sufferer is summarily ridiculed (Mark 15.29; cf. Ps. 22.6–7) and 'invited' to seek rescue, either from God (Ps. 22.8) or by himself (Mark 15.30). The latter distinction, though, is perhaps less material for Mark, because the one invited to save himself (Jesus) has already been portrayed in quasi-divine terms throughout the Gospel. If anything, the allusion to Psalm 22.6–8 and the reallocation of the 'agent' of salvation only serves to confirm that perception – that is, 'Jesus' salvific power *is* the power of God.'[52]

One might also draw attention to other Markan echoes of Psalm 22. Jesus' crucifixion between two robbers (15.27) potentially evokes Psalm 22.16 and its reference to surrounding 'dogs' and villains, particularly in respect of the apparently cruciform imagery of 22.16b. Those crucified with Jesus also mock and revile him (15.32), a further instance perhaps of Psalm 22.6. One might even, in the light of the other connections, conceive of a possible echo of Psalm 22.31 in Mark 15.37 and Jesus' breathing his last.[53] However, the citation of Psalm 22.1 in Mark 15.34 is surely the strongest link to the source text. Indeed, it is perhaps one of the most familiar features of Mark's Passion Narrative, and for many, the centrepiece of the Markan account. The citational form is distinctive in that it equates to, or 'feels like', a direct quotation, but it lacks an introductory formula, since the psalmic text is placed directly on Jesus' lips, so that he seemingly voices David's words. The textual format is also intriguing; Mark actually places an Aramaic paraphrase on Jesus' lips (*Eloi, Eloi, lema sabachthani*), and translates this paraphrase into Greek, rather than citing the Septuagint form of Psalm 21.2. Cilliers Breytenbach concludes thus that Mark has 'taken over a traditional Aramaic quotation as part of the passion narrative, which has been moulded on Ps. 22', rather than explicitly citing the LXX text.[54]

Whatever their exact provenance, the fact that Psalm 22.1 forms Jesus' last words in the gospel account is surely striking. Not only does it underscore the significance of the OT in this regard (i.e. at the climactic point, an OT text is used to 'capture the moment'), but it would also seem to attest, exemplify even, the distinctive portrayal of Jesus as one abandoned, deserted and alone.° At the climax of the Passion retelling, God is the one who finally abandons Jesus.° Thus paraphrasing Martin Kahler's famous Passion Narrative aphorism, Matthew Rindge surmises: 'Mark is also the story of *divine abandonment* with a long introduction.'[55] Like Zechariah 13.7 perhaps, one might say that Psalm 22.1 attests Mark's Passion *in nuce*, and along with the wider narrative of the psalm, it might offer a tapestry for Mark's depiction of Jesus' death. Some further consideration of the role of Psalm 22 is therefore helpful.

What is the psalm?

Psalm 22 is variously described as a psalm of lament or as righteous sufferer psalm. It is potent with material for one who is abandoned. Its opening cry of dereliction continues into 22.1b and 22.2, and the suffering to which the psalmist gives voice is evident (cf. 22.6–7), as is the state of mind they inhabit (cf. 22.14–18). The (righteous) speaker cries out for divine action and deliverance, to elicit some form of intervention that might vindicate the psalmist. This comes (21.21a–31), but in the second, very discrete section

° And confirms the purposes — of a suffering Davidic Messiah — as Davidic authorship is explicitly ascribed. (Cf. p.178-9 But not mentioned or suggested is/are the purpose(s) of this suffering, abandonment. Divine intention - for whatever

or half of the psalm. It is, of course, not the only psalm to exhibit such contrasting voices, particularly in terms of the lament/suffering character (cf. Ps. 69.1–18, 19–36), and other non-lament psalms can similarly exhibit such a binary structure (cf. Ps. 95.1–7a, 7b–11). However, Psalm 22 remains particularly distinctive in this regard, and in manifesting the (apparent) dichotomy of suffering and vindication. The move from dereliction to praise comes in somewhat stark fashion, and some writers conjecture that there may be two separate psalms operative behind the final 'unified' version.[56]

What might we have seen about Mark's allusive use of it?

Mark's familiarity with the whole Psalms corpus is evident, as he had frequent citation from within it (Pss. 2; 118; 110). As we have already noted, the psalms are cited at the supposed three core 'events' of the Markan account: Jesus' baptism (1.11; cf. Ps. 2.7); the transfiguration (9.7; again, cf. Ps. 2.7); and here the crucifixion (15.34; cf. Ps. 22.1). And whereas in the first two citations, the psalm is given *divine* voice, and attests to God's support/'endorsement' of Jesus, the Passion example places the words on Jesus' own lips, and in a way that seemingly implies divine abandonment. In contrast to the previous two encounters, the (divine) silence is somewhat loud, but equally it may be implying something about Jesus and the way Mark characterizes him in divine terms. It is also characteristic for Mark to 'reuse' the material from a particular psalm (as we have seen in Psalm 118, for instance),[57] and such Markan practice would seem to extend to Psalm 22, with Mark 15.34 building on the prior allusions identified above.

What might we say about the 'event'?

A primary question in the use of the psalm is the extent to which it speaks of *both* suffering and vindication – that is, the degree to which Mark has the 'whole' context of the psalm in view. The fact that the psalm is being is used is not in question in 15.34; rather it is *why* and *how* it is used that is more ambiguous, and this raises a number of questions, including:

(In the OT, human suffering & Divine abandonment are closely linked.) 47 The purpose for Jesus' suffering is perhaps a more difficult, even mysterious matter for the early Church. At the very least, it required a more extensive "fabric" of Scriptural texts (cf. Hebrews) than

- What is Mark's 'habit' when citing OT quotations? To what extent is the wider context of the psalm impacting Mark's usage of it?
- What is the overall 'flavour' of Mark's Passion – is it suffering or is it victory? Bearing in mind Mark's ambiguities (the 'fearful' ending, the lack of resurrection appearances), might Mark be steering the reader away from the 'triumph' of the cross and emphasizing its inherent suffering and tragedy?
- To what extent does God 'abandon' Jesus on the cross?
- As such, one might suggest that this is a fulcrum or pivotal question, and the psalm is an entirely apposite one for discerning Mark's essential character, especially when one is pondering the theological questions Mark raises.

What might we say about Jesus' suffering (and vindication)?

Consideration of the psalm also generates questions as to the type or manner of suffering Jesus experiences. It might, for example, shed light on how Mark views Jesus' kingship. Marcus, for example, concludes that every aspect of the Passion Narrative is testimony to the eschatological victory accomplished through Jesus' *righteous* suffering.[58] Others have found such a characterization problematic, however, particularly for the way it might be seen as watering down the psalm's agonizing tone. Indeed, for Stephen Ahearne-Kroll, to draw attention to the vindicatory aspect of the psalm is to misconstrue the character of the psalms of *lament*; for him, Psalm 22 is a *lament* psalm, and he argues that Mark avowedly uses the psalm in that light.[59] It testifies to the genuine suffering and sorrow Jesus endured, and its lament tenor names the explicit harm done to Jesus and the horror of the crucifixion.[60] As with the Gethsemane lament-psalmic allusion (Pss. 42; 43), Psalm 22 similarly attends to God's inaction and takes seriously the dimension of divine abandonment, rather than the vindication that might ultimately ensue. Ahearne-Kroll avers that Jesus is thus far closer to a suffering *David* than a Suffering Servant figure: 'As it is, even after he is raised, Jesus is still "the crucified one" . . . Mark's Jesus is a king like the suffering David of the PssLam.'[61] Such an appeal to the psalm takes seriously the abandonment of Jesus, and the

could readily be ~~cited~~ suggested within the Passion account of Mark or Matthew.

48

faithful sufferer robustly challenges God in the light of the suffering. Similarly, for others, the singular or focused reading of the psalm ensures that Jesus' suffering is genuine and not glossed over by the reader.[62] Psalm 22 emphasizes the reality of the cruciform death, namely that Christ died for sins at real, substantial cost.

Others, however, wish to read the whole of Psalm 22 as operative within Markan usage, both the suffering *and* vindication dimensions. Holly Carey, for example, advocates for such a holistic reading, averring that 'Mark finds in the words the prayer expression of Jesus' own experience.'[63] Carey argues that Mark's readers would have known the full contours of the Jesus story, and would have interpreted the psalm in that light. She surmises that the narrative has prepared the readers to read the full flow of the psalm, and therefore they are expecting a vindication.[64] Rebekah Eklund, likewise, sees the whole psalm as 'foundational . . . to the narrative of Jesus' crucifixion', and this necessitates taking into account the entire psalmic content.[65] As such, it means that the (informed) reader is expectant of the resurrection – or at least some form of vindication – and thus Mark 16 comes as less of a surprise. If so, as potentially with Psalm 118, this would be in tandem with Dodd's proposal that Mark brings the wider context of cited texts 'into play', and that the interpreter should embrace that breadth in order to fully appropriate Mark's portrayal of the Passion event.

Debates will continue as to whether Mark is invoking the whole psalm in 15.34 or just verse 1, and there are merits for both arguments.[66] Marus Borg and John Dominic Crossan surmise that, for Mark, the wider spectrum of the psalm is in view, as it shows the wider framework Mark understands Jesus' death as operative, and without it, the 'good news' dimension is removed. The centurion's confession would act as confirmation of the vindication evidenced within the psalm (15.39).[67] Adopting the more minimalist position, Paul Foster instead opines that, were the vindication aspect Mark's essential point, why does it not cite a more appropriate part of the psalm (e.g. Ps. 22.24)? But of course, that would only send the pendulum the other way, and raise the question as to whether Mark really expected to portray Jesus as 'suffering'. Alternatively, a more *via media* position might be adopted; Mark's citation of Psalm 22.1 could be seen as giving suffering new meaning, what

Ellen Davis calls the 'resymbolization' of the experience of what it means to suffer.

Perhaps it remains a moot point as to whether the *full* psalmic context is brought to the fore, but as we have seen, a lot stands or falls on the citation of Psalm 22 in the Markan Passion Narrative. In view of its repeated citation and usage, it is a key fulcrum or pivot point as to how we might conceive Jesus' suffering and death, and it would be impossible to ignore it. In the previous two citations relating to Jesus' death (12.10–11; 14.27), the implication has been of vindication, and hence one suggests, albeit tentatively, that the same perspective is set forth here.

Other Markan Passion/OT connections

Our discussion of the links is far from exhaustive and the number of potential echoes or allusions in Mark's Passion is huge. O'Brien lists numerous potential examples,[68] of varying significance and genuineness, but we do not have space to address the full gamut of possible OT usage. However, mention might still be made of several other texts or images on which Mark might genuinely – and profitably – have drawn. Mark 15.19, for example, could well be an allusion or echo to Isaiah 50.6, the notion of spitting and scourging being common to both discourses; the allusion would further underscore the Isaianic backdrop to the Markan account, and would show the evangelist drawing on the third Servant Song (Isa. 50.4–9), and therefore also reinforcing the impact of the fourth one. As the links are more thematic than lexical, one might even surmise that Mark 15.19 is an allusion to Isaiah 42.3 (the bruised reed), and therefore invoking the first Servant Song. Similar cases could equally be made for Mark 14.65 and/or 15.15, as they too share the striking/scourging action made to Jesus. The construction of a crown of thorns for Jesus (Mark 15.17) might even be an echo of Psalm 31.4 LXX and the implication that '*I was turned to wretchedness when a thorn was stuck in me*' (NETS).

One might also note the use of Amos 8.9–10 in Mark 15.33 (cf. also Matt. 27.45), and the appeal to darkness covering the earth. It is not also impossible, if there is still some Passover imagery operative here, that Mark has in mind the plague imagery found therein (cf. Exod. 10.21–23), but the Amos source is the more persuasive one. The Amos discourse has an eschatological tone to it and would invest the Markan Passion account with that tenor, and would also pick up the similarly eschatological language of Mark 13.24. Amos 8.10 also expresses the divine mourning for a beloved figure (a 'son' in the Masoretic text form); the allusion would thus highlight the divine sadness and lament over the cruciform activity, an appropriate fit for the Markan context, one might say. Jesus' cry of dereliction comes immediately after the three-hour period of darkness, and the sense of divine – paternal – abandonment seems concordant with that.

Conclusion

Mark's Passion recounting is shaped by the theme of abandonment and by Jesus' desertion by friends, followers and ultimately by God. The theme is sounded at the outset of the Passion through the citation of Zechariah 13.7, and reaches its climax with the allusion to Psalm 22.1 and the expression of divine abandonment. In both instances the declaration is placed on Jesus' lips to underscore the significance. In both too, the statement is drawn from the Jewish Scriptures. To use Goodacre's term, Mark's Passion Narrative is avowedly 'scripturalized', and is imbued throughout with appeal to the Old Testament. Mark's Jesus declares that the Scriptures must be fulfilled (14.49), and the rest of his Passion account sets about telling how that might be.

3

The Old Testament in Matthew's Passion

While Mark may well have been the earliest written Gospel, and might therefore have been the first *textual* form of the Passion material, Matthew's account, much longer and more expansive than that of Mark, quickly became the authoritative Gospel within the Church,[1] and likewise the one positioned at the head of the NT canonical order. Such positioning was doubtless occasioned by several factors and, in the tradition at least, it has tended to be viewed as the most Jewish of the evangelistic testimony. But one of the reasons for its foregrounded location may well have been the way Matthew's use of the OT – and its particular editorial comments concerning the 'fulfilment' of particular OT texts – encouraged its positioning immediately subsequent to the OT material, and thus at the head of the NT canon. Matthew has 11 of these fulfilment quotations, and they are characteristic of its mode of interaction with the OT. More than any of the other gospel accounts, its engagement with the OT material is avowed and direct, no more so perhaps than in its birth narrative (Matt. 1 – 2), in which five OT 'texts' are deemed to be fulfilled (1.22–23; 2.5–6, 15, 17–18, 23), each example showing some rather creative form of interpretative reading.[2]

Most famously perhaps,[3] at the climax of the birth narrative Matthew cites a 'prophetic' text as being fulfilled ('*He will be called a Nazorean*' – 2.23), the source of which we do not have within any known contemporary Jewish textual tradition. Various responses to this lacuna have been offered, for example that 'Nazorean' is a misread of 'Nazarite' or that the cited text incorporates the wider tenor of the Jewish Scriptures (rather than one explicit text).[4] Whatever the explanation, Matthew locates its interpretation of Jesus' birth very much within the Jewish Scriptures, and goes to great lengths to do so.[5] In general these 'fulfilment' editorial glosses are spoken by the narrator rather than by protagonists within the story, and they are drawn generally from the prophetic literature.[6] This is in contrast to the evangelistic appeals to the Psalms corpus, of the kind we have seen in Mark and which Matthew commonly reduplicates; these are generally put on the lips of actual participants, the first-person, direct speech genre of much psalmic discourse enabling such application.

Bearing in mind the birth narrative's predilection for scriptural warrant, however, the Passion Narrative's scriptural appeal seems comparatively muted (at least in terms of material Matthew does not derive from the Markan source). For example, one might have expected scriptural vindication to be found for justifying the securing or guarding of the tomb (27.62–66) or for Pilate's wife's positive affirmation of Jesus (27.19). Likewise the decision to free Barabbas rather than Jesus would seem to be an appropriate situation for which Matthew might have found explicit prophetic confirmation, particularly bearing in mind the 'unusual' prophetic scenarios encountered in the earlier chapters – the Emmanuel prophecy, for example (1.21–23). This apparent reticence for expressing Passion fulfilment is perhaps because Matthew draws so much of its Passion content from Mark and is accordingly dependent on that material. But for whatever reason, in so doing Matthew generally retains – and in the case of 26.54 duplicates – Mark's scriptural patterning (cf. Matt. 26.56; Mark 14.49). Twice, Matthew's Jesus is to declare that the Scriptures must be fulfilled (26.54, 56).

Yet 27.9 aside, Matthew's Passion Narrative still lacks the explicit 'fulfilment' introductory formula configuration associated with the birth narrative, and in short, there is no specified fulfilment text offered by Matthew to explain or signify his death. As such, whereas fulfilment quotations are replete in the birth narrative, and whereas Matthew supposedly needed to demonstrate – however 'creatively' – that Jesus' birth was *kata tas graphas*, it is striking that the Passion Narrative lacks any such determining textual statement. Again, one might have expected, for example, to encounter the explicit declaration that some feature of the crucifixion scene, or the breaking open of the tombs perhaps (Matt. 27.51–53), might have warranted the characteristic Matthean editorial fulfilment citation. Even when Matthew does have extra (non-Markan) material, and when there is some form of appeal to the OT, generally speaking such an appeal tends to be somewhat restrained, more akin to an echo than an allusion. Pilate's washing of his hands (27.24), for example (imagery found in neither Mark nor Luke), perhaps alludes to Psalm 26.6 ('*I wash my hands in innocence*'),[7] but any association is at best implicit, and even the more likely reference to Deuteronomy 21.1–9 remains comparatively 'unsignalled'. Therefore Matthew's initial enthusiasm for explicitly attesting that the Christ event had happened according to the divine will (and thus *kata tas graphas*) seems to have waned by the time one gets to the Passion retelling.

Interestingly, one sees an emphatic use of direct fulfilment language in *John*'s Passion Narrative (in direct contrast to its earlier use of the OT, where such fulfilment imagery is essentially absent), but this is not the case for Matthew (for whom the trajectory is thus the reverse – specific *pleroo* citations reduce in number as the Gospel unfolds. Indeed, for Matthew it is only Judas' death – a comparatively peripheral event, one might say, to the primary cruciform narrative – that receives the *pleroo* designation. Hence one might suggest that, for Matthew's Passion Narrative, it is the *wider* scriptural story – and particularly that of the prophets (26.56) – that is being fulfilled and, interestingly, such testimony is placed on Jesus' lips (26.54, 56) rather than offered as a third-party editorial gloss (as happens in the birth narrative). In this sense then, Matthew's Passion Narrative comes closer to 1 Corinthians 15.3 than to Matthew's own birth account, in the sense of spreading the proverbial 'fulfilment' umbrella as wide as possible and in unspecified fashion. It may equally suggest – although one recognizes the argument from silence – that arguing for Jesus' death from Scripture was more of a 'given' for Matthew's audience and didn't require the evangelist to supplement the explicit scriptural signposting that wasn't already 'present' within the Markan source. Other more controversial aspects of Jesus' life, however, namely his birth, lacked prior understanding or scriptural attestation and required Matthew to provide more explicit scriptural warrant for them.

And, of course, Matthew's use of the OT to unpack the life of Jesus is not limited to the fulfilment quotations. In many ways, Matthew portrays Jesus as a new 'Moses' figure,[8] one who experiences flight to Egypt (2.13–16) and a subsequent 'exodus' from that place (2.19–23). Jesus is seen going up a mountain in a discourse that engages the Law (Matthew 5 — 7), and the five Matthean teaching units have also been seen in terms of establishing a new Pentateuchal pattern (Matt. 5 — 7, 10, 13, 18, 24 — 25). Matthew's Jesus is the one who proposes life or death, distinguishes between sheep and goats, or wise and foolish virgins at the close of the Gospel, a reworking of the blessing/curse language that Moses utters at the end of Deuteronomy. As with the Isaiah tapestry for Mark, but perhaps with an even wider remit, broader OT narratives sit behind Matthew's portrayal and offer insight into its interpretation.

Matthew's Passion Narrative – 'Mark Plus'

Equally significant to assessing Matthew's Passion, of course, is the way Matthew – and Luke, one might surmise – utilizes Mark as a major source for its retelling of the Jesus story. Indeed, the Matthean dependence on Mark, and the comparative *independence* for the birth narrative material, may be a further factor in the relative lack of fulfilment vocabulary in the Passion Narrative. That is not to say that Matthew is uninterested in the OT in terms of Passion explication, but rather that it essentially adopts Mark's approach (with some nuancing), and has only relatively limited additional 'Matthean' flavour.

The so-called Synoptic question – seeking to account for the respective similarities and divergences between Matthew, Mark and Luke – is a long-established and well-worked *topos* within biblical studies, and a recounting of its history is beyond the scope of our inquiry.[9] But we cannot escape its impact here if/when dealing with the respective accounts of Jesus' death. For generally speaking, assuming Markan priority, Matthew adopts much of Mark's material for his own purposes and re-presents it in a new context, but with very similar language and structure. Luke, as we shall see, presents his Passion account in somewhat different terms from that of Mark, and seems to draw significantly on other source material,[10] but Matthew essentially retains the core shape and content of the Markan source. The general trend, therefore, of Matthew's Passion account, and thereby his use of the OT in this regard, is shaped to a significant degree by the Markan material. There are some minor variations to the Markan text, as we shall discuss below, but essentially it remains the case that '[t]hroughout his account Matthew stays remarkably close to what seems to be his primary source, the passion story of Mark.'[11] As such, one might want to characterize Matthew's Passion Narrative as effectively 'Mark plus'; that is, exhibiting the same shape, scope and flavour of the Markan equivalent but supplementing it with some extra – background? – detail.

If the contours and tenor of Matthew's Passion broadly resemble the Markan source, the resemblance likewise extends to their respective uses of the Old Testament. Generally speaking, Matthew retains and reuses Mark's scriptural imagery. Hence we encounter the same reference to Jesus as the rejected stone (Matt. 21.42; Mark 12.10), the same portrayal of desertion (the Zechariah 13.7 citation is preserved in Matthew 26.31, albeit with an additional 'because of me' reference) and the same appeal to righteous sufferer psalms in the Gethsemane narrative (Matt. 26.38; Mark 14.34; cf. Ps. 42.5, 6, 11; 43.5). In particular, Matthew's Passion retains the core focus on Psalm 22 and preserves the various allusions to it that are dotted across the Markan recounting. For example, it keeps the allusion to Psalm 22.18 over the casting of lots for, and division of, Jesus' clothing (Matt. 27.35; Mark 15.24), and to Psalm 22.6, with the derision of the passers-by (Matt. 27.39; Mark 15.29).

However, Matthew also expands on Mark's already extensive use of Psalm 22, and the Matthean appeal to the psalm becomes arguably even more prominent than in its Markan hearing. At one level, the change is stylistic. Matthew offers the Hebrew transliteration of Psalm 22.1 rather than the Markan Aramaic form, the text therefore reading *Eli, Eli, lema sabachthani* (Matt. 27.46, though still requiring the subsequent Greek translation of the text form). The use of the Hebrew *Eli, Eli* – rather than *Eloi, Eloi* – makes the subsequent confusion with Elijah more probable (27.47), and thus may be a further example of Matthew's 'tidying up' of Mark's prose; but as with Mark, the mooted association with Elijah is not subsequently exploited in either account, other than to set up the query as to whether Elijah will come to save Jesus (Matt. 27.49).

More significant perhaps is Matthew's enhancement of other points of connection with Psalm 22, and in particular the further allusion to Psalm 22.8 and the chief priests' mocking invitation to Jesus to let God deliver him (Matt. 27.43). Both Matthew and Mark have the derisive cry for Jesus to save *himself* and come down from the cross (Matt. 27.40; Mark 15.30), though with Matthean addition of '*if you are the Son of God*' (perhaps an echo of the temptation narrative – 4.3, 6). Technically, the mockers of Psalm 22 exhort God to deliver the sufferer (rather than it being a case of self-deliverance), and hence it is the common imagery of Psalm 22.8 and Mark's wider use of the psalm (rather than the explicit language) that justifies the allusion, for Mark 15.30 at least. Matthew, however, offers a further, or expanded, allusion to Psalm 22.8. Where Mark has the chief priests and scribes effectively echoing the derision of the passers-by to *self*-salvation (15.31), Matthew incorporates the psalm's exhortation to *divine* intervention and urges God to deliver the crucified, suffering Jesus (27.43). Where the psalmist portrays the mockers urging the sufferer to commit his cause to YHWH in the expectation of deliverance, Matthew's mockers likewise parody the crucified Jesus that he should similarly put his trust in God in the expectation of divine deliverance. Matthew's allusion to Psalm 22.8 is thus 'louder' than the Markan example and, indeed, becomes more like a quotation in this regard, with a closer lexical and thematic similarity between the text and its source.[12] Like 27.40, it also specifies Jesus as 'God's Son', to add further irony to the challenge for divine deliverance. Commenting on this 'expansion' of the Markan source, Marcus surmises that 'in the transition from Mark to Matthew . . . we can see the narrative growing right before our eyes.'[13] There are even other potential allusions to the psalm, beyond that used by Mark. For example, albeit within the resurrection narrative, it is possible that Jesus' exhortation to go to Galilee so that his brothers might see him (Matt. 28.10) echoes Psalm 22.22–23, particularly as Hebrews 2.12 also picks up such a reference.

It also remains the case that Matthew's Passion Narrative has its own distinctive elements and is not solely an extension of the Markan material. Particular examples include the death of Judas (27.3–10), the dream of Pilate's wife (27.19), the earthquake that opened up the tombs (27.52) and the placement of a guard at the tomb to prevent the theft of Jesus' body (27.62–66). But there is also a particular, potentially anti-Jewish dimension to Matthew's retelling (interestingly so, for a text supposedly written primarily for a Jewish audience), and this has proved troubling for many interpreters. John's Gospel has famously generated questions as to its allegedly anti-Jewish statements and the identity of the *hoi Iudaioi* in this regard, but such questions there permeate the whole of the Gospel, not just the Passion Narrative. Matthew, by contrast, may be seen exhibiting a particular anti-Jewish tone predominantly in its recounting of the events surrounding Jesus' death, manifesting quite sweeping statements regarding the Jews that have been uncomfortable for many modern interpreters. For example, Matthew seemingly apportions 'blame' for Jesus' death to the whole Jewish people (*'His blood be on us* and on our children' – 27.25), and he draws more attention, than Mark at least, to the 'crowd' that has accompanied Judas to arrest Jesus, by attributing the response of 27.25 directly to them. Similarly, the chief priests take the blood money returned by Judas (27.6), and do not accept his repentance (27.4), further 'confirmation' for Matthew of Jewish complicity in Jesus' death.

Similarly, while – and perhaps because – Matthew is very dependent on Mark for his source material, those points at which Matthew does nuance and/or amend the Markan material are interpretatively revealing and contribute to shaping the tenor of the Matthean account, particularly when they relate to the respective usage of the OT. As we have noted, Matthew does place scriptural fulfilment language on Jesus' lips (Matt. 26.54, 56). This parallels the similar attestation in Mark (14.49), but Matthew offers *double* witness or testimony to the fulfilment (again, what we might term 'Mark plus'). Similarly, Matthew 26.31 appeals to the striking of the shepherd and the scattering of the sheep (Zech. 13.7; cf. Mark 14.27), again with Jesus as the shepherd and the disciples implicitly the sheep. However, Matthew denotes the citation as '*it is written*', suggestive of a formal quotation rather than an allusion (so Mark), an aspect complicated by the fact that, as we noted in the previous chapter, the cited form is a paraphrase of Zechariah 13.7 rather than the LXX text form available to us. The Matthean 'scribal' addition here may serve to function as extra reassurance that, even in the moment of betrayal, God's purposes are being outworked and that (explicit) scriptural warrant is being given in this regard (although it is interesting, again, that fulfilment language is *not* used at this point).

Also notable is that Jesus does reassure the disciples of a future re-gathering (26.32, so also Mark 14.28), but this event – as also with Mark – is not given OT 'proof'; only the desertion is ascribed scriptural warrant. Its absence in respect of the re-gathering is particularly notable for Matthew, as it is the fitting climax of the gospel account (Matt. 28.16–20), and thereby an event for which Matthew could have found prophetic justification and therefore 'evidenced' fulfilment. Mark, of course, has no re-gathering – at least not in its short ending (16.8) – and so scriptural approval for it would be counterproductive. But for Matthew, the 'silence' is loud, and perhaps relates to the diverse sources with which Matthew is engaging.

Matthew 27.9 – Zechariah 11.12

Perhaps the most notable Matthean Passion Narrative addition is Matthew's focus on the fate of Judas in the wider Passion account. Judas repents of his actions and returns the thirty pieces of silver (27.3), though when the Temple authorities do not accept the return he subsequently hangs himself (27.5). The chief priests use the returned money to buy the potter's field as a place to bury foreigners. Matthew notes that the place is called 'Field of Blood', partly in respect of this narrative, but more significantly for our purposes, in *fulfilment* of a prophetic text accorded to Jeremiah (Matt. 27.9–10). This is the only explicit 'fulfilment' statement in the Matthean Passion and is notable both for occurring at a point of departure from, or addition to, the Markan account, and for the fact that Matthew only finds explicit 'fulfilment' in an event not directly related to Jesus' actual death. It is the also the final declaration of fulfilment and the last use of *pleroo* in the Gospel.

This begs the question as to why Matthew felt the need both to include Judas' demise within his Passion Narrative and also to attest its fulfilment designation so uniquely. It is possible that the Judas tradition is a secondary development in the early Church's apologetic tradition,[14] its inclusion necessary to show that the betrayal itself was divinely predicated. It may also be that Judas' betrayal, and the high priests' complicity in it, were viewed as among the more problematic aspects of the Passion Narrative and therefore needed scriptural ratification or warrant.[15] But if so, that still does not quite explain the silence in the Markan and Johannine traditions, in whose accounts the betrayal is equally embedded. The reference to the thirty pieces of silver may be drawn from Exodus 21.32 and the sum that an ox's owner had to pay to a master if the ox gored a slave; if so, it is a desultory amount for Jesus' life, and places him on a similar level to a slave.[16] Judas' mode of death, namely that he *hangs* himself, might also warrant further comment, if only that Matthew makes little of it; that is, one might have expected some reference to the cursing associated with hanging from a tree (Deut. 21.22–23) or perhaps some comparison with Haman and his similar death in Esther 7.9–10.

Particularly in the light of such fulfilment designation, Matthew's narration of Judas' death creates problems with the conflicting evidence of Acts 1.16–19, where, although the field is similarly named (Acts 1.19), Judas purchases it himself as a reward for his actions. He is then said to have been engulfed by the field, with all his bowels flowing out (Acts 1.18). The precise 'historical' circumstance of the event is naturally contested but this is not the only point of contrast, for each author offers a different scriptural text(s) as being fulfilled in/by Judas' actions. We shall look at Acts' appeal to the OT shortly, but for the present it suffices to note that such textual origin varies from Matthew's appeal to the prophet Jeremiah in this regard (Matt. 27.9–10). Or at least the appeal is accredited to Jeremiah, but the material instead actually derives predominantly from the prophet Zechariah.

Furthermore, the citation is a paraphrase rather than a direct quotation, and is 'based loosely on Zechariah 11.12–13'.[17] Thus, as elsewhere in Matthew, while presented as a quotation being fulfilled, strictly speaking we don't have the given text in that regard (cf. Matt. 2.23) and, indeed, the 'variance' is more than has been case in previous fulfilment appeals. Matthew's source is cited:

> *And they took the thirty pieces of silver, the price of the one on whom a price had been set, on whom some of the people of Israel had set a price, and they gave them for the potter's field, as the Lord commanded me.* (27.9–10)

Zechariah 11.12–13 sources some of this imagery, but not all of it:

> *And they set my wages at thirty pieces of silver. And the Lord said to me, 'Place them in the smelter, and I will observe whether it is genuine, as I have been proven for them.' And I took the thirty pieces of silver and threw them into the house of the Lord, into the smelter.* (NETS)

One can thus identify the parallels between Matthew and Zechariah – primarily the thirty pieces of silver – and it is also possible that Matthew has read the subsequent reference to Judah (Zech. 11.14) and associated it with Judas' involvement in the incident.

Yet points of difference remain between the text and its proposed *Vorlage*, notably Zechariah's lack of mention of the potter's field, which seems to be such a key detail for Matthew (27.10). Hence while Zechariah 11.12–13 may provide the primary source for the citation, it may equally not exhaust the interpretative possibilities. The Matthean citation also has some affinity with

Jeremiah 18.1–3 and 19.11 (the reference respectively to the potter's house and potter's vessel – cf. Matt. 27.7, 10 and the expression of the potter's field); Jeremiah 32.6–15 also speaks of the purchase of a field for 17 shekels, albeit with no hugely negative connotations. Neither text, though, technically implies the purchase of a potter's field with blood money.

This raises questions, then, as to why the citation is ascribed to Jeremiah, if the majority of it is derived from elsewhere (i.e. Zechariah).[18] Several options are possible. It could be linked to the wider aspect of Jeremiah fulfilment within the Matthean narrative (cf. 2.17–18), though Matthew might have been more explicit or directive if that were the case. Alternatively, it may be that the 'source(s)' of the quotation are less important than modern interpreters might think, and the reference to Jeremiah is sufficiently covered by the 'potter' references. Or, more likely perhaps, the ascription might convey the idea of an amalgam or plurality of Scriptures, with Jeremiah, the proverbial prophet of despair, being assigned as a convenient source. Taking a wider view, Evans describes this as Matthew resignifying the scriptural citations in the Passion context – 'Judas and the temple priests have re-enacted the scriptural story. It is in this sense that the prophecy has been fulfilled.'[19] To push the matter further, the overall dependence of the Passion Narrative on scriptural formulation continues to be attested, so that even the outcome of Judas' betrayal needed to have an OT basis to it. Here, then, we would seem to have an instance where the Passion Narrative has been shaped to make it scriptural, to make the story 'fit' the expectation, even if the 'expectation' wasn't quite what was really expected.[20]

If, then, the similarities to the Zechariah 'source' remain significant, and if it is indeed the primary source of the citation, Matthew 27.9–10 would afford a further instance of Zechariah 9–14 providing a locus for reflection within the overall Passion retelling. As noted in our Markan discussion, Zechariah has been used of the smitten shepherd quotation (Zech. 13.7; cf. Mark 14.27; Matt. 26.31) and also, more specifically, to articulate the triumphal entry (Zech. 9.9; cf. Matt. 21.5). Matthew, as is its habit, takes Mark's material as part of the entry into Jerusalem

(Mark 11.4–7) but expands or develops it, portraying Jesus specifically riding in on a donkey *and* colt (Matt. 21.6–7). The double reference here is striking, and is classed, like Matthew 27.9, as a fulfilment of Scripture, but it has generated widespread enquiry as to the literalness of Matthew's interpretation, and thus whether Jesus entered Jerusalem on two animals or one. Were it the latter, one might surmise that Matthew has overlooked the standard Hebrew parallelism operative in Zechariah 9.9, but such an oversight would be improbable bearing in mind Matthew's general familiarity with scriptural form. More likely is that Matthew merely wants to avoid any misapprehension as to the fulfilment here, and overstates the case accordingly. It just matters that Zechariah 9.9 is shown to be (properly) fulfilled.[21]

The episode raises some tangential methodological questions, such as whether Mark or Luke likewise view Jesus' riding on the donkey as 'fulfilling' prophecy. Mark presents the episode as an allusion of sorts, though mainly through the lens of Psalm 118, but the Scripture is now *fulfilled* in Matthew's account and also formally quoted by John 12.14–15. The event is somewhat strange, one suggests, and worthy of OT comment, but neither Luke nor Mark offer any formal, scriptural commentary on the event; that is, one wonders whether, in respect of Passion Narrative appeal to the Old Testament, the event *itself* is enough to make the (OT) connection or whether one necessarily requires the explicit formula to signal the relationship – a 'let the reader understand . . .' kind of principle. Why do some events get 'fulfilment' ascribed to them and others not?

Matthew's Jesus before Pilate

Matthew offers a longer deliberation between Jesus and Pilate than that found in either Mark or Luke (though John's narration is far more extensive). Within the Matthean retelling, Pilate's wife makes a fleeting 'cameo appearance',[22] and she perhaps expresses some form of oblique belief in Jesus (27.19), particularly as her request arises out of a dream – normally, for Matthew, a means of protection (2.13, 19–20). Indeed, it is possible that Pilate himself also expresses some form of support for Jesus (or at least he comes off better here than in the other evangelists' recounting), such an assessment depending much on how one interprets his hand-washing action, found uniquely in Matthew (27.24). His washing might be construed as cowardice, particularly as he senses an emerging riot (27.24), but equally it might be seen as a pragmatic action in that regard. Whatever the motivation, the laving does seem to be invested with significance.

The action does not seem to have Roman provenance but rather draws on scriptural imagery. As noted above, it may reflect the imagery of Psalm 26.6 but it more probably relates to Deuteronomy 21.1–9 and the sacrificial process described there. The sacrifice is offered in response to death when the person responsible for it is unknown; the Jewish elders would wash their hands over the sacrificed heifer to enact a ritual of cleansing so as not to contract bloodguilt. If Deuteronomy is in Matthew's mind here, there would be the further irony that Israel – in Matthew's example – are the ones who do have Jesus' blood on their hands (27.24). Pilate tries to disassociate himself from guilt in the ceremonial washing of hands, and for Matthew, the people therefore assume responsibility for Jesus' death. This would also resonate with Judas' acknowledgement that he too has betrayed innocent blood (27.4).

Matthew 27.34, 48 – Psalm 69.21

In the previous chapter we noted the allusion to Psalm 69.21 in Mark 15.36, specifically the offering of sour wine/vinegar (*oxos*) to the crucified Jesus. Matthew continues the appeal to the psalm, retaining the Markan material and similarly echoing it with the *oxos* offering to Jesus on the cross (Matt. 27.48). This appeal to a righteous sufferer psalm – whether Psalm 69 or Psalm 22 – is one further instance of Matthew's dependence on the Markan Passion Narrative, particularly bearing in mind Mark's preference for lament/sufferer psalmic material. Matthew also preserves Mark's Gethsemane allusions to Psalms 42 and 43 – further testimony to the righteous sufferer imagery it inherits from Mark. Matthew makes no significant attempt to avoid the sufferer imagery present within such texts.

Indeed, Matthew seems to extend the reference of Psalm 69, potentially to the point of misreading it. Psalm 69.21 is formed of two parallel statements, one the gift of 'food' (gall – *chole*), the other a gift in response to 'thirst' (vinegar – *oxos*), and the parallelism is synchronous, one surmises. Matthew, however, seems to read the two strands as distinct claims, with both parts needing to be manifest; hence while following Mark in terms of the offering of wine (27.48; cf. Mark 15.36), Matthew amends the Markan source at the point of the previous offering of wine mixed with myrrh (Mark 15.23). Instead of the latter, Matthew renders wine mixed with gall as the proffered drink (27.34), so as to ensure both clauses of the psalmic text are present. This is the same synonymous confusion that we get in Matthew 21.4–5 and riding in on the donkey/colt. Having gone out of his way to ensure that Psalm 69.21 is wholly 'fulfilled' – however anachronistically – the lack of a formulaic editorial fulfilment reference is once more striking.

Matthew 27.51–53 – The Opening of the Tombs

As well as the recounting of Jesus' death, a key Matthean addition to the Markan account is its curious narrating of the opening of the tombs of the dead and the raising of bodies of the holy ones (27.52). These events occur as Jesus breathes his last and are occasioned by an earthquake and splitting of rocks (27.51), as well as accompanied by the splitting of the temple curtain (27.51); Mark records the latter event (15.38) but lacks any reference to the seismic activity, and with Luke and John similarly silent on such matters, Matthew's inclusion of them is intriguing. Similarly, Matthew also differs from Mark in that it is the earthquake that occasions the response of the centurion, namely his assertion that Jesus is the Son of God (27.54), rather than, as in Mark, it being a response to Jesus breathing his last (15.39). An added curiosity is Matthew's subsequent comment (27.53) that after Jesus' resurrection, the holy ones entered Jerusalem in a series of their own 'resurrection' appearances, testimony to which, however, we do not elsewhere have access. And this, of course, generates questions as to Matthew's historical integrity, and what it might have meant by including this brief narrative material.

Such action probably, however, draws on OT material or warrant. Matthew may have Daniel 12.1–3 in mind and its anticipated future general resurrection, or it may be alluding to Ezekiel 37.13 ('*And you shall know that I am the* LORD, *when I open your graves, and bring you up from your graves*') or to the apocalyptic Mount of Olives-splitting imagery of Zechariah 14.4–5 (and thus perhaps establishing an *inclusio* with the opening of the Passion Narrative on that mountain). The first two texts have some form of post-mortem expectation to them, but Matthew's reference is so allusive that one cannot identify a precise source for the imagery. And actually worrying about the precise source may miss the significance of Matthew's point here, and the implications of 27.51–53. At one level, the Matthean narration could seem to create confusion between the events of the Friday and those of the Sunday, but it is likely that Matthew sees the Passion-resurrection as an overall whole, with the events of the Sunday already present in, and occasioned by, Jesus' death. At another level, Matthew's inclusion of the material adds further weight to the notion that the retelling of the Passion has been accommodated to or shared by Scripture, in order to demonstrate the outworking of fulfilment. The 'historical' events behind 27.51–53 are secondary or perhaps even only metaphorical; rather, Matthew wishes to continue to show how Jesus' death, and its wider impact, fulfils Scripture – or to put it another way, that Scripture is dictating and shaping the story, rather than the story shaping the Scripture. Perhaps more than any other instance in the Passion Narrative, this episode testifies to Crossan's 'prophecy historicized' lens.

The Burial of Jesus – Matthew 27.57–61

Like Mark (15.43–46), Matthew describes Joseph of Arimathea as assuming responsibility for Jesus' burial (27.57–60), and in both gospel accounts this is Joseph's sole mention. He disappears off the radar of both accounts as quickly as he came on to it. Unlike Mark, though, Matthew describes Joseph as a *disciple* of Jesus (27.57); Mark, however, has him merely *'waiting for the kingdom of God'* (15.43), and in view of Mark 1.14–15, this would suggest that Joseph was not a disciple, at least not at the point of burial.[23] However, Matthew's other additional detail – that is, that Joseph was a *rich* man – may have further OT relevance. The Isaianic servant is said to make his tomb with the rich (Isa. 53.9), and Matthew may be making such an allusion. If so, it would be an intriguing closure to the Matthean Passion, one that finalized it against the backdrop of the fourth Servant Song.

It is difficult, though, to 'gauge' such an allusion, particularly as Matthew does not elsewhere seem to bring further Isaiah 53 material to his Passion, beyond what he would have inherited from Mark; as with many of the mooted allusions in the Passion Narrative, Matthew might have more explicit signposting to the Isaiah 53.9 link, were it genuinely on his radar. And Matthew's appeal to Joseph's wealth may be motivated by Jesus' encounter with the rich young man and the comparison of a rich man entering the kingdom of God and a camel going through the eye of a needle (19.24). Joseph would be the exception to prove that rule. Instead it is possible that it is Luke that has Isaiah 53.9 in mind in respect of Jesus' burial. It does have Isaiah 53 more explicitly foregrounded (Luke 22.37; cf. Isa. 53.12), and makes reference to Joseph's *dikaios* status, which, as we will see, is a key element of Luke's Passion strategy. However, Luke makes no mention of Joseph's wealth, so any link to the Song cannot originate from Isaiah 53.9.

Conclusion

In terms of its Passion retelling, Matthew relies heavily on its Markan source, reflecting its shape, ethos and 'choice' of scriptural citations. In some instances, it tidies up the Markan account to strengthen a 'quieter' allusion (Matt. 27.43; cf. Ps. 22.8) or to make the assumed connection clearer (Matt. 27.46–47). It also adds extra, non-Markan content, which likewise draws on the

Scriptures, sometimes explicitly (in the case of Judas' death – Matt. 27.9; cf. Zech. 11.12), sometimes more subtly (Jesus' encounter with Pilate – Matt. 27.24; cf. Deut. 21.1–9). But perhaps the most striking aspect of Matthew's Passion Narrative is its contrast to the evangelist's account of Jesus' birth, and the comparative lack of fulfilment quotations – Judas' death aside – found within the Passion account. There is no doubt that Matthew presents Jesus dying 'according to the Scriptures', as the frequent appeals to Psalm 22 and other texts imply. But in view of the high expectations for scriptural fulfilment set in the opening chapters, it is surprising that the *kata tas graphas* categorization is not even more explicit.

4

The Old Testament in Luke–Acts' Passion

One of the primary, assumed dictums or givens of NT scholarship is the assertion that Luke lacks a developed soteriology, or rather that it has no *theologia crucis* or 'theology of the cross'.[1] Luke apparently underscores the importance of the cross and the imperative necessity for Jesus to go to it (Luke 9.22; 24.7, 26), but the 'Why?' question remains unanswered or undeveloped, or so it is commonly observed. Hans Conzelmann, for example, in assessing the scope of Luke's theology, spoke of the absence of 'any direct soteriological significance drawn from Jesus' suffering or death. There is no suggestion of a connection with the forgiveness of sins.'[2] Several recent scholars, however, have challenged this negative assessment.[3] In so doing they have notably made supportive appeal to Luke's use of the Jewish Scriptures so as to tease out particular dimensions to the Lucan understanding of the atonement.[4] Either way, though, it remains uncontested that Luke stresses the absolute *necessity* of the cross, and the way the Scriptures attest to this; such scriptural foundation would seem imperative for our concerns. As Green and Baker surmise:

> It is of great interest that Jesus in the third gospel and his witnesses in the book of Acts repeatedly insist that the suffering of the Messiah is declared in Scripture, yet neither Jesus nor his witnesses have much to say about the purpose of that suffering.[5]

Perhaps Luke sees the whole Christ event as in some way salvific rather than just the Passion and/or Jesus' death, but either way, it does so with particular attention to the fulfilment of Scripture.[6]

○ Very important point.

Therefore, while one might to have work harder to 'unearth' the contours of Lucan atonement theology (the absence of a precise parallel to Mark 10.45, for example, is commonly noted, as is an equivalent to Mark 14.24), Luke's articulation of Jesus' death – in both Luke and Acts[7]– is as scripturally founded as it is in Matthew and Mark (albeit in quite different ways). It may be mediated, as we shall see, through different scriptural texts, and in such a way as to be contingent on Luke's particular theological interests and purposes, and it may be that Luke's Passion Narrative evinces a different tenor or 'feel' from that of its Synoptic siblings. But the importance of demonstrating scriptural warrant and necessity for Jesus' death still remains a Lucan priority, particularly so, one might say, in the text of Acts. Peter Doble summarizes the matter succinctly: 'Luke emphasizes Jesus' approaching Passion more than either of the other Synoptists; so why should an evangelist with no *theologia crucis* make so much of the Passion?'[8]

Luke's Use of the Old Testament

Luke's debt to the Old Testament is surely incontestable. Indeed, it 'is safe to say that there is no major concept in the two books that does not to some extent reflect the beliefs and theological vocabulary of the OT'.[9] Perhaps more explicitly than any of the other gospel writers, Luke locates Jesus specifically as the focus or fulfilment of the Jewish Scriptures, and the one to whom they ultimately point (24.25–27). He gives specific scriptural warrant that the Messiah must suffer (24.26), asserting that such matters were the declaration of the prophets (24.25). Luke does not, however, give any further explication of how this is so and, as Hays surmises, one must 'read backwards' – or reread Luke's account with fresh eyes – in order to discern how Jesus might be the one who is encountered within Moses and the prophets.[10] Likewise, in a subsequent meeting with his disciples (24.44–47), Luke's Jesus similarly testifies that the Law, the Prophets and the Psalms are fulfilled in him. Jesus offers them some limited clarification of how this might be so, particularly in respect of the fact that the Christ must suffer (24.46), but the details of such clarification and the associated explanation remain – sadly! – undisclosed. As we noted in Chapter 1, no specific texts are quoted or cited here, and one senses that Luke sees Jesus implying 'that the Scriptures *as a whole* show the necessity of his life, mission, death and resurrection'.[11] And we might further note that Jesus himself is the interpreter of Scripture in this regard; not only is he personified as the fulfilment of Scripture, he is the one who interprets or defines it as such.[12] It is he, for example, who can authoritatively pronounce on the fulfilment of Isaiah 61 (Luke 4.20–21), fulfilment that he himself personifies and embodies.

Luke's appeal to scriptural fulfilment is therefore not limited to the resurrection narratives. From the outset of the Gospel, the evangelist includes several pronouncements that underscore this fulfilment perspective, Mary (1.46–55), Zechariah (1.68–75), Simeon (2.34–35) and Anna (2.38) all voicing quasi-prophetic announcements in respect of Jesus. Such declarations become 'authoritative announcements of what will take place, and thus the equivalent of scripture'.[13] More specifically tied to Jesus' anticipated suffering, prior to his arrival in Jerusalem, Jesus informs his disciples that everything written by the prophets regarding the Son of Man will be accomplished (18.31). Such a prediction would seem to invest the events of Jerusalem in fulfilment terms, and thereby anticipate that Jesus' death should be understood at least in some fashion through the lens of Scripture. Luke 18.31 might therefore function as a precursor, or advance notice perhaps, of the fulfilment claims of 24.25–27 and 24.44–47, and thereby shed a particular light on what the Passion narration might recount. One might find further precedent for this earlier on in the Gospel, in the paradigmatic Nazareth episode (Luke 4.16–30). In his hometown, Jesus is rejected, as 'prophet' (cf. 4.24), by his own people, but such rejection occurs within the context both of the reading of Scripture (Isa. 61.1–2) and of its exposition, particularly in respect of two biblical figures (the widow of Zarephath and Naaman the Syrian – 4.25–28). Here, then, Jesus' fate is inextricably tied both to the encounter with Scripture (4.18–19) and to his claims to its fulfilment (4.21). At a seminal point in the gospel retelling, well in advance of the Passion events, Luke allows the Prophets – or at least the prophet Isaiah – to sound the imminent possibility of

However, for Judeo- christians, quite familiar with Scripture, this "absence" was not necessarily a problem but rather an opportunity for them to create their own "midrash." But it would be a problem f. Gentile Christians ... with Scripture. [cf.179 al

Jesus' rejection (*as prophet*). In view of such prophetic designation, the fact that a prophet cannot be killed outside Jerusalem
(13.33) casts a shadow over Jesus' journey to the holy city, and to
the anticipated, 'necessary' fate that awaits him there.

Overall, then, Luke's use of the OT may be broadly categorized
as a 'promise-fulfilment' hermeneutic; that is, Luke defines and
articulates Jesus' ministry and purpose in terms of scriptural – and
particularly prophetic – fulfilment.[14] The speeches in Acts, particularly the Petrine ones, are then used to exegete what has happened
in and through Jesus' death and resurrection, and demonstrate the
scriptural – and particularly psalmic – 'fulfilment' that has been so
occasioned. While Mark will say that Scripture must be fulfilled
(Mark 14.49), and that Jesus acts so as to bring to completion
what is therefore necessary, this 'fulfilment' dimension is formally
in-built into Luke's account, so as to get to its very heart.[15] It is
notable, then, that Luke omits the Mark 14.49 reference to scriptural fulfilment (where Matthew actually 'duplicates' it – cf. Matt.
26.54, 56), and such an omission surely warrants some comment
or explication. Most probably, its absence impresses on the reader
the voluntary and obedient nature of Jesus' suffering; while his
impending death was commensurate and in tandem with direct
scriptural fulfilment, Jesus' active embrace of suffering is not
merely for such fulfilment purposes.[16]

At the same time, Luke is fairly conservative in his use of the
Old Testament, at least in not greatly extending the scope of his
inherited (Markan) material. Luke adopts far less of its Markan
source than Matthew, particularly in the Passion Narrative, and
this potentially serves to lessen the explicit scriptural backdrop
to the recounting of Jesus' death that we have encountered in the
other Synoptic accounts.[17] In broader terms, where there is Lucan
innovation, where there is new material, it has significant import
(e.g. the Isaianic appeals of Luke 4.17–19; 22.37), but generally there is just less of it, and the number of non-Markan additions is limited.[18] Moreover, Luke contains 25 quotations – half
Matthew's total and about the same as Mark; that is, in terms of
its length, Luke is relatively frugal compared to its Synoptic counterparts when it comes to formal quotation of Scripture. Likewise,
Luke's technique in using the OT is less prescribed or slavish than

Matthew's; it does not have the formal fulfilment quotations that Matthew and John employ (though 22.37 is perhaps the exception to prove the rule), and allusions to Scripture tend to be more embedded in the Lucan account than formally quoted, in the Gospel at least. But equally, when it does include them, Luke's attention is rather focused, and it invariably exploits OT quotations for as much as it can get out of them; they bear some significant explanatory weight or import. The Old Testament citations can therefore assume programmatic value, notably the citation of Isaiah 61.1–2 (mixed in with Isaiah 56), incorporated into the Lucan account in such a way as to make it the statement of purpose or 'manifesto' for the whole gospel enterprise.

More broadly, scholars continue to debate the extent to which either Isaiah or the book of Psalms might be the controlling aspect for Luke's scripturally shaped narrative.[19] We observed that Mark seems to be framed with an essentially Isaianic flavour, but coupled also with psalmic tones. Luke may be said to do the same, and perhaps even more so. For example, it retains the Markan appeal to Isaiah 40.3 and continues to attribute it specifically to the *book* of Isaiah (3.4),[20] but expands the quotation (3.5) to include Isaiah 40.4 and its associated 'levelling' perspective, which fits well with Luke's more inclusive agenda. This addition may thus be shaped by the wider, more universal lens Luke is commonly said to exhibit, and to which the citation in Luke 4.17–19 also attests (and which also explicitly names Isaiah). Interestingly, when Jesus cites Isaiah 56.7 in the Temple clearance scene (Luke 19.46), the 'for all nations' language is omitted (cf. its inclusion in Mark 11.17). The Lucan exclusion is quite loud, as the presence of the phrase would have seemed actually to suit Luke quite well. Moyise suggests it may have been absent from Luke's copy of Mark (for Matthew also omits it),[21] but it may also be a reflection of the Lucan perspective on the effective demise of the Temple – leaving it behind both conceptually and geographically. Luke Timothy Johnson thus remarks of the Temple: 'It has a significant role for Judaism and for the first Jerusalem community, but not an enduring role for the Gentiles.'[22]

Alternatively, the Psalms may be the OT corpus that drives Luke's account, particularly as it moves to the Passion Narrative, and in view of the widespread appeal to the Psalms corpus found in the early chapters of Acts and the Petrine sermons therein. Some of this psalmic usage draws on the Markan source material, notably the familiar appeal to the rejected stone of Psalm 118.22 (20.17–18, albeit in a slightly variant context)[23] or the association of Psalm 2.7 with the baptism and transfiguration scenes (cf. also the explicit use of Ps. 2.7 in Acts 13.33). Luke also includes several of the Markan allusions to Psalm 22 that are dotted across the Passion Narrative (Ps. 22.18, cf. Luke 23.34; Ps. 22.8, cf. Luke 23.35). But Luke adds his own stamp to the use of the Psalms and thus both distances himself from the Markan use and extends the gospel appropriation of the Psalms in particular ways. For example, Psalm 118 is used as part of the lament over Jerusalem (13.35; cf. Ps. 118.26), uniquely so for the evangelistic discourse, before it is also subsequently applied to the triumphal entry scene (19.38). The other Gospels likewise apply Psalm 118.26 in this regard (Matt. 21.9; Mark 11.9–10; John 12.13), but Luke includes the additional designation of 'king' ('*Blessed is the king who comes in the name of the Lord*' – 19.38), perhaps particularly underscoring the Davidic aspect of Jesus' entry. Indeed, Luke also has a wider perception of Jesus as the new David, with links to Hannah, John the Baptist and Elizabeth underscoring his birth narrative discourse. As a broad rule of thumb, where Matthew portrays Jesus as a new Moses figure, Luke adopts a more Davidic 'Jesusology', and patterns his gospel portrayal accordingly. Doble goes as far as to propose that the Psalms are a 'precondition' for Luke's narrative; that is, they are not just tools for it, rather they critically shape the way Luke is drawing out his story of Jesus.[24]

In sum, Luke's use of the OT sets up the necessity of showing how Jesus' suffering fulfils prophetic expectation. Indeed, because of the particular role given to Satan/devil in terms of Jesus' death (4.13; cf. Ps. 22.3, also 22.31), there is the extra necessity to underscore its dependence on OT Scripture; that is, that it forms part of the overall divine plan and is not merely occasioned by Satan's intervention. One might see the Lucan Passion as the climax of the forces of evil against Jesus initiated by and within the temptation narrative (cf. the devil awaiting an opportune time – 4.13),[25] and the scriptural, divine warrant for the Passion needed to be underscored. Therefore, just as Scripture is put on Jesus' lips in the temptation account as a means of vindicating Jesus (4.4, 8, 12), so it is similarly placed on Jesus' lips in the Passion episodes for further vindicatory purposes (22.37; 23.46).

Luke's Passion Narrative

As with the other Synoptic accounts, Luke has prepared the readers for Jesus' death well in advance of the Passion Narrative, and has similar Passion predictions (9.43–44; 17.24–25; 18.31–33), and in the evocative, central scene of Luke 4.16–30, Jesus barely escapes being hurled off the cliff by his fellow townspeople (4.29, perhaps evocative of the second wilderness temptation (4.5–7)). Underscoring such predictions is the core necessity for Jesus to go to the cross. Jerusalem, to which Jesus is heading, is a place that kills its prophets (13.34), and with the Lucan Jesus cast often in prophetic terms, there is an expectant element as Jesus gradually approaches the holy city.

However, although sharing Mark and Matthew's early pre-Passion soundings as to the anticipation of Jesus' death, even a cursory read of Luke's Passion Narrative shows it to be fundamentally 'different' from its Synoptic partners. Whereas it might still possess the same basic shape as the Markan and Matthean accounts (and thereby stand in continuity with the primitive Passion Narrative format), both in its overall tenor and in its inclusion – and exclusion – of particular material, Luke's narration gives shape to a very particular type of discourse. Within Lucan scholarship, this has generated extensive debate as to the extent and nature of Luke's sources.[26] Some have surmised that Luke relies on external, written sources beyond Mark,[27] whereas others have argued that it amends and reworks the Markan material in a way befitting its theological interests.[28] Either way, key points of variation remain. For example, Luke reverses the order of elements within the Passion recounting: the abuse of Jesus (22.63–65) precedes the condemnation scene (22.66–71) whereas Mark places it afterwards; the curtain is torn (23.45) before Jesus' death (23.46)[29] whereas in Mark/Matthew it takes place afterwards (Mark 15.37–38) – further indication, perhaps, of a particular Lucan take on the Temple as institution. There are also other small additional details or inclusions that add flavour to the Lucan account. For example, Jesus heals the ear that has been cut off (22.51), perhaps to indicate that the activity on the Mount of Olives is consistent with the rest of Jesus' (healing) ministry. Or Luke's Jesus prays only once in the Mount of Olives scene (22.41–42),[30] perhaps thereby moderating the agony exhibited by Jesus in the Markan portrait.[31]

More significantly, Luke also includes a large amount of material not found within the other Synoptic equivalents. Unlike Mark or Matthew, for example, Luke has little or no night-time Jewish trial scene. Instead night is the time of Peter's denial (at which Jesus is somehow present – 22.61); daytime sees a trial of sorts (22.66–71) but there are no witnesses as in Mark or Matthew, and no accusation relating to the fall of the Temple. Jesus' response to the council's question as to his messianic status (22.67) is somewhat indirect, more of a non-answer than an answer (22.67–68). Like Mark, it still retains the allusion to Psalm 110.1 and the session at God's right hand, but the corresponding citation of Daniel 7.13 (cf. Mark 14.62) is omitted (the Son of Man is named but is no longer 'coming on the clouds').[32] Even without the full Danielic claim, however, it is a claim to a status that those gathered find reprehensible (22.70–71), even if Jesus is innocent of it.

Similarly, there is no Jewish death sentence pronounced on Jesus. Instead he is taken to Pilate, where he is accused of not paying his taxes and claiming to be a king (23.1–2); that is, Jesus' accusers attempt to locate the arrest in a political context – they have to, because Jesus is 'innocent' (*dikaios*) of Jewish charges. Luke also (uniquely) includes Jesus' interview with Herod (23.4–12), portraying Pilate and Herod 'cosying up' to each other and making for rather unlikely bedfellows (23.12). Such narrative presentation may well be driven by OT considerations, however. The 'two witnesses' principle of Deuteronomy 19.15 could have accounted for the trial with *both* Pilate and Herod – thereby formally confirming the innocence of Jesus. Equally, bearing in mind Luke's liking for the psalm, the double 'trial' may reflect an allusion to

Psalm 2.10 and the respective king and the ruler figures expressed therein – Herod the former, Pilate the latter.

This draws out, then, two key, fundamental distinctives to the Lucan portrayal, both of which shape – and are shaped by – Luke's use of the Old Testament. First, Luke has dispensed with the Markan – and, to a lesser degree, Matthean – focus on the abandonment or desertion of Jesus. All Jesus' supporters are with him at his death, watching on (23.49), albeit from afar (cf. Ps. 38.11).[33] Luke makes no use of the Zechariah 13.7 citation tradition (i.e. Mark 14.27) that encompassed the core Markan desertion motif; it would be inappropriate to include it, as Luke's Jesus is not 'deserted'. The shepherd may still be smitten but the sheep are not abandoning him. Peter may still deny Jesus but his faith will not fail (22.32), and at the point of arrest, the disciples seek to intervene and cut off an ear of the high priest's slave in an attempt to avoid Jesus' arrest (22.50). The omission of the Zechariah 13.7 quotation might also have been occasioned by the subsequent Lucan narrative, as its Markan application requires Jesus to go to Galilee (Mark 14.28), an event that does not find a place in Luke (though equally not in Mark either, of course). In this aspect at least, Luke's (Passion) use of the OT is shaped *by* – rather than shapes – the concerns of that Passion discourse. For aside from the desertion context in which Mark presents it, the Zechariah 13.7 quotation could have been quite useful for Luke, its 'shepherding' connotations commensurate with the wider Davidic/shepherd lens with which Luke works. But unlike Matthew, he does not feel able to use it.

Similarly, unlike Matthew, Luke does not preserve Mark's appeal to Psalm 22.1 (Mark 15.34 – cf. Matt. 27.46), for again, to do so would be contrary to the Lucan 'non-abandonment' portrayal. Luke retains other Passion-related elements of the psalm (Ps. 22.18, cf. Luke 23.34; Ps. 22.8, cf. Luke 23.35) but dispenses with its opening verse. Instead Luke places an alternative psalm on Jesus' lips as his final words (Ps. 31.5, cf. Luke 23.46), and thereby removes the implications of the cry of dereliction; the Lucan Passion Narrative becomes 'a more serene and noble affair'.[34] In other words, the specific OT material Luke employs, and the particular character he wishes to invest in his Passion recounting, are mutually informing.

Second, a core, distinctive feature of Luke's account of Jesus' death is its presentation of Jesus as *dikaios*, normally translated as 'righteous' or 'innocent'. Luke marshals a cast of witnesses to testify to Jesus' *dikaios* status – Pilate, Herod, the good thief – and at the moment of Jesus' death, the centurion at the cross declares that, rather than being a s/Son of God (so Mark 15.39; Matt. 27.54), the crucified figure is *dikaios* (Luke 23.47). This may reflect Luke's pro-Gentile orientation ('son of God' is perhaps a more Jewish appellation), but it more probably reflects Luke's focal emphasis on Jesus' innocence throughout the Passion retelling. Luke also includes the narrative of the 'good thief' and Jesus' interaction with the other, accusatory criminal figure (23.39–43). The good thief is aware both of his own guilt and of Jesus' innocence, and condemns the other crucified figure for *not* recognizing Jesus' righteous state. Other Passion Narrative figures are also shown to be *dikaios*; Joseph of Arimathea for example, is notably exculpated from the Sanhedrin's decision to put Jesus to death (Luke 23.50–51). Likewise, in Acts, Luke draws parallels with Stephen and Paul (and their similar innocence), parallels that serve to underscore the imitation aspect of the presentation of Jesus' death therein.[35] Jesus' wider *dikaios* characterization may evidence Luke drawing on Isaiah 53.11, where the 'righteous' (*dikaios*) servant might make many others similarly righteous (*dikaioo*). But it might equally be derivative of, or echoing, the psalmic *righteous* sufferer that Luke and the other Synoptics draw on (e.g. Pss. 22 and 31), and especially Psalm 34, with its repeated appeal to a *dikaios* figure(s) (Ps. 34.15, 17, 19, 21).[36] Whichever 'source' one finds persuasive in this regard will no doubt mutually inform whether one believes either Isaiah or the Psalms to be Luke's primary OT textual lens.

Luke's Upper-Room Discourse

We have noted that the boundaries of the respective Passion Narratives are necessarily fluid, and there is a good case for arguing that the Lucan Passion Narrative begins at 22.1. It seems to demark a new section of discourse, the explicit naming of Satan's entry into Judas being one such determining factor (22.3), and the setting up of what appears to take the form of a farewell discourse, akin to that found in John 13 – 17. The definition of the contours of the Passion Narrative hence varies between commentators; Doble, for example, clearly demarks the Lucan version as comprising chapters 22 – 23[37] whereas Heather Gorman does not 'initiate' it until 22.66. As with the Markan account, and bearing in mind the fluidity of when the Passion Narrative might be said to begin, there is good reason to consider the discourse of the upper room, and the way it might use the OT to reference Jesus' death.

At one level, Luke retains those aspects of OT reference in the upper room that we located in both Mark and Matthew. The Son of Man's fate is codified or anticipated (22.22); it is conceivable that the betrayal declaration of Luke 22.21 alludes to Psalm 41.9 (formally cited by John in similar circumstances), and the Lucan words of institution (22.19–20) could pick up the imagery of Isaiah 53, verses 6 and 10. Equally, the exhortation to break bread together in Jesus' remembrance (22.19) perhaps echoes the imagery of Passover tradition and the appeal to remembrance found there (Exod. 12.14, 25–27).[38] The inauguration of the New Covenant with blood perhaps likewise recalls Exodus 24.8 or possibly Jeremiah 31.31–34, the core text for Hebrews for such matters. But there are still points of Lucan difference or nuance. Jesus' anticipated death is declared at the outset of the narrative (22.15), and done so more overtly than in the other Synoptic accounts. And the Lucan words of institution famously lack the explicit referral to 'for many' (the so-called 'cup word' – Luke 22.20; cf. Mark 14.24), as does the subsequent declaration of 22.27, which lacks the ransom logion found in Mark 10.45/ Matthew 20.28. Such lacunae, and the implied lack of a vicarious suffering, hence caution against any swift or immediate application of Isaiah 53 to the Lucan Passion account.

Isaiah 53.12 in Luke 22.37

But Isaiah 53 does not go away so easily, as Luke's next formal quotation is drawn from the fourth Servant Song (Isa. 52.13 – 53.12), specifically the citation of Isaiah 53.12 in Luke 22.37.

The discourse picks up prior material, and looks forward, one surmises, to the type of death Luke is going to ascribe to Jesus. We have already flagged the citation in the introductory chapter, remarking both on its inherent oddity and its being a – relatively rare – appeal to the fourth Servant Song, but it warrants further consideration here.

The passage involves a curious exchange between Jesus and the disciples in respect of what they might take with them on their – impending? – journey. Jesus casts their minds back to a previous missional dispatch (Luke 10.1–12), and questions them as to their provision and sufficiency for it (22.35). For this next trip, however, they are to take not just a bag and purse – which they did not require the first time around – but also a sword, if necessary selling their cloak so as to purchase one (22.36). Such a requirement is then given scriptural warrant by Jesus, but in a somewhat striking fashion. First, Jesus declares that the cited Scripture is fulfilled *in him* (22.37), and will effectively reach that fulfilment in the imminent events. Second, the text Luke places on Jesus' lips requiring such christological fulfilment is Isaiah 53.12d (*'And he was counted among the transgressors'*), the final verse of the fourth Servant Song. There is a minor lexical variation from the LXX in Luke's text but the difference is minimal and, accompanied by the 'what is written' introductory formula, there is no reason not to think that the Isaiah text is being cited. Luke stops there, unfortunately, and does not expand or exegete the citation; the final clause of Isaiah 53.12 and the vicarious aspect of the servant's work (cf. *'he bore the sin of many, and made intercession for the transgressors'*) perhaps linger in the background, but they remain unquoted. Such silence has been read both ways. For those wishing to see a meta-Isaianic perspective on the text (the 'maximalists'), Luke has only to mention part of the verse for the whole to come forth. For those of a more minimalist persuasion, the silence is loud; the lack of citation and the lack of developed vicarious discussion cautions against applying a wider Isaiah 53 frame of reference.

Making sense of the citation is thus far from straightforward. The Isaiah text makes no mention of swords, and one struggles to see the immediate connection between the OT quotation and its new context. The disciples reply that they already have two swords (22.38), to which Jesus responds that that is sufficient (22.38). Narratively, there seems to be a subsequent connection to the cutting off of the servant's ear with a sword during Jesus' arrest (22.49–50), and the authorities also come bearing swords (22.52), but it is not evident how either aspect necessarily relates to the Isaiah citation. It is thus difficult to discern why the citation is included, and particularly why the strong introductory formula language of fulfilment is so used. This is the only instance where Luke uses such fulfilment terminology in respect of an OT citation (far less so, therefore, than Matthew or John), and such uniqueness must surely be a significant ingredient for its interpretation. Also distinct is the fact that this is the only gospel text that formally quotes from the fourth Servant Song, and this combination of both 'unique' elements may be decisive. Or rather, it may be that the citation, for all its strangeness (and maybe *because* of it), forms a pivotal moment in unpacking how Luke wishes to portray Jesus' death, especially as it is the final action before the departure from the upper room and thus when the Passion Narrative conceivably begins. (It is striking, then, that there is no discussion of this quotation at all in Hays' recent *Echoes of Scripture in the Gospels*;[39] one might have expected at least some engagement with what appears to be such a significant text).

Bearing in mind its particularity, one suggests that Isaiah 53.12 – and arguably the wider context of the whole Servant Song – offers an interpretative window on to the subsequent Lucan Passion account. Luke has previously used Isaiah 61.1–2 in this regard (Luke 4.17–19), and we might read 22.37 in similar 'programmatic' fashion. One might suggest that Luke's interests here are *christological* rather than soteriological, and that its reading/use of the Isaiah 53 text reflects this.[40] In the Servant Song, Luke finds a pattern for the character or role of Jesus, and cites that particular aspect of the Song (Isa. 53.12c); but it draws back from, or at least is more circumspect about, what that might entail in terms of the Servant's atoning achievement (cf. the absence of Isa. 53.12d). Such a programmatic function, but one perhaps with an even wider scope, is effectively the conclusion of Pao and Schnabel, who contend that:

Placing the quotation from Isaiah 53 at the beginning of the passion narrative, and prefacing the quotation by a long and emphatic introductory formula . . ., Luke wants his readers to understand Isaiah's fourth Servant Song as the hermeneutical key to the narrative of Jesus' suffering and death.[41]

This might be manifest in a number of ways. Luke may be portraying Jesus as self-identifying with the Servant and the experiences that befall him within the Song. This places a significant burden on the fulfilment criterion, and begs the question as to how/when it is fulfilled (Jesus' arrest? The walk to Golgotha? The crucifixion itself?). However, it takes seriously the fact that Jesus claims Isaiah 53.12 is written *about him*. It is in spirit with and, indeed, would significantly contribute to the notion that Jesus dies as *dikaios*, and would give scriptural attestation to that fact. The 'lawful' one must be counted among the 'lawless' ones, and visually so, one might suggest, bearing in mind Luke's particular attention to the two other figures with whom Jesus is crucified (cf. Luke 23.39–43).[42] In sum, one might say that the formal, explicit – and rather strange – citation of Isaiah 53, at such a key point in the Lucan narrative, is of sufficient weight or significance to open up the door to the full extent of the fourth Servant Song.

Johnson adds further weight to this view, venturing that the Isaiah citation confirms that Jesus' death is integral to scriptural fulfilment, rather than occasioned by human activity. There is, he suggests, also something 'vicarious' about the death, in that it is for others, even though Jesus himself will be innocent.[43] Moo likewise thinks this verse starts to give 'Jesus' death redemptive significance'[44] – an important factor bearing in mind those preconceptions as to Luke's undeveloped soteriology. As noted above, attention to the potential full gamut of Lucan use of the OT opens up the possibility for further insights into Luke's *theologia crucis*.[45]

Luke 23.30 – Hosea 10.8: The Daughters of Jerusalem

One of Luke's additions to his Markan source is his account of Jesus' exchange with a group of women as he journeys to his place of crucifixion (Luke 23.27–31). The women are said to be wailing for Jesus and beating their breasts, and Jesus addresses them partly to reassure and partly to challenge. The inclusion of such material may derive from Luke's desire to portray Jesus as *dikaios*, and therefore offer further 'witnesses' in that regard, but Luke also records Jesus' address to the women and the 'reassurance' it gives. This address includes a quotation of Hosea 10.8 (Luke 23.30), a text with which we have thus far had little interaction and similarly not one *directly* linked to Jesus' death.

Technically, the Hosea text seems more of an allusion than a quotation, and the reference seems to be relatively incidental to the overall narrative, not adding much to the portrayal of Jesus himself. However, Hosea's prophetic announcement of judgement, placed on Jesus' lips, may serve as warning, particularly to Jerusalem, of the consequences of rejecting the one who is Messiah, and their impending, resultant distress. Thus while not explicitly tied to Jesus' death, the citation still underscores the Lucan perception of Jesus as a rejected prophet, and particularly one rejected in/by Jerusalem (cf. 13.33–34). It may, though, also refer indirectly to the ensuing crucifixion scene. The question in respect of the green and dry wood (*zulos* – 22.31) may possibly resonate with the ensuing death on a tree/cross (*zulos*),[46] and the dire implications of the event that will shortly take place on a 'dry' tree.

Psalm 31.5 in Luke 23.46

In terms of its use of the OT, perhaps the most significant change Luke makes to the Markan Passion Narrative is the removal of the Psalm 22-derived cry of dereliction (Mark 15.43). Moo observes the shift succinctly: 'a prayer of trust (Ps. 31.5) is substituted for a cry of despair (Ps. 22.1).'[47] Eklund likewise draws attention to Luke's 'peaceful relinquishment rather than an anguished cry'.[48] Other elements of the Psalm 22 matrix remain, notably the division of the garments (23.34b; cf. Ps. 22.18), and it may be that Joseph of Arimathea's patient expectation of the kingdom of God (23.51) is also an echo of Psalm 22.28 (cf. Mark 15.43). There may even be some development or emendation of the Markan tradition; it is the leaders – rather than the more passive people – who engage in the mockery (23.35), but the echo of Psalm 22.8 would still seem to be encompassed,[49] particularly as Matthew 27.43, as we have seen, seems to have made a similar move (Matt. 27.43). The Lucan mockery (23.35–36) may be milder than the Markan variety (Mark 15.30–31) but it is still present in Luke's account and is mediated through a Psalm 22 tapestry, continuing the process begun in the previous verse (23.34b).[50]

Such affinity with Psalm 22, however, does not extend into the first clause of 23.34 (i.e. 23.34a), in which we find a further Lucan word from the cross, or at least an alleged one (*'Father, forgive them; for they do not know what they are doing'*). A number of early manuscripts lack the prayer/citation, hence it is often bracketed off in English translations, indicative of its being a later addition to the Lucan account. However, aside from whether it is 'original' or not,[51] its feel remains quintessentially 'Lucan'; there are parallel appeals to human ignorance later on in Acts (3.17; 13.27), and Stephen appropriates similar language in his prayer for his oppressors (Acts 7.60). Either way, though, the forgiving demeanour fits ill with Psalm 22's depiction of the righteous sufferer, whose intent towards his opponents is generally critical and negative (e.g. 22.12–13, 16, 21) rather than forgiving or merciful. This cautions against moving too quickly to apply the full gamut of Psalm 22 to the Lucan Passion scene;[52] that is, Luke can use Psalm 22 for mockery purposes and for the splitting of clothes, but does so selectively and without utilizing the full 'claim' of the psalm. This likewise cautions, then, for the treatment of Mark, and the automatic assumption that the whole of the psalm is used; Luke would seem to evidence an instance where the gospel writer is selective about which parts are 'appropriate' and which are not.

Instead Luke 23.34a, genuine or otherwise, may be understood as an allusion to Leviticus 5.17–18 and the implications that even sins committed in ignorance necessitate some form of atoning function. As such, it is possible that Isaiah 53.11–12, and its vicarious element, continues to be in Luke's mind here, and/ or it might also perhaps pick up on the forgiveness of sins aspect of the Last Supper and the new covenant imagery therein.[53] More pertinent, though, is the correlation of Luke 23.34a with the ethos and flavour of Psalm 31.5, cited by Luke's Jesus as his last words (23.46), and exhibiting a different tenor or feel from Psalm 22.1. Both texts are addressed to God as 'Father' and pertain to a righteous – or *dikaios* – figure, but Luke 23.34a presents more the ethos of Psalm 31.

Indeed, Psalm 31 is, like the previously encountered Psalms 22 and 69, another example of the righteous sufferer tradition.[54] The sufferer is scorned by his/her adversaries (31.11) but faithfully endures (31.14–15), calls out for help from God (31.16–18) and is vindicated accordingly (31.21–22). Such righteous suffering is akin to that of Psalm 22[55] but with one significant difference, namely that the psalmist of Psalm 31 does not experience abandonment by God. God is privy to, cognisant of the suffering endured (31.6–8), and the psalmist is confident in the divine vindication of the righteous one (31.1–3). Luke's citation of the psalm is therefore in tandem with and contributory to the overall tenor of the Lucan Passion Narrative – it is 'the culmination of Jesus' trust in his Father and his determination to do his will'.[56] It is the very association of Jesus as God's righteous one that shapes Luke's Passion narration, and thereby his choice of OT citation; a Psalm 22.1 – type cry of dereliction would have militated against that, as Luke's Jesus is not abandoned (as we have seen, there has been no citation of Zech. 13.7). Instead placing Psalm 31.5 on Jesus' lips 'intensifies the second part of the Gethsemane prayer: *but* not my will but yours'.[57] The lack of the cry of dereliction also means there no is confusion with Elijah (cf. Mark 15.35–36), and therefore that Passion Narrative element is missing from Luke's account.

Luke's citation of Psalm 31.5 is broadly equivalent to the LXX form except for two lexically minor but interpretatively significant changes.[58] First, the future tense, 'I will commit', has become a present one, 'I commit'; the expectation of the psalm is now 'fulfilled' as Jesus imbibes his role and offers the prayer in the present. Similarly, with the addition of 'Father', Jesus assumes the role of the sufferer but directs the prayer to God as 'Father'; that is, Jesus embraces his – necessary – suffering with due faithfulness as 'son', commensurate with other key moments when he obediently addresses God as Father (10.21; 22.42). There is also probably some wordplay within the citation, with Jesus' commitment of his 'spirit' (*pneuma*) resonant with breath of life (*pneuma* can be similarly used in this regard), and also the possibility of extension to the ongoing work of the Spirit (*pneuma*) in the book of Acts. Furthermore, Jesus' words are echoed at Stephen's death (7.59), and one surmises that Psalm 31.5 is similarly alluded to at this point. This further ties Stephen to Jesus as a successor in *dikaios* suffering, particularly in respect of their respective final words (Acts 7.59/Luke 23.46 and Acts 7.60/Luke 23.34). We also further note that Psalm 22.1/Mark 15.34 is *not* spoken at the moment of Jesus' death – it is a cry, one assumes, in response to the agony of the cruciform moment. Luke's citation, however, comes at point of death, and such death is instant; at Jesus' final moment, he is heard praying *Scripture*.

One further comparative comment might be made. In view of Luke's replacement of Psalm 22.1 with Psalm 31.5, does that mean, as Paul Foster surmises, that Luke has 'corrected' the Markan usage?[59] That is to say, does that mean, as Foster suggests, that Luke 'misunderstood' Mark's appeal to Psalm 22, believing it to espouse only divine abandonment and not the associated vindication, and thus felt it necessary to 'correct' it? On Foster's construal, Luke finds Mark's psalmic appeal one-sided and hence problematic, and therefore necessarily cites instead the more 'righteous' Psalm 31. This is not impossible, of course, and the differences between the evangelists at such a key point certainly warrant explanation; but one wonders if Foster's response is necessarily the case. It is equally possible, more likely perhaps, that Luke's choice of text is merely conditioned by his own perspectives and intentions – Psalm 22.1 simply does not align with Luke's purposes. He has already significantly edited his Markan source, and arguably added to it equally significantly, and the citation of Psalm 31.5 is merely one further instance of this. And is the change of psalm really a 'correction' anyway? Both psalms are righteous sufferer psalms and it would seem legitimate to replace one with a – more suitable – other.

The Acts of the Apostles

In turning to Acts it is harder to extrapolate reflection on Jesus' death from its association with the vindication of the resurrection (cf. 2.35; 5.31, though for an exception, see 20.28). There is a more holistic relationship between Christ's death and resurrection, rather than the demarcation into two separate or distinct events. But there is still merit in seeking to focus (primarily) on how the OT is used to speak of Jesus' death, as this will equally be the tenor of our later chapters. Citation of the Old Testament in Acts invariably occurs within the context of preaching and prayer, particularly the former, and we will explore some of the references to Jesus' death presented within such discourses.[60] Acts continues, though, to uphold the necessity for the Messiah to suffer, and for the way the Scriptures testify to that fact. Luke gives particular designation to the prophets in this regard (Acts 3.18) but does so – as is characteristic elsewhere in the NT – without naming specific Scriptures in this regard. We find, for example, a further instance of the Lucan 'prophetic expectation' hermeneutic in Paul's sermon at Pisidian Antioch (13.27, 29), again stressing the scriptural warrant for Jesus' death (but with the Jerusalem authorities complicit in the fulfilment of the expectation through their rejection of Jesus).

Acts 1.20 – Psalm 69.25

Like Matthew, Luke finds OT fulfilment in Judas' death, again, one surmises, to demonstrate the divine purpose within the betrayal episode (Acts 1.15–20). Luke's narrative of Judas' death – and its rather evocative bowel-splitting consequences – are somewhat in tension with the Matthean portrayal, and the respective authors find different scriptural sources with which to endorse the event. But it remains interesting that both Matthew and Acts root Judas' wider action in terms of OT fulfilment, albeit with different texts and in different forms.[61] Luke's scriptural appeal (Acts 1.20) is ascribed to David and is cast as Scripture to be fulfilled, David thereby in some sense foretelling the action of Judas (1.16). Whereas Matthew's Judas citation was a paraphrase of both Zechariah and Jeremiah imagery, Luke's source text is a composite quotation, drawing on both Psalm 69.25 (cf. Rom. 11.9–10; 15.3) and Psalm 109.8.

In the latter, Psalm 109-derived part, Luke emphasizes the need for a replacement for Judas, and that may, however figuratively, underscore the significance of the Twelve and the OT testimony to their role and function (i.e. the figurative aspect of the twelve tribes of Israel). Psalm 109.8 has no apparent cruciform reference though; it is merely a designation of the imminent need for a replacement. The first part, however, quoting Psalm 69.25 (Luke amends the plural 'their' of the LXX to the singular 'his'), seems more pertinent in this regard. It draws on a psalm we have seen used in Luke's Passion narration (23.36; cf. Ps. 69.21), and interestingly, it is a further righteous sufferer one, commensurate with that corpus which shapes the portrayal of Jesus in his suffering and death. The appeal to the psalm would seem to locate the Judas episode within the wider Passion Narrative, and 'locate' it within the scope of Jesus' death as a righteous sufferer. As we have seen, Luke's key interest is in finding scriptural fulfilment for Christ's sufferings (and resurrection), but he can also find similar justification for more 'secondary' events like Judas' death. This is in contrast to Matthew who, while still finding scriptural fulfilment for Judas' demise, does not draw the same parallel in terms of the righteous sufferer corpus but instead looks to Zechariah and Jeremiah.

Acts 2.25–31 – Psalm 16.8–11

Peter's Pentecost speech (2.14–40) begins with the citation of Joel 2.28–32 and finds within that text the promise or prophecy fulfilled by the Pentecost event. Peter then turns to a recounting of those recent occurrences that have occasioned Pentecost, and cites Jesus' death (2.23) and resurrection (2.24), before appealing to a direct citation of Psalm 16.8–11 (2.25–28) as testimony to both events (with subsequent appeals also to Ps. 132.11 (Acts 2.30) and Ps. 110.1 (Acts 2.34–35)). The handing over was part of God's plan and foreknowledge (2.23), and this is juxtaposed with scriptural warrant (2.25–28), effectively equating Scripture as the means by which such divine foreknowledge is manifest.

Peter steps through the claims of Psalm 16, and from it finds scriptural authentication for Jesus' death and resurrection. He reasons that David wrote the psalm (such Davidic authorship is key for Luke's argument), but must have done so prophetically, for David died and his tomb is still with them (2.29). Since David must thus have (properly) died, he must therefore have been speaking prophetically about a future 'other' who would not (like David) be abandoned to Hades or whose flesh would not experience corruption (Acts 2.27; cf. Ps. 16.10). Luke therefore reads David as speaking concerning Jesus (2.25), and anticipates what will subsequently befall Jesus – and thus that the messiah will never lose sight of God (2.25). Scriptural precedent is therefore found for the idea that after death Jesus will not experience corruption. Just as the resurrection may be shown to be according to Scripture, Jesus' death is likewise so by logical extension.

It is ambiguous within Psalm 16 as to whether the sufferer avoids death or overcomes it by some means, or perhaps even experiences direct heavenly entry, akin to figures such as Enoch or Elisha. Luke removes some of that ambiguity; he is clear that Jesus has died but stresses that death could not contain or control him (2.24). Luke seems to understand the psalm as showing that Jesus is not *abandoned* to Hades (death), and/or to experience its corruption (2.27). Indeed, the psalm's emphasis on such 'non-abandonment' gives further warrant for Luke's removal of such imagery from the gospel Passion Narrative (e.g. Mark 15.34); it is incompatible with the wider portrait of Jesus' death across both Lucan texts.

Psalm 16 is cited again in Acts 2.31 (Ps. 16.10), but specifically in terms of the resurrection, and thus the latter emerges as a primary lens through which Luke is reading the Scripture. One might suggest therefore that Psalm 16 functions as a kind of 'script' for Luke on which to map or demonstrate the resurrection (cf. Acts 13.35, where Psalm 16.10 is similarly cited in this regard), but it has implications for Jesus' death too, and specifically God's vindication of Jesus in and through it. Scripture is used to demonstrate that the crucified Jesus was (now) *not* dead. This is subsequently backed up with an allusion to Psalm 132.11 (2.30), which affirms David's prophetic credentials and the divine oath, made with David, of a messianic figure who would sit on David's throne and, in light of Psalm 16, not be abandoned to death.[62] Peter's Pentecost address continues with further scriptural citation (2.34–35, quoting Psalm 110.1), and this is also linked with

Jesus' death, but again essentially from the perspective of Jesus' resurrection and exaltation. The psalm testifies to the vindication of the one crucified (2.27); God has acted and exalted him (just as Jesus attests before the council – Luke 22.69).

Acts 3.12–26

Peter's second speech (3.12–26) comes after the healing at Temple's Beautiful Gate (Acts 3.1–10). It gives a second recounting of the events of the Passion, but a more kerygmatic focus, and with emphasis on those present having rejected the holy, *righteous* one (3.14). This revisits the language of *dikaios* as seen in the gospel account, and recognizes Luke's continued emphasis on that dimension of Jesus' death. Once again, Luke underscores that the event is God's fulfilment of what had been promised through the prophets, namely that the Messiah would suffer (3.18). Luke garners no evidence for this, though, and it may be that 3.18 merely reflects 'a dogmatic early Christian presumption to biblical exegesis: the prophetic tradition in its entirety had announced that the Messiah would suffer'.[63] It is interesting, though, that bearing in mind Luke's previous dependence on the Psalms for outworking Jesus' passion, the 'prophets' (only) are named in this regard. There are a number of scriptural allusions present throughout the speech that derive from outside the prophetic or psalmic corpuses (e.g. Exod. 3.6, cf. Acts 3.13; Deut. 18.15–19, cf. Acts 3.22–23), and the reference to 'all the prophets' may therefore reflect a more general 'all Scripture' designation (cf. Luke 24.25–27, 44–47). At the same time, Jesus is – just as in the Gospel – implicitly cast in prophetic terms, as a 'prophet like Moses',[64] and Peter sounds a severe warning about the implications of not listening to a prophet (3.22–23). Jesus' 'prophetic' character therefore seems to matter here.

The background to the affirmation of 3.18 is more ambiguous perhaps. The reference to God's glorification of his *servant* Jesus (3.13), when set against this backdrop of prophetic fulfilment, may be an allusion to Isaiah's servant, particularly as the language of glorification (Acts 3.13) is similarly applied to the Isaianic figure (Isa. 52.13). This would lend further credence to the notion that the Fourth Servant Song shapes Luke's Passion understanding. However, Moses can also be described in servant terms (cf. Josh. 1.7, 13), and David equally so by Acts itself (4.25), prior to two affirmations of Jesus in that regard (4.27, 30), so the case for Isaianic dependency is far from proven. Indeed, the ambiguity of the servant reference may be indicative of the way Luke draws on *both* psalmic and Isaianic material, rather than of his being dependent exclusively on only one of the respective sources.

Either way, the fulfilment aspect of 3.18 is critical. One might surmise, for example, that for Scripture to be fulfilled in terms of a suffering Messiah, the absence of the latter necessarily required a default to a Suffering *Servant* figure, as no other such figure would have emerged. On the other hand, bearing mind the prior appeal to Davidic/psalmic material, it is possible, particularly bearing in mind the polemical nature of Peter's address, that Luke is advocating a new, or specific reading of David's sufferings, and thereby articulating the sense of a suffering, 'quasi-Christ' figure.

Acts 4.11 – Psalm 118.22

The 'rejected stone' quotation (Psalm 118.2) is a familiar one from the other Synoptic accounts (Matt. 21.42; Mark 12.10; Luke 20.17), and 1 Peter will likewise employ it within its catena of stone-themed imagery (1 Peter 2.4–8). Luke appeals to the psalm prior to Jesus' death (20.17) but also reuses the citation in his second volume (Acts 4.11), in a restatement of what seems to have been an established text in relation to Jesus' death. In this latter instance, however, Luke replaces the notion of rejection with a different verbal idea, that of 'scorning' (cf. Luke 18.9), perhaps to underscore the full extent of the verdict against Jesus. He also inserts 'by you' into the psalmic text to emphasize the leaders' complicity in the action. The sense of the original citation still stands, though; a familiar Scripture is applied against the leaders in respect of Jesus' death, and therefore restates and compounds the accusation against the Council. The structural differences between a capstone or a cornerstone are not insignificant, of course, and builders may wish to comment accordingly (!), but the key point remains that a central 'stone' has been rejected, and Psalm 118.22 remains a core text for the interpretation of Jesus' death.

Acts 8.32–33 – Isaiah 53.7–8

It is in the narration of Philip's encounter with the Ethiopian eunuch (Acts 8.26–39) that we find a further Lucan quotation of Isaiah 53. The narrative evokes a number of OT parallels, but it is the Isaiah text that is the one formally cited (8.32–33) and which occasions the scriptural reasoning in which Philip and the eunuch begin to engage. The citation is from Isaiah 53.7–8, and it is the only OT text that Luke actually 'writes' in Acts (the other citations are 'voiced' by the speechmaker), and this would seem a not insignificant detail.[65] The eunuch questions the identity of the figure about whom Isaiah speaks, and explicitly as to whether the prophet is speaking about himself or another figure (8.34). The eunuch's query is a presenting one both for himself and for biblical interpreters; the pericope might appear to shed light on contemporary perceptions of the Isaiah figure, and the extent of any expectation as to the 'fulfilment' of such prophetic texts.

As with our previous discussion of Isaiah 53, there is some ambiguity as to what interpretative significance the citation might generate. The eunuch is found reading the passage, and Philip uses the Isaiah text as the starting point for some kerygmatic explanation (8.35), but strictly speaking, he does not apply it specifically to Jesus' death, nor offer any exposition of it in that regard. The Scripture is thus presented more as a launch pad for discussion, and the implication is that other Scriptures were likewise used. This seems not dissimilar to the kind of exposition Jesus engages in in Luke 24.27, when he appeals to the wider contours of the Jewish Scriptures.[66] Similarly, as with other instances of potential Isaiah 53–Jesus association, Luke applies neither vicarious suffering language nor imposes any explicit sacrificial aspect to the sheep/lamb figure, omitting the critical last part of Isaiah 53.8 ('*he was led to death on account of the acts of lawlessness of my people*'). This cautions against interpreting wider Isaianic reference into the citation, as it is only the demeanour of the Servant's suffering that Luke attests here.[67] Bearing in mind the fulfilment language elsewhere in terms of Lucan use of the OT, its absence here is notable, as it would seem to have been a primary citation with which to draw such fulfilment implications. It is too much, then, to say explicitly that 'Philip explains that this prophecy has been *fulfilled* in Jesus.'[68]

On a glass-half-full reading, however, the Isaianic text is still the one cited, and at least highlights the *possibility* of innocent – or righteous – suffering in respect of Jesus' death, and in that sense is resonant with the wider Lucan Passion explication.[69] It is, of course, conceptually quite plausible that Luke/Philip here is applying Isaiah 53 within the wider context of Jesus' death, even if that is not quite what Luke specifically states, and one might suggest that there is something *purposeful* to the implied suffering.[70] And in the light of 8.35, one has to ask whether, if it is *not* Jesus' death being discussed, then what else did Philip and the eunuch's conversation comprise? The citation's association of the Servant's fate with humiliation (8.33) might also resonate with the claims of the Christ hymn of Philippians 2.5–11, which, as we shall see, both maps Jesus' death on the cross and does so in ways associated with Isaiah 53. We might say then that, while it remains contested as to whether the use in Acts 8.28–35 of Isaiah 53 can fully bear the soteriological burden of vicarious suffering, as a minimum, it accords the principle that Scripture was being read in an attempt to make sense of Jesus' death, and that it needed to be read with some christological lens.

Other instances in Acts

Within the rest of Acts we see further association between Jesus' death and the OT's testimony to it. In Paul's word of exhortation in the synagogue at Pisidian Antioch, essentially a retelling of the story of Israel, he places particular emphasis on the scriptural precedent for the rejection of Jesus (13.27, 29). Jerusalem's leaders' and residents' failure to understand the Scriptures – that is, the prophets – meant that they inadvertently fulfilled those Scriptures by their rejection of him (13.27). Again, the identities of the prophets are not formally specified, and the essential innocence of Jesus continues to be upheld (13.28), but there are some potential points of specificity. For example, the narrative of being taken down from the tree – rather than the cross – probably reflects an allusion to Deuteronomy 21.22–23. And Paul's warning in respect of neglecting God's action in Christ's death and resurrection is attributed both generally to the prophets but also specifically to the prophet Habakkuk in the citation of 1.5 (Acts 13.41). The latter quotation is not explicitly about Jesus' death, but it does extend to its ramifications.

We might also mention other examples of wider appeal to prophetic testimony. Acts 10.43, and its appeal to the prophetic testimony to the reception of forgiveness of sins for everyone who 'believes', may be an allusion to Isaiah 53.1, 5–6, and the believe/transgressions language found there (even if it is 'all' the prophets who so testify – 10.43). Peter's preceding account of the Passion also applies scriptural imagery to Jesus' death, with a further appeal to the Deuteronomic imagery of hanging from a tree. Later on, in Thessalonica, Paul is found proving from the Scriptures that it was necessary for the Messiah to suffer (17.2). And one surmises that even under house arrest, when seeking to explain the message of Jesus in terms of the Law and the Prophets (28.23–24), a key feature of that explanation would surely have been that Jesus' death was *kata tas graphas*.

Conclusion

Luke's use of the Jewish Scriptures in respect of Jesus' death is both similar to, and different from, its Synoptic counterparts, but the points of contrast outnumber the similarities. Luke may continue to draw in part on Psalm 22 or Psalm 110, and its Passion Narrative may still have the same basic shape as the Markan variety, but Luke put its own 'stamp' on the retelling of Jesus' death. Jesus' *dikaios* status is emphasized, as is the way his death was both in obedience to the Father and the fulfilment of prophetic expectation. Luke's retelling is shaped by an extensive appeal to the Psalms corpus, but also, more elusively perhaps, to the Suffering Servant of Isaiah 53. As with both Matthew and Mark, there can be no doubt that, for Luke, Jesus' death was 'according to the Scriptures'.

5

The Old Testament in John's Passion

John's dependence on OT quotation and allusion is sounded from the outset of the gospel account, its opening declaration of '*In the beginning* . . .' (1.1) sending the reader back to the opening chapter of Genesis and the creation narrative found therein. The rest of the gospel account is similarly embedded with OT imagery and points of reference, whether in terms of formal citation (the appeal to Isaiah 54.13 in John 6.45, for instance), wider narratival representation (such as the parallels between the heavenly feedings of Exodus and the Bread of Life discourse – John 6.25–65) or the broad comparison between the Sinai generation and the era inaugurated by the Jesus event (cf. e.g. 1.17). Elsewhere in the Gospel, the Scriptures are said to testify to Jesus (5.39), and Jesus himself claims that he was the one about whom Moses wrote (5.46).[1] One might surmise even that John puts Jesus' words on the same level as Scripture; the disciples' recollection of the scriptural testimony in John 2.17 (Ps. 69.9), and their 'belief' in it, is put in equivalent terms to their remembrance of Jesus' words (2.22). 'Scripture' and 'Jesus' word(s)' become effectively equivalent in terms of their perceived authority, and 'fulfilment' expectation is ascribed not just to Scripture but to Jesus' own words and predictions (18.9, 32).[2] From the outset, then, one might suggest that John's high Christology impacts on its perception of the scriptural texts; whereas Scripture was traditionally indicative of the divine will (and of course still remained so for John), in the Fourth Gospel it also becomes indicative of the will *of Jesus*, as the figure who is one with the Father (10.30; cf. also 17.21).[3]

It is thus both unsurprising and characteristic of its *modus operandi* for John to – continue to – appeal to the OT when narrating the events around Jesus' death, and Scripture 'forms the foundational narrative on which the Fourth Gospel is built'.[4] This may be mediated through direct quotation of OT Scriptures (1.23; 2.17; 6.31), but John is less dependent on such direct citation than either Matthew or Luke–Acts, and indeed has significantly fewer quotations than either of them. While the so-called Book of Signs (John's first 12 chapters) has occasional OT quotations, it is really only in the Passion account that the direct quotation mode of citation is extensively exploited, and the language of 'fulfilment' properly adopted. One might suggest, therefore, that just as John's retelling of the Passion account manifests some sort of narrative heightening, so also the 'volume' of scriptural citation likewise increases, and comes to a head to 'intensify' that (Passion) narrative situation, especially, as we shall see, in terms of the notion of fulfilment. Like Matthew, John has a number of explicit fulfilment quotations, each pointing to a particular text or nugget of Scripture. In contrast to Matthew, however, these fulfilment quotations feature towards the end of the gospel account rather than at the beginning. Where Matthew made – surprisingly – little direct fulfilment appeal in his Passion Narrative, John ventures in the opposite direction, loading his Passion with scriptural fulfilment, even if in quite surprising fashion, as we shall see. Graham Stanton surmises that the evangelists' contrasting use/location of fulfilment quotations offers an appropriate window on how they are respectively using the Old Testament: 'whereas the Johannine citations set the "world's" hostile reaction to Jesus and his work in the light of prophecy, the Matthean quotations portray the person Jesus and the nature of his sending.'[5]

John's Passion Narrative

John's Passion Narrative has a substantially different flavour or tenor from that we have encountered in the Synoptic accounts, and particularly that found in the Markan portrayal. This is perhaps most apparent in the overall indication of the cross as the moment of Jesus' glory; the cross embodies triumph rather than defeat (John 17.1).[6] As with Luke, gone is the Markan cry of desolation

(Mark 15.34) and the abandonment by his disciples (Mark 14.50); in its place comes the presentation of the cross as Jesus' victory, a crucifixion in the presence of his family and friends (19.26–27), with new familial relationships so formed as the Beloved Disciple welcomes Jesus' mother into his home (19.27). Again as with Luke, John makes no appeal to Zechariah 13.7 (cf. Mark 14.27); even more than in the Lucan instance, to do so would run counter to the very ethos or core of the Johannine Passion, and its essential 'non-abandonment' portrayal. The actual crucifixion scene is recounted in comparatively brief terms (19.16–30), notably so in terms of the implied – glorious – importance of the event, and the repeated appeal to scriptural fulfilment found within it. The 'trial' before Pilate (18.28 – 19.16), by contrast, is an extended, quasi-comical affair, and is thus much longer than the crucifixion scene it directly precedes.

John's account also varies from its peers in a number of other aspects. Most notable, particularly for historical-Jesus scholars, is the different timescales that the respective traditions utilize. Whereas the Synoptics adopt a Holy Week calendar whereby a Passover meal is eaten on the Thursday evening (cf. Mark 14.12; Matt. 26.17; Luke 22.15), and hence Jesus dies on the Friday (still the Passover), John depicts an alternative chronology for these events. There is no eucharistic inauguration – no Passover meal is eaten (cf. 18.28); as we shall see, for John, Jesus is – and thus dies as – the Passover Lamb (cf. 19.29; 1.35), ahead of the Passover feast. Similarly, John lacks any Gethsemane exchange between Jesus and his disciples. John 17 is often spoken of as evoking the 'spirit' of Gethsemane, at least in terms of narrative sequence compared to the Synoptics,[7] but 12.27–36 is perhaps the closest Johannine equivalent, interestingly so bearing in mind the citation of Psalm 6.3–4 in John 12.27. The Markan Passion Narrative placed Psalms 42 and 43 on Jesus' lips at this point in Gethsemane, whereas John appeals to Psalm 6 instead. Jesus poses the question as to whether he should 'pray' the request that he might be saved from death, but declines to do so (12.27), and fittingly so, for in the Johannine Passion there is no sense of Jesus exhibiting uncertainty about his mission.[8] Indeed, for John to have Jesus praying the hesitant, or uncertain Gethsemane prayer within the Passion account would fit ill with John's portrayal of Jesus as the good shepherd who – avowedly – lays down his life for the sheep (10.11), and this may have occasioned the absence of 'Gethsemane-type' material later on in the gospel account.[9] For John's Jesus confidently embraces his ultimate glorious task. Where Mark's Jesus prays that the 'hour' might pass for him (Mark 14.35), John's Jesus confidently announces that the hour of his glorification has come (John 12.23); he is expecting Judas and the events that will subsequently unfold (18.4). As such, Jesus can rebuke Peter for cutting off Malchus' ear (or earlobe – 18.11), because he is supremely confident of his destiny (notably only John identifies Peter as the one who enacts the incident). The irony, of course, is that Judas and the authorities come with lanterns to seek after the one who is the light of the world (8.12; 9.5) . . .

Likewise, John's Jesus carries his own cross and does not require the crucifer assistance of Simon of Cyrene (19.17). One might draw connections here with the sacrifice of Isaac, with Jesus, like Isaac, carrying the wood for his impending death (Gen. 22.6), but John does not really signal or exploit such an association. John also lacks any formal trial before the Sanhedrin; it is really an early morning conversation between Annas and Jesus (18.19–24), not even the Lucan short gathering (22.66–71). A confident Jesus asserts his position without fear, before being dispatched to Caiaphas and Pilate; indeed, John seems to portray *Pilate* as being on 'trial' rather than Jesus, with the governor frequently dispatched in and out, to deal with both Jesus and those seeking his death. As Carroll and Green surmise: 'the cursed prisoner becomes the judge'.[10] One might surmise, though, that a trial scene is not necessary, as Jesus has been on trial for the whole of the gospel account; indeed, many Johannine scholars have speculated that the structure or shape of the Gospel is an overall trial scene.[11] And a trial scene of sorts has already taken place, in which the Sanhedrin gathers, in response to the raising of Lazarus, to plot and agree to put Jesus to death (11.47–53).

In sum, therefore, while there is a recognizable similarity between the Johannine and the Synoptic Passion Narratives (the basic contours and framework remain the same), their respective attentions to key elements vary significantly, and hence we have different stories or episodes in this regard. Such a combination of similarity and variance extends also to their respective use of the Old Testament and the particular texts and interpretation they so draw in this regard.

John's use of the OT and the Farewell Address

As we have already seen, John generates questions as to when its Passion Narrative starts or when it is appropriate to view it as starting, particularly if one is looking at the influence of the OT in this regard. The extended, so-called Farewell Address of John 13—17 is a prolonged narrative of Jesus' final moments with his disciples, but it is not until 18.1 that Jesus and the disciples exit the upper room, even though the bidding to leave was given as early as 14.31. However, there are significant OT-related elements of the pre-John 18 discourse that warrant further comment, particularly for how they shed light on John's overall perspective on Jesus' death, and not just its explicit narration within the Passion retelling. John has used the OT previously to speak of Jesus' death (1.36) or to speak of the implications of belief in him (3.11–14; cf. Num. 21.4–9), so such discourse is not restricted to its Passion account (just as we saw in the case of Mark and Luke). Jesus predicts his death in terms of being *'lifted up'* (8.28; 12.32–33; cf. 18.32), a play on the way the cross is the moment of triumph when Jesus is *'raised up'*, but also an image drawn from OT narration (3.14) and the lifting up of the Son of Man (12.34). Furthermore, John is distinctive for the way it patterns Jesus' ministry in relation to – and potentially in fulfilment of – Jewish festivals (notably the Passover but also Tabernacles and the Feast of Dedication), and this gives a further dimension to its engagement with the OT. Hence while John has rightly been divided up into the so-called Book of Signs and a Book of Farewell (the latter culminating in a Passion sequence), there is good reason to see the Passion as a fitting climax to the whole gospel account – or even that 'the Passion in John encompasses nearly the whole of the Gospel.'[12]

John 12.38–41

Key in this regard is John 12.38–41. The unit is located within the pre-Passion context but it acts as a building block between the prior signs discourse and the farewell, Passion material that is about to ensue. In 12.38–40, John includes two Isaiah quotations as a framework or window for interpreting particular aspects of Jesus' death. The first of these (12.38) draws from the Fourth Servant Song (Isa. 53.1) but does not explore the vicarious or suffering aspect of Jesus' death in this regard, suggesting instead that the Song might be seen as having a wider frame of reference than just those matters. The second citation (12.40) quotes Isaiah 6.10, a text also used by Mark 4.12. John ventures that Isaiah has seen Jesus' glory (12.41), probably a reference to the preceding verses where the prophet sees the enthroned Lord (Isa. 6.1–3), but with Jesus understood as the enthroned one;[13] that is, for John, when Isaiah spoke the words of the prophecy, he was speaking specifically about Jesus.

One might make two further observations about this pericope. First, John's concern seems to be to discern OT precedent or testimony for the 'non-response' to Jesus; that is, why, despite the signs, do people not believe in Jesus (12.37)? Just as scriptural warrant will be sought for Jesus' death, so is it likewise sought to confirm the 'response' of those who do *not* believe in him and his death. This resonates with the earlier debates Jesus has with his opponents over scriptural witness; they think they understand Scripture as the source of eternal life (5.39), but it is Scripture that testifies against them, as it testifies to Jesus (5.40) and was written about him (5.46). Second, John here introduces fulfilment language for the first time in respect of his mode of OT citation; that is, in 12.38, John moves from an '*it is written*' introductory formula in the first half of the Gospel (cf. 2.17), and on to the notion of 'fulfilment' in its later chapters.[14] This signals, as we shall see, a different or heightened lens for interpreting the way the OT is being used to interpret Jesus' death, and particularly to underscore its anticipation in the Jewish Scriptures. Indeed, by using the language of fulfilment, John implies that the 'true meaning of Scripture cannot be found within the text itself, but only *in its fulfilment in Jesus* and in the sending of the Spirit'.[15]

This also has ramifications for what John understands by the term 'Scripture'. For example, in the light of 12.38–41, Johannes Beutler notes that 'in all instances [from 12.38 onwards], "scripture" gives witness to details of the passion and death of Jesus',[16] so focused is John on the associations between Jesus' death and scriptural fulfilment. Likewise it generally matters more for John that 'Scripture' is fulfilled rather than for particular passages to be specifically cited. Beutler also appeals to John 19.36–37 in this regard, for example, and the two quotations found therein; as we will see, neither is especially specific in terms of referent, and thus John seems to have in mind a wider purview of scriptural discourse here rather than particular, specific texts.

John 13.18

One might speak similarly of John 13.18 and the citation of Psalm 41.9 (Ps. 40.10 LXX) therein. While technically part of the upper-room discourse, and thus prior to the Passion, the psalmic citation heralds the betrayal that is to come and can thus can hardly be detached from the impending Passion retelling. Several points are of note here. First, the introductory formula for the citation is, as with 12.38, the language of fulfilment. We have noted an equivalent, possible allusion to Psalm 41.9 in Mark 14.18–21, but the Johannine example here is presented as a formal quotation, and one being directly *fulfilled* in the imminent betrayal. John's text form is emended from that of the LXX (e.g. the verb 'to eat' is different), but the presentation as a fulfilment quotation adds weight and significance to the anticipated event. To emphasize the fulfilment aspect, John reiterates Judas' partaking of the bread (13.26–27, 30), removing any ambiguity as to the identity of the betrayer. John therefore actually explicates *and* narrates the fulfilment, thereby underscoring for him the significance of the fulfilment aspect. Jesus is thus seen to know the referent of the Scripture, *and* to enact and direct its fulfilment (13.18). He also restates the necessity for its fulfilment later on in the farewell account (17.12), emphasizing the requisite nature of the betrayal. The scriptural referent in 17.12 is left unspecified (the only designation is that it might be fulfilled), and is generally thought to reflect back to 13.18 and, by association, to Psalm 41.9.[17]

Second, Jesus' contextualization of the Psalm 41.9 citation – that is, that he announces the betrayal prior to its occurrence so that when it ultimately happens the disciples will believe (13.19) – effectively casts the psalmic text in *evidential* fashion. This puts further weight on the text; it can bear the confirmatory authority as testimony to the nature of the imminent betrayal (and by extension, to the resultant death). In short, when John's Jesus wants to proffer evidential proof of his imminent death, it is Scripture that is so used; that is, John finds in Psalm 41.9 both fulfilment *and* evidential capacity. Such evidencing may also have a wider referent. Bearing in mind that a meal has yet to be eaten, the reference to '*ate my bread*' (13.18) may seem initially misplaced. However, it may also refer back to John 6 and the Bread of Life discourse; the verb John uses in 13.18 (*trogo*) is only used elsewhere in John in relation to that discourse (four times – John 6.54, 56–58), and the echo back to chapter 6 may thus have occasioned the verbal change in 13.18.

Third, the wider context of the psalm – if taken into account – deepens the sense of betrayal Jesus predicts (and maybe also extends a pointer to Jesus' resurrection). On the one hand, the one who is '*lifting their heel*' against Jesus (Ps. 41.9b) is more than merely the one who dined with him (John 13.18); the psalmist describes the betraying individual as his '*bosom friend*' (Ps. 41.9a) and thus adds extra poignancy to the betraying relationship. There are perhaps further OT parallels here, with the betrayal of David by Ahithophel, who leaves the king and joins up with Absalom (cf. 2 Sam. 15.12). Elsewhere John will portray Jesus as a quasi-Davidic, royal sufferer, and Ahithophel's betrayal, that of a trusted counsellor, may serve as a precedent for that experienced by Jesus in the case of Judas. On the other hand, the surrounding verses of the cited text – that is, Psalm 41.8 and 41.10 – pick up potential imagery of 'rising up', the imagery to which John frequently refers in respect of the final resurrection (6.39–40, 45, 54; 11.23–24), and also of Jesus' own (20.9). Such references draw on the same Bread of Life discourse to which John 13.18/Psalm 41.9 might have alluded back, and a biblically literate audience familiar with the whole psalm might thus hear in 41.8–10 an anticipation of Jesus' resurrection and vindication.

John 15.25

One further pre-Passion Narrative quotation is worthy of discussion, and perhaps requires it, and that is the textual citation in John 15.25. Its citation is striking at a number of levels, with A. T. Hanson calling it 'an unusually explicit reference to the fulfilment of scripture'.[18] Jesus is speaking of the opposition – the hatred even – he experiences as being a fulfilment of Scripture (15.24), but in doing so he describes the cited text as originating from 'their' law (i.e. that of his (Jewish?) opponents and not 'his' own – cf. also 10.34). This is not only strange in historical-Jesus terms (is not Jesus Jewish?), and the particular phrasing probably reflects the redactional voice of the so-called Johannine community, but it also poses interesting questions as to how John will subsequently use the Jewish Scriptures to speak of Jesus' death. It could be seen as setting Jesus – and his subsequent crucifixion – apart from, or *outside* of the Scriptures, but that view seems most unlikely bearing in mind the 'fulfilment' hermeneutic found so explicitly here and in the subsequent Passion account. It might also, bearing in mind that John 15 relates to the anticipation of the Paraclete/Spirit, imply some replacement agenda in respect of reception of the Paraclete.[19] In such a way the Spirit – as the ongoing remembering of Jesus' words (14.26) – could be seen as 'replacing' the prior 'textual' authority found within John, especially as Jesus' words themselves are being accorded quasi-scriptural status by John. But again this view seems unlikely; not only does it fail to take account of the other ways John positively appropriates the Scriptures, it misses the polemical or provocative perspective on scriptural interpretation that John seems to inscribe here. In this sense the Paraclete will lead the believer into all truth, into a fuller understanding of the Scriptures, rather than into the 'inferior' understanding demonstrated by the 'others' – be they the Jews or otherwise.

As such, the polemical 'their' probably pertains to John's assessment of the scriptural *misunderstanding* that Jesus' opponents exhibit; that is, they search the Scriptures but do not understand the way their own Scriptures attest to the divine attestation of the righteous figure that they oppose. The interpretation of the Jewish Scriptures is foundational for discerning who Jesus is, and John consistently offers a critique of those whose interpretation of the Scriptures fails to embrace Jesus (cf. Nicodemus in 3.1–10 or the Jewish authorities in 5.39–40). As such Margaret Daly-Denton surmises that the quotation in 15.25 attests Jesus – and the Johannine community – having superior understanding of the Scriptures, rather than Jesus denigrating them. For those Johannine readers who have experienced suffering and persecution (cf. 9.22; 12.42; 16.2), they may be reassured by the parallel between Jesus' experience and their own, and the fact that Jesus has given scriptural warrant/interpretation to this effect.[20] Jaime Clark-Soles takes the argument one stage further, contending that the citation in John 15.25 is effectively a 'hate' command rather than a 'love' one, John being a notable exception in not citing Leviticus 19.18. Rather than loving *the neighbour*, it is the more inward-focused appeal to love *one another* that functions as a mark of enforcing the boundaries of community membership. Those who are outside the community do not 'love' Jesus and instead 'hate' him, and effectively do so in a manner foretold by the Scriptures. Jesus' opponents are thus not law *breakers*, rather law *fulfillers*; as Clark-Soles observes: 'they have indeed fulfilled *their* law, but in the most tragic of ways.'[21] Scripture – and its interpretation – thus become used as markers of sectarian identity, of determining who is 'in' and who is not.

One further possibility is that John 15.25 is a polemic on a particular form or section of scriptural text; that is, Torah. John does not quote directly from Torah and that may be a factor; the Passion fulfilment citations, as we shall see, derive from the Psalms and from Zechariah. There is the Passover imagery, of course, in respect of the Paschal lamb, and it is possible that John 15.25 may be offering a critique that Jesus' opponents do not understand what 'the Law' is in this regard. However, this may be putting too much burden on the text and thus 'L/law' here probably means the fall gamut of the Scriptures rather than any individual portion within them.[22]

Whatever the significance of the introductory formula, the *Vorlage* of the signalled quotation is not entirely clear, or at least may derive from a couple of potential sources. Psalm 69.4 ('*those who hate me without cause*') is one such possibility. The psalm is used elsewhere by John, in instances broadly relating to his death (Ps. 69.9, cf. John 2.17; Psalm 69.21, cf. John 19.28–29); its use here in the Farewell discourse might suggest that the wider narrative of the psalm as a righteous sufferer text formed a core ingredient of John's purposes, interestingly so bearing in mind the psalm's similar usage in the Synoptic Passion accounts. Alternatively, Psalm 35.19 (likewise '*those who hate me without cause*') might also offer a potential source text. It represents a further righteous sufferer psalm, and there are wider aspects of Psalm 35 that might pertain to Jesus' subsequent death/rejection (35.4, 11, 16); one can see how such texts could inform the Johannine Passion depiction.[23] Ultimately, though, the precise origins of the quotation are less significant than the hermeneutical questions so raised. The polemical nature of the citation's delivery, and its implied consequences, are what remain particularly significant. It is the *effect* of the citation, as direct scriptural appeal, that is ultimately determinative, and Scripture becomes one of the media by which the Johannine community define themselves. How a person reads or appropriates Scripture, and thus how they respond to its testimony to Jesus and his (righteous sufferer) death, function as an identity marker as to membership of and involvement in the Community.

Passion Citations

The OT citations become more frequent as the Passion ensues, with four direct appeals to fulfilment in the crucifixion scene of 19.16–37. John narrates the death of Jesus very succinctly, particularly bearing in mind its climactic aspect. The prior exchange with Pilate, for example, is notable for both its greater length and its general lack of OT citation, the latter feature somewhat striking bearing mind the volume of scriptural association in the second half of the Gospel. At the same time, this only serves to underscore the – comparative – emphasis John places on the crucifixion scene as the climax for the fulfilling of Scripture, and its primary locus, three of the four citations in the unit being cast in explicit fulfilment terms.

Psalm 22.18 in John 19.24

The first of the Johannine Passion direct fulfilment quotations is the most extended of the four and thus appears to have particular significance, especially in view of its seemingly 'forced' application to the narrative at hand. A direct appeal to Psalm 22.18, it finds formal scriptural precedent in the soldiers' division of various parts of Jesus' clothing. This division of clothes is scripturally echoed throughout all the gospel Passion Narratives (Mark 15.24; Matt. 27.35; Luke 23.34), with the allusion accordingly to Psalm 22.18, and this suggests the association was well embedded within and across early Passion tradition. John's usage, however, differs from its Synoptic counterparts. Not only does it utilize a formal fulfilment quotation rather than a more embedded allusion to make the point, it also, unlike the Synoptics, uses the first-person voice to heighten the significance of the reference (*'they divided my clothes . . ., and for my clothing'*), further inculcating the Johannine notion that Jesus is the one about whom Scripture speaks. Furthermore, in quite awkward fashion, John (mis?)reads the apparent parallelism of Psalm 22.18 as incorporating two distinct actions rather than as comprising one and the same activity. It is possible, of course, that John has failed to understand the parallelism of 22.18 (akin perhaps to Matthew's apparent portrayal of Jesus' triumphal entry on a donkey and a colt (Matt. 21.5), thereby similarly 'misreading' the parallelism citation of Zech. 9.9), but it seems more probable that John's intention is to remove any suggestion that the incident was *not* in fulfilment of Scripture, and to ensure that every dimension of the text is thereby properly fulfilled. Either way, John's concern for scriptural fulfilment would seem somewhat 'overexact'.[24]

It remains the case, though, that the choice of this text as one being 'fulfilled' remains somewhat strange. The Synoptic accounts – notably Matthew – do not see the need to formally quote Psalm 22.18 in this regard; and in terms of texts to which to appeal as vindicating the crucifixion as being in fulfilment of Scripture, Psalm 22.18 would seem to be more at the incidental rather than evidential end of things. However, John characteristically portrays the crucifixion scene as Jesus' royal triumph (John

19.19), rather than the locus of defeat, and this may have likewise shaped his use of the psalmic tradition, causing him to read the Psalm differently from the Synoptics. Daly-Denton argues for this more triumphal reading, finding echoes here of David's tearing of Saul's robe (1 Sam. 24.1–22) and the effective vindication of David's impending kingship.[25] Similarly, it is not really clear what interpretative significance is drawn from the seamless tunic for which lots are cast. Some have surmised that this is a reference to the unity of the Christian – or Johannine – community, or alternatively the tunic might be said to allude to the clothing worn by the high priest (Lev. 21.10), and that Jesus is being depicted in sacerdotal terms (and thus as superior to the high priest). However, if that is the case, there is little other reference in John to support portraying Jesus as a priest figure (king rather than priest seems to be the primary role John has in mind). Overall, then, it is evident that Psalm 22.18 – and its 'fulfilment' – matter for John, but it remains less evident as to specifically why/how so.

More generally, the citation of Psalm 22.18 underscores the way there seems to be a corpus of 'common' OT texts that are functioning consistently in the Passion recounting, and whose usage can serve to bridge any John–Synoptic divide. We might similarly note that Psalm 118 – and probably Psalm 69 – are used across all four evangelistic accounts, and give further basis for the existence of a 'core' corpus of OT texts used consistently across the Gospels in seeking to explicate the significance of Jesus' death. As was the case with Luke (who appealed instead to Psalm 31.5), John does not use Psalm 22.1 at the high point of the crucifixion scene. Indeed, again like Luke, any appeal to Psalm 22.1 would be counter-intuitive for John's purposes; there is no agony here for Jesus, and to admit so would be contrary to the particularly Johannine portrayal. And there is likewise no taunt episode (Ps. 22.8) akin to that found in Matthew and Mark. It is possible that John 19.18 has Psalm 22.16 in mind, but that is really only a faint echo. More significant perhaps are possible links between Psalm 22.17 and John 19.36, with John's emphasis on none of Jesus' bones being broken and hence their 'countability' (Ps. 22.17); or alternatively, there may be a further allusion to Psalm 22.15 in John 19.28 (see below). At the same time, there is a limit to the extent to which John uses Psalm 22 in that its remit does not – indeed it *cannot* – include reference to Psalm 22.1, as that runs contrary to the Johannine depiction of the crucifixion as 'glorious'. Such selectivity – or limitation – in the use of the psalm might then sound a note of restraint when mooting the application of the whole of Psalm 22 to the Markan Passion. There is, as we have suggested above, good reason for such application, but the Johannine usage cautions against applying it without due attention.

Psalm 69 (or Psalm 22.15) in John 19.28–29

In contrast to 19.24, John 19.28–29 offers no specific OT text as cited, or at best does so only minimally, yet it still exhibits a formal declaration of the fulfilment of Scripture.[26] It is possible that the fulfilment clause is associated with the preceding declaration that Jesus knew that all was finished (19.28; cf. also 19.30) and, if so, one might read the verse as a summative declaration of the 'complete fulfilment of Scripture'; that is, in Christ's glorious death, all is finished in terms of scriptural expectation.[27] Even at the moment of death, Jesus is in control, and knows/confirms the climax of the scriptural witness to his death. More strongly than that, perhaps, Jesus takes the lead and 'gives the cue, as it were, for the fulfilment of the scriptures to be enacted'.[28]

Most commentators, though, associate the fulfilment declaration with Jesus' subsequent declaration that he is thirsty (19.28), and look therefore to a textual location to which John might be referring in this regard. It is possible that John has in mind Psalm 22.15, particularly bearing in mind both the psalm's wider Passion association and the fact that the succeeding verses (22.16–18) have just been on John's radar. The psalmist's declaration of thirst also occurs when laid *'in the dust of death'* (22.15b), and are thus potentially commensurate with the crucifixion scene. A more likely candidate, though, is Psalm 69.3, John thereby making another appeal to the lament psalm tradition, and to one it has previously cited (John 2.17, cf. Ps. 69.9; John 15.25, cf. Ps. 69.4).[29] The case for Psalm 69.3 is further premised on the gift of sour wine (*oxus*) that is offered in response to Jesus' declaration of thirst (19.29). In similar fashion to Mark 15.36/

Matthew 27.48/Luke 23.36, John seems to allude to Psalm 69.21 and the gift of sour wine (*oxus*) found there given to the suffering figure. one might further note that, of the four Gospels, only John has Jesus declare his thirst; this is partly further indicative of the way John's Jesus is 'in control' of events, but also consistent with how – as in 19.24 – John expands or develops the OT citation more than its Synoptic equivalents.

The wine is proffered to Jesus on a branch of hyssop (19.29), a historical detail that is often queried bearing in mind the insufficient stiffness within hyssop to perform the task. The Synoptics offer an alternative means for the distribution (cf. Mark 15.36), but John's choice of hyssop seems deliberate even if historically implausible. As part of the Passover, hyssop was dipped in the lamb's blood to mark the door (Exod. 12.22), and it would seem John wishes to underscore the Passover association in this regard. Thus Scripture and story are here mutually informing. John wishes to portray Jesus' death as the Passover lamb; Jesus is handed over to be crucified at the very time the Passover lamb is to be killed (19.14–16; cf. 1.29, 36), the scriptural imagery thereby shaping the way John recounts the story.[30]

Exodus 12.46 (or Psalm 34.20) in John 19.36

The third fulfilment citation is as ambiguous as the second but builds further on its predecessor's Passover imagery. Unlike the previous citation, however, it lacks Synoptic precedent. The context for the quotation is the soldiers' efforts to ensure Jesus had died; having confirmed he had done so, they did not need to break his legs to expedite the death (John 19.31–33). Unsurprisingly for the Johannine Jesus, he is able even to control when and how he dies. John can hence appeal that this fulfilled the scriptural citation, namely that '*none of his bones shall be broken*' (19.36). As with the previous citation, there are several possibilities for the source text. But bearing in mind the presenting Passover imagery, 19.36 is probably an allusion to the scriptural tradition that the Passover lamb's bones would not be broken (Exod. 12.46; cf. Num. 9.12), and it serves to reinforce the Paschal lamb lens through which John portrays Jesus' death.[31] Alternatively, the source text might be Psalm 34.20, as the verbal idea is closer here, even though the thematic association is more general, enhancing further notions of righteous suffering. C. K. Barrett surmises that both traditions might be operative here, namely that the actual 'source' text is psalmic because of the lexical correspondence, but that the usage of it is through the Passover lens.[32]

Zechariah 12.10 in John 19.37

The second part of what is presented effectively as a composite citation takes the reader from Passover imagery and on to the narrative of Zechariah, and to the text of Zechariah 12.10. Forms of the Zechariah text may be found elsewhere in early Christian writing, but normally in the context of the second coming rather than Jesus' death (cf. Matt. 24.30; Rev. 1.7), so its use here in relation to Jesus' death is striking. In the light of this change of 'context', Hanson avers that John might have meant: '[t]his prophecy has already been fulfilled. You do not need to wait until the parousia.'[33]Also significant is the mode of citation, as it is the second element of a composite quotation (with John 19.36, as we have just seen). The placement of such a composite citation here seems significant, at the climax of the Passion account, and it may manifest an *inclusio* with the previous composite citation we observed in 12.38–40 (of Isa. 53.1 and 6.10), thereby book-ending the discourse in respect of Jesus' death.[34] If so, it would be the case that Scripture is not merely being *fulfilled* by Jesus' death, it would also be being used to demark the boundaries of the recounting of that death.

While the form of citation is more allusive, and while there is some textual variation in effect, it 'is evident that, at a minimum, John was in some sense including the Zechariah 9—14 material in his meditation on the significance of the passion of Christ'.[35] This is in synchronicity with the similar use of Zechariah 9—14 material in the Markan and Matthean evangelistic Passion Narratives, and further suggests that that textual unit proved to be a suitable source for making sense of Jesus' death. It is similarly possible that Zechariah 9—14 provides bookends to John's Passion, with Zechariah 9.9 quoted in respect of the triumphal entry (12.15) and Zechariah 12.10 similarly cited here (19.37), at the end of the Passion scene, thereby establishing a 'Zechariah *inclusio*',[36] a contrasting one that moves from celebration (Zech. 9.9) to piercing (Zech. 12.10). The jubilation of the triumphal entry contrasts with the mourning of the Passion.

In this second element of the composite citation, it is – merely – the *saying* of the citation that matters, rather than its fulfilment, and thus the Zechariah element could be viewed as subsidiary or lesser in that regard. However, it is equally possible, particularly in view of the composite nature of the citation, that this second reference also anticipates 'fulfilment' by extension. The respective source texts are not aligned so closely elsewhere in contemporary literature, and thus it seems likely that John juxtaposes them for interpretative gain, expecting that they will both be viewed as being, in some way, 'fulfilled'. Quite what specific significance one might draw from this citation, though, remains more elusive. The text form is not one to which we presently have access; Zechariah 12.10 LXX reads 'mocked' rather than 'pierced' (i.e. '*they look on the one whom they have mocked*'), and John has instead used a Greek version that follows the Masoretic form of Zechariah 12.10.[37] The use of 'pierced' therefore seem particularly pointed (no pun intended . . .), as the LXX form of 'mocked' might have fitted equally well, though John does lack explicit reference to the mockery voiced by onlookers and leading figures (cf. Mark 15.29–32). Hence one assumes that the verbal/text form is driven by the need to find 'fulfilment' in the 'piercing' actions of 19.34, and it could be that the Scripture merely fulfils that piercing aspect. However, that would seem to limit John's particular crafting of the Zechariah text; the citation may have a more ironic tone in that the soldiers – by piercing Jesus – inadvertently fulfil Scripture, and thereby participate in a divinely approved action.

It is also not clear who John anticipates being the ones who look on the pierced Jesus (19.37). The referent may include the eyewitness of 19.35 (probably the Beloved Disciple), but more probably it extends to a wider audience, those whom John invites to consider their response to Jesus, and ideally from the perspective of belief in him (cf. 20.30–31). Whoever the implied 'seer' is, though, their focus is on the pierced Jesus; as with the entire

Passion Narrative, Jesus is the focal point of the episode and the one on whom fulfilment has come.

What is also striking is the way the fulfilment citations of 19.36–37 do not build on or exegete the claim that blood and water came out of Jesus' side when soldiers pierced him with a spear (19.34). The incident seems imbued with symbolism and significance, both in terms of the importance John ascribes to the Beloved Disciple's eyewitness testimony to it (19.35) and the extensive discussion of the potential sacramental imagery the scene supposedly manifested. Bearing in mind the intensive attention to fulfilment imagery within the crucifixion pericope, one might have expected John to frame 19.34 in similar terms, but he only does so with reference to the visualization of the piercing (19.37), not in respect of the actual outflow from Jesus' side. It is possible that John might be making an allusion here to Zechariah 14.8 and the imagery therein of rivers of live flowing out from Jerusalem. This would be a further link to the Zechariah 9–14 imagery we have encountered elsewhere in the Gospels, and would correlate well with the living water imagery John elsewhere utilizes, particularly for how John connects that imagery with the gift of the Paraclete and the Spirit's advent after the glorification – that is, death – of Jesus (7.37–39; 14.26). It might also build on Jesus' prior declaration of 19.28; that is, the invitation for anyone who is thirsty to come to him who is living water (7.37). But the 'blood' outflow would not be referenced, and John still does not signpost the allusion, so one is hesitant about building too much on the Zechariah 14.8 link.

Passion Citations: Summary

What might we say more broadly, then, about John's use of the OT in terms of the crucifixion scene? Evidently, scriptural testimony and fulfilment matter for John, and they find a particular heightening or resonance in the crucifixion account. However, one might equally say that for all John's emphasis on fulfilment, Psalm 22.18 apart, the sources for such fulfilment are ambiguous, with several potential 'candidate' sources. On the one hand, this might be seen as opening up a wider pattern or matrix of

OT fulfilment, with such a variety of voices so present. This is potentially the case for John 19.36, where the righteous sufferer imagery and the Passover lamb motif can be 'comfortably' juxtaposed and this may deepen the interpretative satisfaction. On the other hand, it may be further testimony to the principle that John is less bothered as to the precise sources – or otherwise – of the citations and instead focuses essentially on their fulfilment *as Scripture*.[38] John 19.24 would be the exception that proved the rule; that is, it renders a complete or explicit citation of Psalm 22.18 in order to underscore the fact that the psalmic text was being fulfilled. To put it another way, John only cites as much of the OT as it needs to do to demonstrate that the fulfilment has been achieved.

Furthermore, it is not exactly clear *why* these particular texts are being fulfilled or, more particularly, why it is these specific events that require OT attestation. It is notable that the four citations are in close proximity to each other and, course, they are at the high point or climax of John's narrative. It would seem appropriate, one surmises, for the actual moment of death to receive scriptural fulfilment (19.28–30), but the appeal to scriptural warrant for the casting of lots might seem unnecessarily pedantic. Or at least it is not evident why that event per se – rather than, for instance, the passing of Jesus' mother on to the Beloved Disciple (19.26–27) – required such explicit fulfilment confirmation. But 'fulfilled' these texts must be, and that is the lens through which John reads them, not by putting them on the lips of Jesus but more as an editorial, third-party explanation. Matthew Scott sums up John's hermeneutic well, saying its 'teleological approach to quotation licenses a reworking of the scriptural voice that it speaks in the mode of its fulfilment'.[39]

One further observation is perhaps required, namely the extent to which the use of the OT in John's Passion Narrative informs comparisons with the Synoptic accounts. We have noted the very contrasting flavours of Mark and John's Passion accounts, and the distinction surely remains significant. John *explicitly* cites Scripture and seeks to demonstrate its fulfilment whereas Mark tends merely to allude to or echo it (Mark 14.26 notwithstanding). John does not wish to depend on allusive echoes – he seeks to make his point robustly... *

① ②

* Ie. John cites relatively peripheral aspects of the Passion as fulfilling Scripture and is relatively more explicit in his use of Scriptural citation/quotation. Moreover it is Jesus' prophecy that is most significant...

to make his point robustly, and say 'this is Scripture' and thereby reinforce the notion that Jesus' death *kata tas graphas* is no accident or misapprehension.[40]

It is possible, though, that consideration of their comparative use of OT citation may give good grounds for finding more 'consistency' or common ground between the respective gospel accounts. For example, taking Jesus' thirst in more 'spiritual' than 'physical' terms, and thirst for God thereby equating with spiritual dryness (and thus the absence of God – cf. Ps. 22.1), Michael Licona suggests that John 19.28 is a 'dynamic equivalent translation' of the Markan testimony. He surmises that 'John has redacted Jesus' words but has retained their meaning'.[41] Hence John 19.28 becomes a 'fulfilment' of Psalm 22.1 rather than of Psalm 69.3, and John 19.28 and Mark 15.34 become effectively equivalent expressions. Licona makes a similar claim in respect of John 19.30 and Jesus' cry that '*it is finished*'. While not named as a fulfilment citation by John (and such silence should not be dismissed lightly, bearing in mind the high percentage of quotations in the crucifixion scene), Jesus' declaration might equate to the Lucan Jesus' confession '*into your hands I commit my spirit*' (Luke 23.46; cf. Ps. 31.5). Thus whereas 19.30 is not described as fulfilment, it would effectively equate as such, and offer further endorsement of the outworking of God's purposes.[42] Alternatively, John 19.30 might replay the last line of Psalm 22, the declarative '*the Lord has done it*' (Ps. 22.31) equating to John's '*it is finished*' assessment.[43] Certainty is not achievable in such matters, but one might still aver that the wider Passion discourse opens up a number of possible inter-gospel connections, such connections being particularly located within the evangelists' respective use of the lament or righteous sufferer discourse.

The Passion and the wider Johannine Corpus

What contribution do the Johannine epistles make to our question? Relatively little, one might conclude. The second and third epistles make no mention of Jesus' death, nor do they signal any formal citation of the OT, and therefore they can proverbially be

3 factors lead in a direction quite *opposite* from the fulfillment references in Synoptics–Acts: much less mystery regarding Scriptural fulfillment, much more clarity as to the purpose of the crucifixion, too much less temptation for Gentile Christians to Judaize in synagogues.

set to one side for our purposes. The first Johannine epistle, however, does make some appeal to Jesus' death, even if there is no formal OT quotation cited in this regard. The wider Jesus 'event', for example (or the revelation of the Son of God), was enacted to destroy the works of the devil (3.8). More directly perhaps, Jesus' death is described as atoning sacrifice (*hilasmos* – 2.2; 4.10; cf. Lev. 25.9; Num. 5.8), implicitly connecting it to the sacrificial discourse of the OT and perhaps even the Day of Atonement imagery found in Hebrews (see Chapter 7). Likewise the claim that Jesus' death cleanses the readers from their sin (1 John 1.7) might also have sacrificial connotations (cf. Lev. 16.30), even to the point of another implicit reference to Yom Kippur.[44] But these examples are fairly limited in number, and UBS4 lists no formal quotations of the Old Testament in 1 John. The writer may claim that Jesus' self-offering was an act of love (1 John 3.16), but offers no particular OT warrant for the assertion. As such, 1 John seems able to speak of Jesus' death and its impact without finding the necessity of its being *kata tas graphas*. While it does not say that it is *counter* to scriptural testimony, bearing in mind the evangelist's association of Jesus' death and the fulfilment of Scripture, the epistle's relative silence on the matter is somewhat striking. Indeed, rather than the letter exhibiting deliberations around the interpretation of Scripture, it is the interpretation of John's Gospel that provides the locus for the epistolary debate.[45]

The Book of Revelation

What, though, of the text of Revelation? How does one assess the contribution of a text that never formally *quotes* the Old Testament[46] but is imbued with OT allusions and echoes, most of which are integral – critical, even – to the sensible exposition and interpretation of the text? The volume of appeal to Jewish scriptural imagery would suggest that the recipients or audience of Revelation were well versed in the Scriptures and regarded the texts as in some way 'authoritative', but discerning how this might pertain to our particular enquiry is not straightforward. On the one hand, Revelation's use of the OT goes well beyond just finding scriptural warrant for Jesus' death. Its eschatological orientation is more concerned with matters future (Rev. 1.1), and with a wider frame of reference than the Passion tradition. Revelation is arguably more concerned with the eschatological or heavenly implications of Jesus' death,[47] and less with defending how that death might be according to the Scriptures. On the other hand, Jesus' death remains central for Revelation's outworking, and the symbolism used to evoke or explicate this is steeped in Scripture. Consider, for example, Revelation's appeal to the language of sacrifice. The blood of the Lamb has conquered (12.11) and brought forth sacrificial cleansing (7.14), and the Lamb is the recipient of worship on the basis of the achievements of its slaughter/death (5.9, 12).

One may point to further 'Jesus' death' associations. The Son of Man figure – whose portrayal in Revelation 1 is soaked with Daniel 7 imagery – holds the keys of death (1.18) and is the one who was once dead and is now alive (1.18). Jesus is also the faithful witness, the firstborn of the dead (1.5), a possible allusion to Psalm 89.27, 37; it juxtaposes the psalm's high Davidic, messianic claims ('*I will make him the firstborn, the highest of the kings of the earth*' – Ps. 89.27) and appeal to '*enduring witness*' (Ps. 89. 37) with the reality of the 'glory' of the cross.[48] If this is a 'genuine' allusion, it would offer one instance of Psalm 89 – the text Juel believed lay at the heart of NT messianic exegesis – being used, albeit loosely, in respect of Jesus' death. Similarly, Psalm 69, another righteous sufferer psalm but one of which we have identified more NT usage, may be the source of an allusion in Revelation 3.5 (Ps. 69.28), and the reference to being blotted out of the book of life. The faithful 'sufferers' of Revelation 3 are implicitly associated with the psalm's righteous/faithful sufferer and with the achievements of that 'suffering'. If so, it would be an instance of a text (Ps. 69) that was widely associated with Passion Narrative tradition also being used in the Apocalypse in not dissimilar fashion. But at the same time, we also encounter some citational variance. A case in point may be Revelation 1.7, probably a paraphrase or reworking of Zechariah 12.10 (also cited in John 19.37, as noted above). The same (Zech. 12.10) text that was embedded in the Gospel's Passion account, and used evocatively of Jesus' death on the cross (John 19.37), is reused in an alternative 'eschatological' context within the Apocalypse. The recollection of the piercing of Jesus becomes associated with the Parousia moment.

Hence at the very least, interpretation of Revelation necessitates an approach that is in some way *kata tas graphas*,[49] but to do full justice to this in respect of Jesus' death would require an extended volume in and of itself, well beyond our scope or capability. Instead we might take one portion of the Apocalypse and use it as a window on, or sample of, the type of wide-ranging appropriation of biblical imagery it adopts. Revelation 5 may serve as one such example. The scene opens in the heavenly throne room, continuing the narrative of chapter 4 – itself laden with OT-sourced imagery – and the concern over who would be able to break open the scroll.[50] The opening of the scroll or book may allude to similar, mysterious imagery in Daniel 12.1–4. One of the elders reassures John that the Lion of Judah (cf. Gen. 49.9) is able to fulfil the task. This imagery, framed in terms of conquering victory, would seem to reflect the achievements of Jesus' death and casts Jesus in leonine terms. There is no formal citation in this regard, not even an allusion or echo to a triumphant righteous sufferer psalm, but the root of David reference (5.5) probably derives from the '*root of Jesse*' motif (Isa. 11.10) and, when coupled with the victorious characterization, invests the discourse with some messianic flavour. It may even reflect the development of the branch that will come out of the stump of Jesse, and the fruit therefore from that line, with the establishment of an eternal throne of David (cf. Isa. 9.7). As such, 'Jesus is seen as the true fulfilment of the promise that a descendent (*sic*) of David would be the Messiah.'[51]

The scene shifts quickly, however, and John sees the figure of the Lamb standing between the four living creatures – imagery probably drawn from Ezekiel – and the throne. The Lamb's capacity to open the scroll is premised on its death, and the nature of it; it has been slaughtered (5.6, 9, 12), but now stands – and, by its blood, humanity is ransomed. The blood-related imagery, and its associated efficacy, is evocative of the covenant-making process (Exod. 24.8), and its frequent repetition underscores the sacrificial aspect to Jesus' death. Just as in the gospel account, it might also evoke Passover lamb imagery and the redemptive action of that event. It is also possible that Revelation 5.9 alludes to Isaiah 53.7, thereby fusing together the Passover and Suffering Servant traditions.[52] There is no significant lexical reason to make that association, beyond the lamb motif, but the sinlessness of the Servant (Isa. 53.11) is broadly resonant of the Lamb's ascribed worthiness (Rev. 5.9).[53] And the whole scene, and particularly the worship context, may draw on the seraphs' praise found in Isaiah 6.3.[54]

Conclusion

Scripture is the context in which, and against which, John recounts the narrative and significance of Jesus' death, and it 'seems the most *alttestamentlich* of New Testament books'.[55] There is a particular dependency on the Psalms, with half of John's quotations drawn from that corpus and particularly from those characterized as righteous sufferer texts. We have also seen that the Passion Narrative – however loosely defined or articulated – itself shapes the way John interprets and utilizes Scripture. The signs that Jesus does at the beginning of the Gospel – or in its first half – are commensurate with Scripture, but they cannot be said to fulfil it. Instead it is the Passion events that see Scripture brought to completion or find its true meaning, and '[i]t is in Jesus' rejection and crucifixion that the Scriptures find their ultimate fulfilment'.[56] The cross is the primary locus of Jesus' glorification, and hence the climactic place of scriptural fulfilment. Hence John's usage of scriptural witness is in some sense dialogical; that is, the scriptural testimony shapes and informs the narration of the Passion account, but it is also shaped by the particular form or understanding of the Passion with which John is working. The Old Testament and Johannine testimony are mutually informing.

6

The Old Testament in Paul's Depiction of Jesus' Death

Introduction

At this point in our discussion we must change direction in terms of our consideration of how the Old Testament is used to address or unpack the portrayal of Jesus' death. Having focused primarily thus far on the way the OT functions within the *narration* of Jesus' death – through what we have termed the Passion Narrative discourse – we now turn to Paul, whose textual form is self-evidently different; that is, epistolary rather than narrative. Of course, we might well have started our reflection on the scriptural portrayal of Jesus' death here; Paul's epistles probably pre-date the textual form of the Gospels (as our prior discussion of 1 Corinthians 15.3 seemingly attests), but the different genres of literature have shaped the structure of our discussion thus far. Hence while we will still be focusing in this, and in the subsequent chapters, on the way the Old Testament functions to address Jesus' death, it will no longer be through primarily *narrative* ways (although, as will become clear, narrative readings of the Pauline literature have become more popular in recent years).[1] This will mean a different form of engagement with the material, and as with any interaction with Pauline theology, it will necessarily be piecemeal and/or selective, drawing from various texts rather than from one primary locus of inquiry.

At the same time, we should not be bereft of loci of engagement. If Luke is said to lack any *theologia crucis*, Paul tends to the opposite extreme, with Jesus' death on the cross surely integral or core to his theological understanding.[2] Indeed, Paul cannot speak of Christ *without* doing so in respect of the cross, as one particular rendering of 1 Corinthians 2.2 testifies: '*I resolved to know nothing among you except Jesus Christ – that is, him crucified.*' The cross fulfils a pivotal role in Paul's theology (cf. the 'word' or 'message' of the cross – 1 Cor. 1.18), and Jesus' death is thus central to Paul's epistolary formulation. As such, for Paul, Jesus Christ and the cross are inextricably intertwined; as with the gospel writers, and in notable distinction from other sources such as Thomas or Q, Jesus' death is the climax or zenith of his mission. It remains, then, to examine the ways the OT might have shaped or informed that perspective for Paul, and what light such OT usage might shed on Paul's Christology.

Paul's Use of the Old Testament

To say that the Old Testament was integral to Paul's letters and theology is surely a self-evident truism. Paul's epistolary correspondence abounds with scriptural resonances, drawn mainly from the Septuagint – sometimes explicit, sometimes implicit – with approximately a hundred direct quotations of the OT, and a large number of further direct allusion or echoes.[3] Paul also habitually signals his quotations, customarily with an introductory formula like 'it is written' (Rom. 1.17; Gal. 3.10) or 'Isaiah says' (cf. Rom. 15.12). He can also speak of a Messiah promised by the prophets and in the Scriptures (Rom. 1.2), thereby setting the OT as the framework for his kerygmatic and epistolary discourse, comparable perhaps to how Mark uses the Isaiah designation at the outset of his Gospel to establish its scriptural foundation.[4] But more than Mark, Romans 1.2 establishes a wider OT scope for its christological exploration, and is less specific in that regard; it is closer to the 'broader experience of the scriptures of Israel'[5] as attested in 1 Corinthians 15.3. The gospel/Christ mystery has also been disclosed through the prophets *to the Gentiles* (Rom. 16.26), the absence of reference to Torah presumably commensurate with Paul's emphasis on Jew–Gentile unity ('one body' – cf. Rom. 12.1–8), and thereby omitting the ethnically specific implications of the 'Law'.

While there are diverse views as to the relative volume of OT citation between the respective letters (e.g. Philippians has strikingly less explicit OT usage, with arguably no formal citations, likewise perhaps 1 Thessalonians), it is surely fair to say that no aspect of Pauline theology can be divorced from, or discussed without reference to, the Jewish Scriptures and the apostle's employment of them. Surveying Paul's use of the OT and its relationship to major themes within Pauline theological formulation, Moyise concludes that it is possible 'to give a substantial account of Paul's theology by summarizing his use of Scripture',[6] and Paul's articulation and exposition of Jesus' death is no exception to this rule. Indeed, one surmises that it is totally immersed in the vocabulary, imagery and assumptions of Jewish Scriptures. It is striking, then, that the one who announces that Christ is the end – or technically the 'goal' – of the Law (Rom. 10.4) can derive so much kerygmatic formulation from 'the Law', and/or can confirm that the declaration of the righteousness of God (surely in some way related to Jesus' death) is attested to by the Law and the Prophets (Rom. 3.21 – again, notably in general rather than specific, terms). Those texts that had fed Paul's development and training as a Pharisee continued to have authority for him, but were now, in the light of Jesus' death and resurrection, to be read with a different lens or optic.[7]

We might then venture three summary statements in this regard:

1   At the risk of stating the obvious, it has long been recognized that Paul's primary interest has been in the death and resurrection of Jesus Christ rather than in the life and teaching of Jesus. While this dichotomy has been challenged in recent years,[8] it remains the case that it is hard to avoid the fact that Christ's death is an integral element to Paul's theologizing. Where Luke allegedly has no *theologia crucis*, Paul's writing is integrally shaped and formed by it.

2   Likewise, Paul's role as an interpreter of the Jewish Scriptures is foregrounded and worthy of attention in and of itself, beyond any specific emphasis on Jesus' death. Paul's use of Scripture is a focus of extended scholarly research and there is a wide discourse on the subject, varying from large-scale examinations through to detailed focus on individual units of scriptural and

intertextual play.[9] Different lenses for Paul's engagement with Scripture have been identified, including his use of intertextual echoes,[10] his rhetorical use of Scripture,[11] the nature of Paul as a *reader* of Scripture[12] or the way he utilizes Scripture as the fulfilment of Israel's hopes, and an end to exile.[13]

3 As we have observed, it is the Pauline attestation (1 Cor. 15.3–4) that seemingly points us to the fact that the early Church found a way of speaking about Jesus' death in Old Testament terms. Paul, it seems, had inherited that tradition and was concerned to faithfully pass it on; indeed, the appropriate transmission of such tradition is described as being of 'primary import' (1 Cor. 15.3). It is ambiguous as to whether such significance specifically pertained to the security of the handover process, or to the fact that Jesus' death – and resurrection – were *kata tas graphas*. Either way, the centrality of scriptural testimony in relation to Jesus' death is surely an integral Pauline – and early Church – phenomenon.

One might also add three further qualifying or contextualizing statements. First, much of Paul's use of Scripture goes well beyond his depiction or portrayal of Jesus' death. One thinks of the extensive forensic language in terms of justification, for example, notably the citation of Habakkuk 2.4, and its contribution to the 'justification by faith' dynamic. This has connections, of course, with the outcome of Jesus' death, but implications well beyond that in terms of Christology and ecclesiology. Likewise the debates around speaking in tongues, and the curious appeal to Isaiah 28.11 in respect of glossolalia (1 Cor. 14.21), have little to do with Jesus' death but remain intriguing loci for engagement on Paul's practice of scriptural interpretation.

Second, the ways of measuring or evaluating Paul's use of Scripture are manifold, as are the ways one categorizes such usage. Various concepts abound, such as 'narrative criticism' or 'intertextual approaches', and techniques similarly vary, perhaps focused on detailed textual criticism and/or debates about the presence (or otherwise) of a citation. The methodologies so used are all fruitful places of exploration, and each can generate interpretative solutions. They can also occasion key questions of 'principle', notably whether Scripture shapes Paul's understanding of Jesus' death[14] or whether Paul's – pre-established – theology shapes his use of Scripture.[15] This parallels the discourse we noted in the introduction, and the contrasting approaches of Lindars and Juel, namely as to whether the kerygma or Scripture itself formed the starting point for messianic proclamation.

Third, and perhaps most significantly for our concerns, Paul can speak of Jesus' death *without* explicit scriptural allusion. This would seem to be the case in Colossians 2.12–15, for example, where the recounting of the events of Jesus' death seems to lack a formal citation of Scripture.[16] Hanson suggests that it might form an allusion to Numbers 25.1–5,[17] but the point of connection for any putative echo is minimal at best, and Paul gives no explicit – or even implicit – basis for making any such association. That said, if one were looking for ways to demonstrate how a cruciform death was *kata tas graphas*, then Numbers 25.1–5 would seem to provide a suitable source text, and it is surprising, perhaps, that the NT authors do not seem to avail themselves of it in this regard.[18]

We might also wish to note that Pauline material that is pre-existing 'tradition' – handed on to and via Paul, and that may exhibit a pre-existing catechetical or confessional form – is still worthy of comment in respect of its OT usage. Alexander Wedderburn notes, for example: 'It is clear that in many passages where Paul refers to Christ's death he may well be dependent on shared early Christian traditions and that he has therefore inherited and taken over from others ways of interpreting that death.'[19] The so-called Christ hymn of Philippians 2.6–11, itself a key locus of thinking in relation to Christ's death, would be a case in point. Many argue that it derives from a pre-existing, poetic or hymnic tradition, bespeaking a particular christological formula with which Paul 'agrees' and thereby 're-confirms' in his epistle.[20] Others are less persuaded, and aver that the material remains quintessentially Pauline, and therefore the creation of the apostle himself. Either way, the text/hymn is still of interest for how it might reflect OT imagery, particularly as to how it might draw on Isaiah 5 (see below); whoever its 'author' may be, it would still offer early Christian testimony as to how Scripture was being used in respect of Jesus' death. And of course, as we have already seen, 1 Corinthians 15.3–8 is surely 'traditional' material, and likewise raises questions about what OT texts lie behind the process of forming that *kata tas graphas* tradition.

A Pauline Passion Narrative?

Of course, we do not possess a Passion Narrative in Paul, or at least not a formulaic one. Instead we possess more of a jigsaw option, images relating to Jesus' death being drawn from a variety of Pauline texts and utilized for a variety of heuristic purposes. This can create ambiguities as to how/when Jesus' death is being referred to, and – as with Acts – it can be difficult to disentangle claims about crucifixion from Paul's fundamental belief in the resurrected Christ who appeared to him on the Damascus Road (Gal. 1.13–17). Paul's reflection on Jesus' death is therefore part of a wider Pauline theology and is not so 'discrete' as in the Gospels, for obvious reasons.

As observed above, the use of Scripture to articulate Jesus' death on the cross was not something begun *ex nihilo* by Paul. Rather there was, it seems, an inherited tradition that was seeking to make sense of Jesus' death through reflection on, and by interpretation of, the Scriptures, and it would seem appropriate for that reflection to be premised on or informed by some form of pre-existing Passion Narrative.[21] While we may not have formal access to such a Passion Narrative, the Pauline texts would still seem to allude to aspects of what it might have comprised. Indeed, as Dale Allison observes, if we did not possess the evangelistic Passion accounts and were therefore dependent only on Pauline testimony, we might still construct a reasonably coherent account of what a primitive Passion Narrative might have contained.[22] For example, we would know that Christ was crucified (1 Cor. 2.8; Col. 2.13–14), under or by Roman authorities (1 Cor. 2.6–8; conceivably Pontius Pilate – 1 Tim. 6.13) and nailed to a cross so that blood was yielded (Rom. 3.25) because of his messianic claims (Rom. 1.3–4; 15.12). Paul articulates some form of Jewish responsibility for Jesus' death (1 Thess. 2.14–16), he locates it in Judea (1 Thess. 2.14–16) and ascribes to it some action of '*handing over*' or '*betrayal*'

(1 Cor. 11.23). It culminates with Jesus' death and burial (1 Cor. 15.3–4), with perhaps Paul's references to being 'crucified with Christ' (Rom. 6.6; Gal. 2.19) indicative of Paul's knowledge of the tradition that Jesus died among others (cf. Mark 15.27, 32). However, critically for our purposes, in these instances that Allison records, we do not encounter any accompanying explicit, scriptural citation or any *kata tas graphas* signification. Hence we can compile a Passion Narrative 'of sorts' but it is one that lacks explicit OT commentary (particularly when compared to the evangelistic testimony), and one without any concrete, direct fulfilment of particular texts. One therefore has to read more between the lines. We might, for example hear sacrificial OT echoes in Romans 3.25 or, later on in Romans 4.25, there would seem to be an allusion to Isaiah 53 imagery; but in both instances this is manifest in a far subtler form than we see in certain parts of the Gospels. As such, we might say that the Christ dying 'according to the Scriptures' is a datum Paul tends to assert rather than explicitly *evidence* within his epistolary corpus, and the direct association with OT fulfilment we encountered in the gospel accounts is actually far from prominent within Pauline discourse.

Or it may be that we need to look at the question in a different way. In Romans 9—11, for example, Paul is grappling with the soteriological implications of Jesus' death, especially in relation to the Jew–Gentile matters and the implications of the Christ event for those Jews who do not embrace Jesus as Messiah (cf. Rom. 9.1–5). The unit is replete with scriptural citation – abundantly so – but its soteriological reflection, while premised around Jesus' death, is concerned with its ramifications, and one must read somewhat 'between the lines' to discern the contours of the OT–Jesus' death relationship.[23] Similarly, when Paul alludes to Jesus tradition in terms of the words of institution (1 Cor. 11.23–26), they comprise a reference, one surmises, to Jeremiah 31 or Exodus 24.8, and the (new) covenant inauguration in the Pauline words of institution; or they may be a further reference to Isaiah 53.6, 12 and the invocation there of dying for sins. Again, what we do not have is a *direct* quotation, and the source is probably the wider Jesus tradition rather than – directly – the OT, but the citation represents at least *some* intertextual association with an OT text, and its application to Jesus' death (or indeed the Passion tradition). But it remains the case that such connections are more interpretatively complex than standard fulfilment quotations we found in either Matthew or John.

What texts does Paul use in this regard?

In spite, then, of the abundance both of Paul's discourse about the cross and his appeal to the OT Scriptures, there is strikingly little *formal* association between these respective areas, and relatively little attempt by Paul to present christological 'proof texts' referring to the cross. There is only one quasi-Matthean or quasi-Johannine 'fulfilment' quotation pertaining to Jesus' death (1 Cor. 15.54–55), and this is only tangentially relevant, as its claim that *'death has been swallowed up in victory'* – a composite quotation of Isaiah 25.8 and Hosea 13.14 – speaks of future fulfilment rather than a present one. This – relative – silence is rather striking, and one may want to ponder why Paul does not have more *explicit* quotations in this regard, particularly bearing in mind their presence in other so-called theological discourses. With Moyise, 'Paul's use of scripture springs from the *consequences* of Christ's death and resurrection',[24] but there is less direct explication of that death, no absolute, explicit scriptural citation. Hays essentially concurs with this conclusion and argues that Paul is effectively uninterested in proof texts that christologize Jesus' identity.[25] Instead there are what he terms 'ecclesiological hermeneutics' at play in Paul: 'What Paul finds in Scripture, above all else, is a prefiguration of the *church* as the people of God.'[26] Hence there are less direct statements about Jesus' death fulfilling certain christological categories, the exceptions being, Hays proposes, Romans 15.3 and 1 Corinthians 15.3–4. To these texts we now turn.

1 Corinthians 15.3

We might begin our consideration of Paul by going back to the key creedal, confessional text, which in many ways occasioned the discussion in question, and the essential acknowledgement that Christ died according to the Scriptures (1 Cor. 15.3). This declaration is something Paul has inherited and passed on to the Corinthians, and is duly continuing to uphold (cf. also 1 Cor. 8.4–6). The technical term Paul uses here for 'handing on' (*paradidomai*) suggests that this is secure tradition and already well established as such; the idea of dying for 'sins' (plural) is an unusual one for Paul, further suggesting that it is material he has inherited rather than coined himself.[27] It would seem, as such, to be a central kerygmatic statement for Paul; indeed, Gathercole opines that '1 Corinthians 15.3–4 might have just as good a claim (if not better) than Romans 1.16–17 to be a distillation of the gospel'.[28] Thus, on the basis of 1 Corinthians 15.1 (cf. also 15.11), it would have formed the fundamental *euangellion* that Paul had preached to the church in Corinth.[29] We have commented earlier on in the introductory chapter as to the affinities of 1 Corinthians 15.3 with Isaiah 53, and the latter text is probably the best individual case for evidencing the 'for our sins' aspect of the creedal formulation, but the remit of the OT tradition is probably wider than this, and incorporates a more general scriptural spectrum.

It is also notable that the *kata tas graphas* declaration is made to a predominantly *Gentile* church, and within an epistolary text that expresses little to no interest in the Jew–Gentile questions that permeate so much else of the Pauline corpus. Yet it is to the testimony of the *Jewish* Scriptures that Paul appeals when seeking to undergird so fundamental a premise as Christ's death and resurrection. Elsewhere in 1 Corinthians, Paul seems to appeal to other sources (e.g. Menander in 1 Cor. 15.33), but for what seems to be the central aspect of his gospel, it is the Old Testament to which he turns. As an essentially Gentile church, this is striking, as is likewise the volume of other OT (non-'death related') material Paul uses in the letter.[30] It would seem, therefore, that the Corinthians were reasonably well versed in the Scriptures, and/or that Paul thought them sufficiently so. Moreover, there is no sense that the Corinthians are disputing the essential tenor or basis of these creedal confessions – Paul neither needs to 'justify' the 15.3–8 tradition nor offer further explanation of the confessions' scriptural warrant. The implication therefore is that the

Jewish Scriptures formed the basis of what the Corinthians now understood as the basic elements for their understanding of Jesus' death. The rest of chapter 15 builds on this creedal/scriptural consensus. It is the outworking or implications of the confessional statements of 1 Corinthians 15.3–4 that Paul effectively seeks to address (though primarily in terms of the resurrection rather than the crucifixion).[31]

We might also note that Paul refers here to *Christ* rather than Jesus, to the role rather than the name (1 Cor. 15.3). There is no need to make the claim here that Jesus *is* the Christ[32] – and thus, it seems, that that particular appeal is not an integral part of Paul's use of the Jewish Scriptures. What, however, is scripturally mandated for Paul is that Jesus dies (for us) '*as Christ*', referring to the messiah's crucifixion. And likewise, it is not (just) that Jesus died according to the Scriptures, but that he died *as Christ* according to the Scriptures; that is, Scripture attests that Jesus dies in messianic character – the 'crucified messiah' is given scriptural attestation. It is *Christ* crucified – not Jesus crucified – that Paul preaches (1 Cor. 2.2) and that is the stumbling block to the Corinthians (1 Cor. 1.23; cf. 1 Cor. 1.17).

This will become significant in Galatians 3.10–14, where Paul explores further the OT-related implications of the crucifixion. In this tightly packed unit of theologizing, Paul grapples with the differing processes of living by faith and by works of the law, and does so by juxtaposing scriptural testimony to each mode of living. The righteous live by faith (3.11, citing Hab. 2.4), while those who pursue life according to the law do so outside of the life of faith (3.12, citing Lev. 18.5). However, by implication, those who live by the law are under a curse, because the law itself cannot be kept; again Paul finds scriptural reference for this (Deut. 27.26), and life under the law becomes effectively a 'dead end'.[33] However, Paul finds resolution for the impact of the 'curse' in Jesus' death, and thus the cross is the means of extension of Abraham's blessing to the Gentiles (3.13–14); that is, Paul is able to make lexical and conceptual connection between the 'curse' imposed on the one who hung on a tree (Deut. 21.22–23 – the arboreal reference is thus critical) and the 'curse' that befalls those who cannot live up to the demands of the law (Gal. 3.10). In N. T. Wright's reading, the crucified Christ 'bears' the curse and uses it up, releasing the person(s) who should rightly be cursed.[34] It is not entirely clear whether Paul's theologizing starts with the 'cursedness' of the cross or the 'cursedness' of not meeting the law's requirements, but either way it is scriptural interpretation that enables Paul to find the resolution. And it is the OT-attested problem of the *crucified* Messiah (i.e. Deut. 21.22–23), the presenting problem with which the early Church was forced to grapple, that actually contributes to the resolution. The scriptural problem enables the scriptural solution, one might say.

Returning to the Corinthian testimony, one might further note that only the *resurrection* tradition is taken up in the rest of 1 Corinthians 15; that is, Christ's death is mentioned but its implications are not expanded on or developed in any way. As such, there appears to be no explicit reason why Paul includes the reference to Jesus' death *kata tas graphas*, other than that it was so integrally linked to the tradition that it was present by default. It was perhaps so intrinsic to the earliest kerygmatic pronouncements that it shaped the missional process, and one might suppose that Paul's missionary preaching may well have included a narration of the Passion. It would seem probable, then, that this included allusion to or citations of the OT, and hence that 'the scriptural shape of Jesus' death . . . was part of Paul's missionary preaching.'[35] Paul emphasizes that it was before the Galatians' very eyes that Christ is crucified (Gal. 3.1), suggestive therefore of some public – or performative? – re-enactment of the Passion events. Assuming, likewise, the principle of 1 Corinthians 15.3, one might extend the same principle to the Corinthian church, and concur with Jon Weatherly's assessment:

> In the case of the Corinthian church, at least, it appears that the relative lack of allusions to the Passion events bespeaks not a lack of interest in them but the assumption that they are well known and do not need repeating.[36]

Such familiarity elsewhere may then equally explain the lack of direct Pauline appeal to the Old Testament in order to *explain* Jesus' death. In 1 Thessalonians 2.14–15, for example, reference is made to Jesus' death in a way that might have invited some reflection on its scriptural significance or warrant, but Paul does not pursue that option.

The contribution of Isaiah 53

Paul further claims that Jesus' death *kata tas graphas* is 'for us' (1 Cor. 15.3); that is, it possessed an inherent, vicarious dimension. While Paul does not name any specific Scripture in this regard, one possible candidate, particularly in view of its potential use elsewhere in the Passion Narrative, is the fourth Servant Song of Isaiah 52.13 − 53.12. Gathercole ventures such a possibility, averring that the respective texts share a significant amount of common imagery: 'Paul . . . has no trouble in using the language of Isaiah 53 to describe Jesus' death', and demonstrably does so in the case of 1 Corinthians 15.3. Gathercole identifies a number of family resemblances between the two texts and advocates that Paul, with Isaiah 53.12 and its vicarious suffering in mind, is casting Jesus' death in substitutionary terms (cf. 1 Thess. 5.10).[37] Similarly, Otfried Hofius surmises that the scriptural *kata tas graphas* 'must be referred to Isaiah 53',[38] though he contends that the reading is first and foremost a christological one: 'the fourth Servant Song by no means provides the hermeneutical key for understanding Jesus and for interpreting his death on a cross.'[39] Paul does, of course, quote from Isaiah more than any other OT text, particularly in Romans, and an Isaiah 53 backdrop to Jesus' death would seem appropriate. In the light of such widespread Isaianic citation, Shiu-Lun Shum makes a strong argument for the impact of Isaiah 53 on Pauline soteriology: 'Paul was familiar with the so-called Fourth Servant Song . . . when composing or dictating Romans, *and subject to its influence in reflecting on God's salvific plan through Jesus' death*'.[40]

The case for the dependency of 1 Corinthians 15.3 on Isaiah 53 probably remains contestable, however. The fundamental problem still remains, particularly that for Paul, Jesus dies as the *Christ*, not as a *servant*. There is also the issue that Isaiah 53.11 LXX has a convoluted textual tradition and it is not straightforward to map potential points of connection to its claim that the Servant 'bore their iniquities' (53.11). And dying *for* someone, the vicarious element to which scholars often point when drawing NT links to Isaiah 53.11–12, may have origins in other, non-biblical sources (Greek tragedy perhaps), and thus one must be cautious of automatically assuming that the Isaiah narrative informed Pauline thinking.[41] Thus even as 'maximalist' an OT/NT interpreter as Hays has to conclude that it 'is possible that Paul may have read Isaiah 53 as a prophecy of Christ's vicarious suffering, but it is hard to substantiate this claim'.[42] David Horrell similarly surmises that the Servant Song 'is hardly prominent in his [i.e. Paul's] christological reflection'.[43]

Of course, it is equally the case that Paul can cite from Isaiah 53 without necessarily referencing Jesus' death. Romans 10.16, for example, quotes Isaiah 53.1 and thus shows Pauline knowledge of the Song, but it need imply no more than Jewish unbelief in the gospel and offer scriptural warrant for that (cf. the similar use of Isaiah 53.1 in John 12.38).[44] One might make the same observation in respect of Romans 15.21 and its quotation of Isaiah 52.15. The citation does not directly address Jesus' death, but evidences Pauline awareness of the Song and the capacity to extend its 'reference' or add 'significance' to wider gospel matters. Alternatively it may be that such Isaiah 53 allusions in Romans offer a lens on how Paul perceives Christ's death in respect of his own mission. For example, Paul seems to appropriate a more 'positive' aspect of the Isaianic witness (Isa. 52.7) in Romans 10.15, and this immediately prior to the hesitation in 10.16 (Isa. 53.1) that not all will believe the gospel message. He also alludes to Isaiah 52.5 earlier on in the epistle (Rom. 2.24) in respect of Israel's relations with Gentiles. In respect of these various citations of Isaiah 52—53, Ross Wagner concludes that they 'provide strong evidence that Paul's understanding of his own mission as apostle to the gentiles has been fundamentally shaped by careful and sustained reflection on this portion of Isaiah as a whole'.[45] The missional dimension to Jesus' death might therefore be said to be *kata tas graphas* for Paul, with Isaiah 53 prominent in this regard.

But in terms of Paul referencing Isaiah 53 directly in respect of the soteriological meaning of Jesus' death, one might instead turn to Romans 4.25 and Paul's claim that Jesus was handed over to death for our trespasses (and raised for our justification). The language of handing over (*paradidomai* – 4.25) would draw on the claim that the Servant's soul was handed (*paradidomai*) over to death (53.12d),[46] echoing similar imagery in the gospel testimony (Mark 9.31; 10.33; 14.21). Likewise the Servant was given over (*paradidomai*) because (*dia*) of sins (53.12f.), just as Jesus was handed over because (*dia*) of sins (4.25). Indeed, in the midst of wider scholarly scepticism as to the Passion import of Isaiah 53, there now seems to be near unanimity that Romans 4.25 properly draws on the Servant Song imagery.[47] The verse may further be pre-existing creedal tradition that Paul is merely restating; the couplet structure of the statement points in that direction, and there is also something of a family resemblance to the other creedal tradition of 1 Corinthians 15.3–4. If so, and if there were an allusion here to Isaiah 53.12, Romans 4.25 would offer fairly secure evidence of the use of the Servant Song in relation to Jesus' death, and – dating Romans to the late 50s CE – from relatively early in the tradition.

If it is the case that Romans 4.25 alludes to Isaiah 53.12, then one might make the same suggestion of other Pauline texts. Romans 5.19 shares a similar catechetical and couplet shape to 4.25, along with its reference to Christ's vicarious achievements. Christ's obedience makes many righteous, echoing the work of the Servant in this regard (Isa. 53.11). Likewise Romans 5.8 speaks of Christ dying for (*huper*) us/sinners, which resonates with Isaiah 53.6, 12, as does Galatians 1.4, itself often compared to 1 Corinthians 15.3 for sharing the same reference to plural 'sins'.[48] In terms of Deutero-Pauline texts, we might also see the influence of Isaiah 53 on Titus 2.14 or 1 Timothy 2.6, particularly as they exhibit language similar to that of Mark 10.45 and the potential Isaianic imagery manifest there. One might even mention Romans 8.32 and its vicarious claims, but this text could equally refer to Genesis 22 and the sacrifice of Isaac therein.[49] In the Targum tradition it is Isaac's fate that is stressed for Genesis 22, not that of Abraham, and Paul may be reflecting that particular tradition. Furthermore we might note, of course, that Paul states that Jesus himself views his death as an offering '*for you*', or on '*your behalf*'

(1 Cor. 11.24). It could therefore be that Jesus tradition, as much as Isaianic content, shaped his thinking in this regard, or at least that the two strands might be in some way connected.[50]

Other potential 'Pauline Servant' texts might be suggested. Paul's claim that God made Christ who knew no sin to be sin (2 Cor. 5.21) is a possible contender. Lim, for instance, contends that this text 'constitutes a statement that conforms to the traditional expectation of the Messiah as well as the description of the Suffering Servant in Isaiah 53'.[51] The concept of Christ being made sin could be an echo of the crucifixion scene, and thus be working, like Galatians 3.13, with the Deuteronomic curse imagery (Deut. 21.22–23). 1 Corinthians 1.18 could allude to Isaiah 52.14–53.2, and if so, shed a fourth Servant Song light on the scandal or stumbling block of the cross; the lexical similarity is fairly minimal but their thematic association – the fundamental implausibility of both cross and Servant – is somewhat stronger.

A further example may be found in Philippians 2.6–11; significantly so, one might suggest, as the Christ hymn is often surmised as being the 'story of Christ' for Paul and an integral summary of Pauline Christology. Hooker, though, unsurprisingly refutes the association, and her grounds are not unreasonable. The respective words for 'servant' differ (Isaiah – *pais*; Paul – *doulos*), and the emphasis on Christ's self-emptying in the hymn pertains to the whole incarnation and not just to Jesus' death.[52] At the same time, such differences are not insurmountable, and one may still find Isaiah 53 echoes prevalent within the hymn, and many commentators end up doing so. The imagery of being *'humbled and obedient unto death'* (Phil. 2.8) could well evoke Isaiah 53.12c, and the hymn's portrayal of Christ's obedience (2.8) is resonant with the Servant's righteous characterization (53.11). The Servant is also exalted in the light of his action (52.13), consistent with the vindication and authority that God places on Christ (2.9–11). In terms of thematic rather than lexical similarity, the relationship is therefore quite strong. As Fowl observes: 'if . . . one is concerned to find conceptual backgrounds for 2.6–11 and not direct literary sources, there is much to commend Isaiah 53.'[53] The hymn's subsequent allusion to Isaiah 45.23 potentially gives further grounds for the Servant association, Isaiah 40–55 providing a wider lens against which to interpret the hymn.[54] But perhaps Gordon Fee provides the strongest endorsement of the relationship of Philippians 2.6–11 to the Servant Song:

> It is hard to imagine that early Christians . . . would not rather automatically have heard this passage with that background [i.e. the fourth Servant Song] in view, especially since that passage begins (52.13) the way this one ends, with the Servant's exaltation by God.[55]

One might say that Philippians 2 and Isaiah 53 are cut from the same proverbial cloth, and if one were looking for a framework or tapestry for which Paul might be outworking his understanding of Jesus' death, Isaiah 53 and/or Isaiah 40–55 would seem appropriate candidates to consider. As with Mark, there is sufficient Isaiah 53 'association' to generate interest but probably not enough to satisfy.

1 Corinthians 2.9

While we might struggle to find one definitive example – beyond 1 Corinthians 15.3 – where Paul explicitly evidences the *kata tas graphas* principle, there are still perhaps instances to which we might point. There may be one interesting example or further exception that proves the rule (1 Cor. 2.9, and the attested quotation found therein). The identification of the source of the quotation remains contested, however.[56] Isaiah 64.4 (Isa. 64.3 LXX) may be mooted as a possibility in this regard, but there are not insignificant differences from 2.9, and thus the source may well be an amalgam with that and Isaiah 65.17, or a 'scriptural' source text not known to us.[57] Bearing in mind also that 1 Corinthians 2.6–16 has other questions relating to it, as to its originality, some element of interpretative caution is undoubtedly appropriate.

Nonetheless, for our purposes, and assuming Pauline authorship, it seems evident that Paul thinks he is citing *Scripture* (the 'as it is written' introductory formula would seem to imply that, as it is the same form as that found in Romans 15.3), and this surely warrants some consideration, especially as the citation follows the confirmation of Jesus crucified (2.8). The wider discourse probably relates to what Anthony Thiselton terms a 'redefinition of wisdom',[58] but such wisdom redefinition is done with/through Scripture, and contextually in the light of the cross; that is, in 2.9, Paul is drawing a distinction between divine wisdom and worldly wisdom, and the way the cross manifests the former. In so doing, Paul is not so much exegeting the crucifixion as expounding its effect or context; this age does not understand God's secret purposes, otherwise they would not have crucified Jesus. There is an outcome or impact to Jesus' crucifixion – some consequence to its being 'on a cross' – and Scripture is used to affirm and explain this. As such, 1 Corinthians 2.9 potentially offers a 'scriptural' (or scripturally created?) assessment of the impact of Jesus' death for Paul, even if one is not confident as to its precise *Vorlage*.

Romans 9.33 – Isaiah 8.14; 28.16

In Romans 9.30–33, Paul continues to build on the Israel/Gentile questions that dominate chapters 9–11, and the implications therein for those Jews who do not embrace Jesus as Messiah. At various stages of Romans 9–11 (a unit Hays characterizes as a 'broadly analogous to a lament [or righteous sufferer?] psalm'[59]), Paul turns to Scripture to discern or articulate why Israel do not embrace the good news. Isaiah is his most frequent dialogue partner and citational source. Core to the scandal of Romans 9.30–33 is the way Gentiles have attained righteousness (by faith – cf. 9.30), whereas Israel has not, by virtue of their striving being premised on works (9.31). In seeking righteousness on the basis of works rather than faith, Israel has stumbled, and stumbled over a stone (*proskumma* – 9.32) effectively comprising Christ's death and resurrection.

Paul sets forth scriptural evidence of, or for, such stumbling in 9.33, with a composite citation of two texts presented as one; Isaiah 8.14 is placed 'inside' Isaiah 28.16, thereby rendering one conflated quotation. The two Isaianic chapters are suitable sources for Paul's theologizing here, since they 'both speak of a sharp division within Israel between a faithful minority who trust in the Lord and the majority who refuse to rely on God'.[60] First Peter makes a similar connection of the two texts (1 Pet. 2.6, 8), but presents them as discrete citations, juxtaposing them also with Psalm 118.22.[61] Paul also cites Isaiah 28.16 without 8.14 in Romans 10.11, suggestive perhaps that it was an integral or key kerygmatic text for him. In the Petrine instances, the textual tradition is complex, and it is similarly so here in Romans 9.33.[62] In particular, Paul's text form differs from the Isaiah 28.16 LXX *Vorlage*, and is closer to that of the Masoretic tradition, causing Dane Ortlund to suggest that there might have been an early pre-Pauline form of the text on which Paul is dependent here.[63] If so, it would confirm that, from early on in Christian practice, a kerygmatic formula or expression, one loosely tied to the OT citation, had emerged and become associated with Jesus' death, equivalent perhaps to some form of *testimonium*.[64]

The composite, conflated citation is able to fulfil a dual purpose for Paul. On the one hand, the stone is the cause of the stumbling; it is that which makes Israel fall (9.33a). On the other hand, that same stone is equally the locus of hope or vindication (9.33b); the believer will not be put to shame by embracing this stone (cf. Rom. 1.16–17). Paul does not name the stone here, of course, and one should not automatically jump to the conclusion that it is the crucified – and resurrected – Jesus. Peter makes that connection (particularly in the light of the addition of Psalm 118, already associated with Jesus' death), but Paul is more ambiguous, at least at first sight. The stone could possibly be God (this would be conversant with Isaiah 8.14), or it could be a pejorative reference to the Law (cf. Rom. 9.31). However, it is surely difficult not to read the stone as embracing the crucified Christ, and the response thereby to his death. Paul applies similar 'blockage' language elsewhere in respect of Christ (Rom. 10.21; 11.8), and the logic would seem to extend to Romans 9.33. If so, it would certainly qualify as an apologetic use of the Isaiah texts, a reading *backwards*, one might say, that sees the Christ event operative in this regard; but it would also set the framework for the Petrine appropriation of the tradition in 1 Peter 2.6, 8. Whatever the conclusion, though, integral to Paul's argument – and at the climax of the argument – is that the Scriptures of Isaiah are utilized in this regard. Romans 9.30–33 would seem to be a discrete example of Christ's death being interpreted *kata tas graphas*, and with particular attention to the way the *response* to it was similarly informed by Scripture.

Paul is therefore also able to use the OT to bring out the inherent irony of Jesus' death and the way that informs his own mission. What causes Jews – that is, those who do walk not 'by faith' – to stumble is similarly the grounds of salvation for those who *do* walk by faith. Such duality seems to be consonant with the context of Isaiah 8.14, whereby God is simultaneously the origin of the stumbling and also a place a sanctuary (Isa. 8.14a) – *both the cause of stumbling and also the locus of refuge and salvation*. This is in contrast to the LXX form of Isaiah 8.14, which stresses that the sanctuary is *not* a place of stumbling. The citation of Romans 9.33 is thus closer to the Masoretic text form that finds the sanctuary and the stumbling block in the same 'place'; it sets forth both aspects – judgement and hope – in respect of Jesus' death, and arguably establishes the anchor point for Paul's argument in the wider pericope.

One final thought on this passage: the imagery of Romans 9.30–33 is not dissimilar to that found in 1 Corinthians 1.18–31 (the *skandalon* imagery is broadly consistent, even if it has become a more literal 'stone of stumbling'), and the stone is thus the *skandalon* set before Jews, the stumbling block that is the crucified Christ. Likewise, in ways not dissimilar to 1 Corinthians 2.9, albeit in a very different context, the grounds for Israel's difficulty are found in Scripture, and the problematic aspect of Jesus' death is set forth. Hence Scripture is not being used to articulate the details of Christ's death, but it does function to set forth its effect or consequences, and to yield an explanation in this regard. It is interesting, therefore, that Paul does not appeal to the 'stone' text(s) in 1 Corinthians 1–2 to support the scandalizing aspect of Jesus' death there (perhaps because of the presenting ethnic questions of Romans 9–11 or perhaps because the Zion appellation (9.33) is too 'Jewish' for the Corinthian context).

Jesus' Death as Sacrifice

It is commonplace in recent theologizing to reduce the attention to sacrificial material found within the Pauline literature in relation to explaining Jesus' death.[65] Such reticence can often derive from the essential 'foreignness' of sacrificial language, but might also be occasioned by affront at notions of divine appeasement and/or the propitiation of divine wrath. However, a wide range of sacrificial language is still used to speak of the atonement, and this draws on OT imagery. Green and Baker summarily conclude that 'for Paul, Jesus' death is best interpreted in sacrificial terms' and suggest this is consistent with the evangelist's declaration that Jesus' death is a ransom for sins (cf. Mark 10.45).[66] It is difficult to dismiss their conclusions. Old Testament sacrificial imagery and vocabulary are used to unpack the significance of Jesus' death, even if not through explicit quotation or formal allusion.

Paul can describe Jesus as a Passover Lamb (1 Cor. 5.7) but does not develop the image in detail. Elsewhere the connotations of Romans 8.3 are that God sent Jesus effectively as a sacrifice for sin. More explicitly, one might look at Paul's clam that Jesus died as a *hilasterion* (Rom. 3.25), part of a pericope focused on the implications of Jesus' death that could be said to be 'the single most important text in Pauline soteriology'.[67] The OT and/or sacrificial background to this term would seem to be evident, but it is not quite clear what the *hilasterion* is. Some have seen it as a propitiatory sacrifice, others as an expiatory one. Alternatively, it may be the actual location of the sacrificial act; that is, the mercy seat (cf. Heb. 9.5), the lid of the Ark of the Covenant. But whatever particular form of sacrificial practice one identifies within it, it is hard to avoid some form of sacrificial aspect to Romans 3.25.

Jesus' death as Exemplary

At this point we might move to consider the way Paul uses the OT to underscore or elucidate the exemplary nature of Jesus' death. Christ's death may have had atoning significance ('*for us*' – 1 Cor. 15.3), but such atoning efficacy does not exhaust

Paul's usage of Christ's suffering, and in several instances Paul appropriates crucifixion language to portray his own actions and practice (Rom. 6.6; Gal. 6.14), in a way that seems to invest the crucifixion with some paradigmatic or mimetic aspect. We have already noted how Luke patterns Stephen's death after that of Jesus, notably in the same OT allusion (Luke 23.46; Acts 7.59; cf. Ps. 31.5), and Paul's manifestation is not dissimilar.

A Pauline mimetic appeal to Jesus' death is unsurprising when we consider how frequently Paul appeals to Christ as an example figure. Larry W. Hurtado acknowledges this aspect within Pauline thinking, averring: 'Jesus . . . functions as the inspiring model of the ethical qualities that are to characterize the present life of the redeemed and of the eschatological outcome of their redemption as well'.[68] Paul urges the Roman Christians to '*put on Jesus Christ*' (Rom. 13.14), or to embrace the same attitude as Jesus Christ (Phil. 2.5). Such mimesis is particularly pertinent for Paul himself, and he seems to go out of his way to portray himself as akin to Jesus, embracing an *imitatio Christi* pattern or mode of encounter, and can therefore exhort the Corinthian church to imitate him as he imitates Christ (1 Cor. 11.1; cf. also 1 Thess. 1.6; 1 Cor. 4.16–17). Integral to such mimesis is the exemplary aspect of Jesus' death. Paul can declare that he has been crucified with Christ (Gal. 2.19), or express how he is partaking in Christ's sufferings (2 Cor. 12.3–7) and how he knows Christ most intimately in his suffering and death (Phil. 3.10). Likewise, Paul claims that he carries the death of Jesus in his body (2 Cor. 4.7–12) and has the rhetorical stigmata, or marks of Jesus branded on him (Gal. 6.17). The curious comment that Paul bears a thorn in his flesh, one that plagues him in ongoing fashion (2 Cor. 12.7), could well be a further, oblique reference to his sharing in Jesus' suffering, and therefore effectively another instance of Paul exhibiting an 'exemplary' mode of behaviour.

As such, Paul does seem to have in mind a pattern/story of the living Jesus that he calls his readers to embrace. A key element of the 'story' is Jesus' obedience, especially his obedience unto death (Phil 2.8), and it is that central aspect of Jesus' character that Paul seeks to mimic or replicate. *How* Jesus dies, as well as the event of his death, remains crucial for Paul. Unsurprisingly then, the exemplary aspect of Jesus' death is associated with some form of appeal to the Jewish Scriptures. One such instance would be 2 Corinthians 4.7–12, where Paul directly juxtaposes, and implicitly connects, his own sufferings (2 Cor. 4.8–9) with Jesus' death (2 Cor. 4.10–11), so that Jesus' death becomes efficacious in him. While there is no formal OT citation operative in verses 7–12, there are potential echoes of the righteous sufferer psalms, and if these psalms have already become associated with Passion traditions, it is probable that Paul might have them in mind when explicating the exemplary role of Jesus' death, conceiving of 'his own experience as a recapitulation of the christological paradigm'.[69] The language of being *persecuted, but not forsaken* (4.9) echoes the common expression of the sufferer (the verb *egkataleipo* is the same one used in the psalmic appeals of Matt. 27.46; Mark 15.34; Acts 2.27, 31). Paul also contextualizes these reflections on his/Jesus' sufferings in 2 Corinthians 4.13 with a direct reference to Psalm 116.10 and its imagery that draws on wider righteous sufferer texts. In Psalm 116, the psalmist faces death (116.3) and calls out to God for rescue and vindication (116.4); he receives such rescue, and is able to evaluate the suffering he has experienced (116.8–11) and declare himself approved as God's servant (116.16). Paul is thus able to apply the logic of the psalm to his own experience, and that of Christ; just as Christ's (righteous) sufferings vindicated him as God's faithful servant, so also Paul's own suffering should be seen in such terms. As such, one might surmise that:

> *Paul's reliance on this scriptural worldview* reveals his understanding that his sufferings are not a matter of coincidence, but, like Jesus' own experience on the cross, are part of God's sovereign plan to reveal power by sustaining Paul in the midst of his afflictions.[70]

If Paul has so imbibed the principle that Jesus died 'according to Scriptures', then it follows that the hortatory application of Jesus' death is also consistent with, occasioned and demonstrated by Scripture. Just as the gospel writers found the righteous sufferer motif a convivial one for explicating Jesus' death, so Paul similarly finds it a suitable template for reflecting on his own experience of suffering and distress. It may therefore be in the background of Paul's other theologizing on his experience of suffering, with the reflection of Philippians 1.19 potentially one such example,[71] or likewise 2 Timothy 4.17 and Paul's recollection of being rescued from the lion's mouth (2 Tim. 4.17), probably also an echo of Daniel 6.

But perhaps the most explicit instance of this exemplary appeal occurs in Romans 15.3, this time with a more formal OT quotation attested.[72] Paul holds up Christ's selfless behaviour as a model for his readers, but does so with a direct citation of Psalm 69.9b.[73] Although the Scripture is 'written' (15.3; cf. 1 Cor. 2.9), it is perceived in some way to be on Christ's lips; that is, Christ is giving voice to it[74] and, on Paul's reading, effectively becomes the one 'praying' the psalm to God. Paul has already cited Psalm 69.22–23 in Romans 11.9–10 but attributed it there to David; in 15.3 it becomes the prayer of Christ and enables Paul to portray 'the suffering of Jesus as a paradigm for obedience, emulation, and even participation'.[75] The previous part of Psalm 69.9 is cited in John 2.17 (Ps. 69.9a), but Paul's use differs from his Johannine counterpart; John's context is that the disciples remember Jesus' words in this regard, whereas Paul effectively imposes the words on Jesus' lips,[76] a process Hays terms 'christological ventriloquism'.[77] In Paul's perspective, Jesus 'owns' the psalm, one might say – he has authority for it and for its usage and interpretation, particularly in respect of his suffering and death.

As with 2 Corinthians 4.13, Paul therefore utilizes the psalm to portray Christ as a righteous sufferer, and from that position, to exploit the exemplary ramifications of such suffering. Romans 15.4 sets the citation in context, with Paul proposing that whatever was written in former days – that is, Scripture – offers the basis for ethical instruction; Christ's suffering, voiced by Christ himself in the psalm, provides such a basis. Furthermore, the quotation of Psalm 69.9 suggests Pauline awareness not just of the righteous sufferer tradition – and its capacity to be used in this exemplary fashion – but also the association of that tradition specifically *with Jesus' death*. Paul does not need to justify or explain the connection he is making; there is no expansion as to why/how he might be appealing to the psalm, it is merely presented as an accepted given. Wright thus contends that Romans 15.3 captures the 'basic story of Jesus', and particularly the Gethsemane narrative where Jesus apprehensively awaits his fate.[78] This would suggest, then, that Psalm 69 – and the wider righteous sufferer tradition – has become so intertwined with the Passion tradition that it cannot be 'cited' without hearing Christ's inhabiting of the role.[79] Indeed, in view of such association, Hays surmises that the righteous sufferer psalms were embedded into early Church tradition, prior to the writing of Romans, and therefore that Psalms 22 and 69 – and perhaps 116 too – could well be the texts understood within the *kata tas graphas* designation of 1 Corinthians 15.3.[80]

This may also extend to Paul's use of the Suffering Servant motif. Whereas, as we have observed, scholarly discussion has tended to focus on the appropriation (or otherwise) of Isaiah 52.13 – 53.12 for soteriological/vicarious reasons (i.e. '*for our sins*' – 1 Cor. 15.3), it is possible that such texts are also being deployed by Paul for heuristic purposes as well, to – typologically? – indicate the kind of suffering he has experienced. It could be seen to inform the ethical practice espoused in Romans 12.12–21, the call to bless those who persecute you (12.14), weep with those who weep (12.15) and to overcome evil with good (12.21).[81] We will see similar usage of Isaiah 53 in this regard in 1 Peter 2.22–25, and Paul might offer prior evidence of such practice. The Servant Song, and particularly its suffering dimension, provides a framework of self-understanding that enables – or causes? – Paul to conceive of himself in the light of Isaianic servant, and follow on from Jesus in that light.

Conclusion

Whereas Paul has a prominent *theologia crucis*, and whereas he is heavily dependent on the Jewish Scriptures for his theologizing, he has remarkably little direct, explicit appeal to the Old Testament to authenticate Jesus' death as being according to the Scriptures. His epistolary corpus is an important testimony to the early Church's view on the scriptural warrant for Jesus' death (1 Corinthian 15.3), but there is surprisingly little articulation of the 'nitty-gritty' aspect of this in his letters (1 Corinthians 2.9 perhaps being the exception that proves the rule). It is likely that such association was made as part of his missionary preaching (cf. Gal. 3.1), but it is not foregrounded in the extant Pauline literature.

Thus Paul does not use the OT to resource or scripturalize the 'events' of the Passion, even when he makes reference to them. It may be, then, that the OT 'fulfilment' we find in the Gospels, in relation to particular aspects of the Passion, derives more from the individual writers rather than being the 'core' of the tradition being passed down. Instead the scriptural backdrop to Jesus' death is more implicit but still impactful. We have seen that it might inform three elements of Paul's understanding:

1 *Soteriological* – drawing to a degree on Isaiah 53, that Christ died for our sins.

2 *Missional/Ecclesiological* – drawing particularly on texts from Isaiah in terms of the acceptance/rejection of Jesus' death.

3 *Ethical* – using the image of Christ as the Righteous Sufferer – notably Romans 15.3; cf. Psalm 69.9 – as a model for imitating Christ.

7

The Old Testament in
Hebrews' Passion

In terms of the New Testament's appropriation of Old Testament material in relation to the significance of Jesus' death, the so-called Letter to the Hebrews warrants particular engagement in its own right. One might point to three core reasons for this. First, OT citation and allusion form and shape the heartbeat of Hebrews' discourse, and it is hard – perhaps impossible – to extrapolate Hebrews' argument, or its mode of interpretation, from the scriptural material that provides its interpretative ingredients. When reading Hebrews, one cannot help but encounter a tapestry of OT images and citations; indeed, the interpreter may feel easily confused if she cannot sufficiently grasp or comprehend its core OT imagery.[1] Second, the interpretative or hermeneutical mode Hebrews uses in this regard is sufficiently distinct or discrete, and lacks any particularly close parallels or equivalents. For example, its characteristic mode of portraying Scripture as divine speech, thereby creating divinely voiced introductory formulae (i.e. 'God says'), is a key feature of the epistle's 'DNA', and one that warrants further hermeneutical consideration, particularly in terms of how Hebrews conceives of the OT as 'Scripture' or 'text'.[2] Jesus 'speaks' in Hebrews, but speaks only Scripture. Third, the particular doctrinal focus of the letter, namely Christ's once and for all high-priestly offering – of himself – places Jesus' death at the centre of Hebrews' theologizing. While Christ's death is not the sole 'issue' within the letter (the repeated warnings against apostasy are surely also core to the tenor of the text – cf. 6.4–8; 10.27–31), and while the OT likewise contributes to the author's reflections on these other matters, it is something of a given to say that OT interpretation shapes the implementation of a major epistolary theme.[3]

As such, the text of Hebrews is riddled with references to Jesus' death that are associated with, or generated by, OT imagery. Jesus dies as Son (1.5; 5.7–8; cf. Ps. 2.7; 2 Sam. 7.14), as high priest (5.6; cf. Ps. 110.4) and as the one who offers his own body in terms of his death (10.5–10; cf. Ps. 40.6–8), and Hebrews finds scriptural warrant for all these respective lenses. Likewise the epistle can draw on a variety of scriptural motifs in respect of Jesus' death, but without using formal quotation to do so. The wider context of the letter's discourse is the inability of the old covenant to achieve forgiveness of sins (10.1–4), a reversal of which was achieved by Christ's death, an event conceived of as the new, or better covenant (8.6–13). The portrayal of Jesus' death is hence set against the tapestry of the Day of Atonement (9.6–14), and Jesus' high-priestly actions are compared with those of the Aaronic predecessors (7.11–28). The centrepiece, for many, of Hebrews' doctrinal discourse is 7.1 – 10.18[4] and the exposition of the New Covenant therein. Such exposition includes comparison and engagement with a wide array of Mosaic and Aaronic images – the construction of the tabernacle system as the 'location' for Jesus' offering (9.1–10), or the sacrificial practices within the respective covenantal orders (9.23–28). Each of these is directly compared with the practice and achievements of Jesus' death, with sacrifice a focal theme; without shedding of blood, says Hebrews, there is not forgiveness of sins (9.22). There is also the wider comparison of Jesus' high-priestly function in terms of Melchizedek, in part with reference to Genesis 14.17–24 but more explicitly in terms of Psalm 110.4 (cf. Heb. 7.1–10). More specifically, Jesus' sacrificial blood speaks a better word than the blood of Abel (12.24), and the shedding of blood inaugurates the new covenant, just as it did the first one (9.18). There is even some OT reference in terms of the resurrection, with the *Akedah* perhaps seen in these terms (11.19), indicative therefore that Genesis 22 was in some – limited – way linked with the Passion. At the same time, Hebrews can seem to overly focus on Jesus' death, and move directly from crucifixion and on to the Ascension (i.e. without apparent reference to the resurrection – though cf. 13.20). Its use of the OT has traditionally been seen as reinforcing this, though recent scholarship has offered a rebuttal of that view, particularly in paying due attention to the life-giving aspect of blood within the OT sacrificial system.[5]

Hence there is no *one* 'text' or schema on which Hebrews draws in this regard, rather a matrix or amalgam of a number of sources or traditions, notably Psalms 110, 40 and Jeremiah 31, and Hebrews combines and juxtaposes such interaction to unpack the significance of Jesus' death. Indeed, many have averred that Hebrews' use of the OT is rather like a set of mini-sermons on these given passages; the biblical text – normally in its Septuagintal form – is cited and the writer of Hebrews then offers something akin to an exposition on that text, or on certain key words or themes within it.[6] This can mean some quite long textual citations, but limited interaction with them; the citation of Jeremiah 31.31–34 (Heb. 8.8–12), for example, is the longest quotation in the NT, but Hebrews' interaction with it is more minimal, concentrating foremost on the *new* aspect of the covenant and the impact for what now becomes 'old' covenantal thinking (8.13).

Hebrews also adopts the contemporary interpretative practice of focusing on one word or phrase within a citation, as the concentrated locus for exegesis.[7] For example, in its citation of Psalm 95.7–11 (Heb. 3.7–11), Hebrews exploits the semantic possibility of the word 'Today' in this regard (Heb. 3.13, 15–19), and likewise the notion of 'rest' (Heb. 3.11; 4.1–11). Hebrews' prologue may also shape this hermeneutic. God has spoken previously through and by the prophets but has now spoken by his Son (1.1–2). While there is discontinuity here, there is also a notable *continuity* – a continuity of divine speech, whereby the prophetic promise and expectations are now realized.[8] As David deSilva opines of Hebrews' OT hermeneutic: 'since the final word was spoken through the Son, the earlier words can frequently find their "true" meaning when spoken by him as well.'[9]

Furthermore, Hebrews' use of the OT, while premised on significant, specific citation of actual scriptural texts, is also founded on an appeal to a wider scriptural *narrative*. The account of the

Day of Atonement, for example, is so embedded into Hebrews' theology, it is not 'cited' as a quotation or allusion, but the cultic event becomes the tapestry on which Christ's death is explicated and explored. To put it another way: Christ dying 'according to the Scriptures' for Hebrews is part of an appeal to a wider story rather than to explicit specific citations, and in that sense is conversant with the broader perspective we suggested for 1 Corinthians 15.3. At the same time, Hooker offers an alternative – though not necessarily contrasting – view on that point. She makes the interesting observation that Hebrews effectively names or identifies those Scriptures that are left *unnamed* in 1 Corinthians 15.3, and thus that the latter text 'could stand as the text of his [Hebrews'] epistle'.[10] Whereas Paul remains implicit or silent, Hebrews identifies those very Scriptures that *do* show how Christ could be seen as 'dying for our sins'. Or to put it another way, Hebrews seeks to fill in the gaps of what Paul – and those from whom he inherited the *kata tas graphas* tradition – might have meant by Christ dying according to the Scriptures. As such, Hebrews offers the strongest, or most articulated aspect as to *how* Jesus' death interprets the Scriptures.

Let us consider one presenting textual example. We have seen that Isaiah 53 has been used to some degree by all our previous NT authors, and that there is some sense that it shaped each of their respective assessments of Jesus' death (but without doing so in a dominant or exclusive fashion). Hebrews is probably a further such instance, alluding sufficiently to the Fourth Servant Song – but only secondarily so, perhaps, other texts being more formally quoted in this regard (Pss. 110; 40; Jer. 31; perhaps Ps. 8). The most probable allusion to the Song is found in Hebrews 9.28 and Christ's offering – once for all – to '*bear the sins of many*', a reworking of the same phrase found in Isaiah 53.12.[11] It may also echo Isaiah 53.4 and its assertion of the sin-bearing characterization of the Servant therein. The Servant Song also opens with its key figure's exaltation (Isa. 52.13), just like Hebrews (1.1–4), and only then moves to their humiliation, again like Hebrews, and to a death that deals with sin in some vicarious sense. However, 9.28 would seem to be the only place in the letter in which any Isaiah 53 formal allusion may be found (there may be an echo of Isa.

53.12 in Heb. 13.12–13, but it is faint, at best), and such limited use is striking, particularly for a text so focused both on Jesus' death and its scriptural attestation. And the Song gives no particular grounds for the *high-priestly* dimension for Jesus' death, so central for Hebrews' explication of the event. Were Isaiah 53 really so embedded as the Passion Narrative's primary *kata tas graphas* text, should one not expect a greater frequency to its usage? Evans surmises that the limited use derives from the text's being so established within the tradition, and its role is therefore assured;[12] but that is an argument from silence. While such a 'given' characterization is certainly possible, it may equally be the case that the Servant Song was merely one of a wider repertoire of scriptural texts of which Hebrews could avail itself, but without any implication that it was the 'go to' text in this regard.

One might also make the point that Hebrews reads – or can read – Christ *back* into the OT, not dissimilar perhaps to aspects of the Johannine tendency to view the Scriptures speaking directly about Jesus (John 5.39; 12.41). While this is not explicitly related to Christ's *death*, it is notable that Moses is said to experience sufferings *'for Christ'* while in Egypt (Heb. 11.24–26). This not only reads Christ back into the scriptural account but also does so in relation to Christ's sufferings – one might say his death, bearing in mind Hebrews' focal interest in that regard. Moreover, the christological link with Moses seems particularly significant. On the one hand, Hebrews uses the same term for Moses' suffering (*oneidismos* – 11.26) as for the abuse Jesus bore in his death (13.13), and which the audience are likewise encouraged to embrace. Such lexical similarity would seem to offer a broad Mosaic lens to Jesus' death (or perhaps, more exactly, portray Moses in Jesus terms, rather than vice versa). On the other hand, this same word (*oneidismos*) is frequently used in Psalm 69 (69.7, 9–10, 19–20) which, as we have seen, is a core 'righteous sufferer' text for the gospel Passion Narratives, and also cited in Romans 15.3 (Ps. 69.9), placed on Christ's lips. Hence it is quite possible that Hebrews' use of such language, in both 11.24–26 and 13.12–13, reflects its awareness of, or familiarity with, the OT sources that informed wider evangelistic/Passion Narrative tradition.

Hebrews' Portrayal of Jesus' death

This view carries further weight when one considers Hebrews' depiction of the Passion. While the letter lacks a formal, extended narration of Jesus' death, and while it is not extensively interested in Jesus' pre-mortem earthly ministry, it still has a number of references to the events contained within a putative Passion Narrative, and these would seemingly attest to the author's awareness of some form of such Passion-related traditions. The death is explicitly described as by crucifixion and shame-bearing (12.2), and in a way so as to shed blood (cf. 12.4). The allusive reference to Jesus' enduring hostility from sinners (12.3), embedded with the references to crucifixion and shedding of blood, may reflect the abuse tradition, either on the part of the Roman soldiers (cf. Mark 15.16–20) or of the wider crowds (Mark 15.29–32). Likewise the subsequent reference to lifting weak knees may be an echo of the Johannine Passion tradition of ensuring Jesus' legs were not broken (John 19.31–33).

Hebrews records Jesus offering up prayers and supplications to God to the 'one who could save him from death' (5.7), and this would seem to draw on the Gethsemane narrative and associated tradition. The lexical variation from the Synoptic tradition has caused some to suggest that Hebrews 5.7 is independent of their Passion Narratives,[13] but the wider context surely permits some connection with the Gethsemane account.[14] Jesus' prayers are tearfully accompanied (5.7), and the implied depiction bears a close resemblance to the Markan portrayal, with Jesus in anguish as to his impending fate and seemingly abandoned by those around him (cf. Mark 14.34–36).[15] Some scholars, perhaps because of these Gethsemane parallels, have even proposed that OT righteous sufferer psalms might have formed the backdrop to Hebrews 5.7–8, with either Psalm 22 (cf. Ps. 22.24) or Psalm 31 (cf. Ps. 31.23) operative in this manner.[16] Unlike Mark, though, there is no formal citation of Psalms 42 and 43, and it is possible, therefore, that the Lucan account of the episode (Luke 22.41–44) might be more in Hebrews' mind, the loud cries (5.7) expressing confidence rather than hesitancy, and with Jesus not necessarily apprehensive as to his imminent fate (i.e. 5.7–8 are not *necessarily* portraying Jesus as anxious in this regard).[17] Alternatively, if Hebrews is emphasizing the volume of Jesus' cries, 5.7–8 may be alluding to the crucifixion scene itself and Jesus' crying out from the cross, perhaps the Markan cry of dereliction (Mark 15.34; cf. Ps. 22.1).[18] Whatever the specific part of the Passion Narrative, Hebrews emphasizes the reality of Jesus' suffering and its associated efficacious, formative aspect. Jesus learnt obedience through such suffering (5.8) and was perfected or completed by it (5.9). The tenor of this is commensurate, one suggests, with the psalmic righteous sufferer tradition.

Hebrews is also aware of Passion tradition relating to the location of the crucifixion scene and aspects of its broader retelling. Hebrews exhorts its readers to follow Jesus outside the city/camp, and to embrace the suffering he so endured (13.12–13). This seems to be a plausible historical reference, is consistent with John's location of Jesus' death (John 19.16–18; cf. also Mark 15.20–22), and the reference to abuse (13.13) potentially includes the verbal mockery Jesus experienced (Mark 15.29–32; cf. Ps. 22.6–8) as well as the physical suffering. Hebrews' tangential reference to crucifying Christ again and holding him up to contempt (6.6) might also echo this public, shaming imagery.

This reference to the Passion account might also be shaped or informed by broader OT imagery, particularly as 13.10–16 return the reader back to the sacrificial and cultic themes that dominate the epistle's prior discourse (inter alia 'altar' – 13.10; sanctuary – 13.11). Some have surmised, for example, that the location of Jesus' death 'outside the gate' reflects the imagery of the Day of Atonement and the taking of the animal outside the camp (cf. Lev. 16.27).[19] The language may be similar but there are key points of difference, notably that the death of Jesus takes place outside the city/camp, whereas the sacrificial victims of the Day of Atonement die *inside* the camp, and their carcasses are only subsequently taken outside. Hence it is likely that Leviticus 17.1–9 may equally be part of the OT matrix in 13.10–16; the passage follows on from the Yom Kippur narrative of Leviticus 16, but importantly, it addresses the sacrifice of an animal whose death occurs *outside* the camp (like that of Jesus – 13.12). Hebrews 13.10–16 may even pick up the narrative of Exodus 33.7–11, and Moses pitching the Tent of Meeting outside the camp. As an alternative place of sacrifice to the tabernacle, and external to the camp confines, it is a place where encounter with God occurs (33.9–10). Hebrews may see in that Exodus account a different mode of divine engagement that is 'better' than that espoused in the tabernacle sacrificial system.[20]

Jesus' death as Priestly Action – Psalm 110.1, 4

If there is one text around which Hebrews seeks to unpack its understanding of Jesus' death, it would probably be Psalm 110.[21] Hebrews is able to draw on its dual claim, namely that the one seated at God's right hand (Ps. 110.1) is the same (royal) figure who is a priest for ever in the order of Melchizedeck (Ps. 110.4). Verse 1 pertains to the Son's role and authority (i.e. being greater than angels – cf. Heb. 1.13–14), but as the text goes on, its remit is extended to imply the completion of the Christ's work. To 'sit down', particularly at God's right hand, is to indicate the success-ful achievement of Christ's work, and especially the once/once for all dimension to it (1.3; 8.1; 10.12).

Psalm 110.4 is perhaps more directly related to Jesus' death, as it is the launch pad both for the Son's priestly characterization and for the eternal nature of his priestly function. Because he is an eternal high priest, and a 'successful' one, Jesus is able to become the source of 'eternal salvation' (5.9) for all who believe him. In the light of Psalm 110.4, Hebrews makes mention of Melchizedeck and refers briefly to Genesis 14 (7.1–10), but it ends up making little of that association, particularly in respect of Jesus' death. Instead the comparison is made with the earthly, Aaronic high priesthood, which is always subject to death and change (7.23–28), and Jesus' high priesthood is thus presented as superior – it is *eternal*. But in terms of its use of Scripture, Hebrews does exercise some degree of exegetical licence here; for all its sacerdo-tal interest, the psalm makes no claim to *high* priesthood, the very form of priestly practice with which Hebrews seeks to engage. Instead, as with the Aaronic high priesthood, it is God who calls the high priest (5.4), and it is the Father's appointment of the Son to this role (5.5, citing Ps. 2.7) that vindicates the status of the designation. As the (high) priest for ever (5.6, citing Ps. 110.4), Jesus is then able, in his death, to make the once and for all Day of Atonement sacrifice (9.11–12), the once and for all offering of himself (10.4–10).

Jesus' death as New Covenant – Jeremiah 31

Scot McKnight pithily surmises that 'If Paul crossed the threshold by sorting out the relationship of the old to the new in terms of covenant, the author of Hebrews set up shop and made the category his home to an unprecedented degree.'[22] McKnight's interest lies primarily in mapping the evolution of covenant thinking in terms of the Christ event, but he rightly underscores the centrality of the New Covenant for Hebrews, particularly as a lens or motif for explicating Jesus' death.[23] What has occasioned this focus is not self-evident but it may, as with the Synoptic rehearsals of the Passion Narrative, have origins in the ritual or cultic context.[24] Either way, the (new) covenant discourse is central; Jesus is announced as the mediator of the New Covenant (8.6) and also the guarantor of it (7.22), his sacrificial death core to its inception. The central discourse of Hebrews 7—10 provides the focus for explicating the contours of this New Covenant (a better high priesthood, a better tabernacle, a better sacrifice), with the citation of Jeremiah 31 the launch pad for it and effectively 'the programmatic statement for the remainder of Hebrews'.[25] The citation follows the LXX form and is, as noted, the longest OT quotation in the New Testament. The Jeremiah text has no particular association with death, christological or otherwise, but Hebrews views the Christ event, and Jesus' self-offering, as the fulfilment of the prophecy. It would seem that the shedding of blood is associated with New Covenant inauguration, again drawing on OT imagery, and Hebrews reads the event in that light.

Despite the lengthy quotation, Hebrews does not engage extensively with the Jeremiah text. Instead what matters for Hebrews is that the covenant is *new* (8.7, 13). Jesus' death has consequences for the former covenant, which is now rendered 'old' by the inauguration of its successor. The attribution of Jesus' death as New Covenant thus becomes the key that unlocks the various other elements within the first covenant (priesthood, sacrifice, tabernacle), and Christ's death redeems the believer from the sins committed under the first covenant (9.16).

Scripture as Jesus' speech

Characteristic of Hebrews' understanding and usage of the OT is its presentation of Scripture as divine speech; that is, it is explicitly voiced by God (4.3), by Jesus (2.12–13) and even by the Holy Spirit (3.7). Hermeneutic-wise, the OT is conceived literally as the word(s) of God rather than merely a textual or written medium, and the vocalization functions as the introductory formula designating that a quotation is being used. In two of these divine-utterance instances (2.12–13; 10.5–7), Jesus is the one voicing Scripture, and in a fashion that sheds light on how the OT is being used to portray his death (akin to Pauline examples such as Rom. 15.3). The first occurrence derives from a text foregrounded within the Passion Narrative but the second one is from a less familiar text or at least one that is not so obviously present there. Both texts are declared in the midst of the congregation (cf. Ps. 40.10). Either way, though, when Hebrews' Jesus uses direct speech, he uses the language of Scripture. We might note that the letter's further reference to Jesus speaking – 5.7, as discussed above – is connected to the portrayal of his death, and warrants further consideration in that regard. It is notable, though, that Hebrews does not explicitly place Scripture on the *earthly* Jesus' lips here – in contrast to the evangelistic testimony.

Hebrews 2.12 – Psalm 22.22

The first instance of Jesus speaking Scripture is the citation of Psalm 22.22 (LXX 21.23) in Hebrews 2.12. It is the first citation of a double or effectively composite quotation, with Hebrews likewise placing the words of Isaiah 8.17–18 on Jesus' lips (2.13). We have noted already, of course, that Psalm 22 is a significant text in respect of the Gospels' Passion portrayals, but its usage here is not explicitly related to Jesus' death. The context is instead Jesus' intermediary declaration of God's name in the assembled congregation of his siblings, probably a post-exaltation proclamation, and tied more to Jesus' resurrection than to his death. As the one who is declared 'Son' by God (1.5), the Son responds with an affirmation of his resultant filial and fraternal identity.

However, while the primary citational context may be the sibling one (2.11), it remains intriguing that, in order to explicate the familial efficacy of Jesus' death, Hebrews appeals to the same psalm the gospel writers use to narrate and frame the Passion encounter. What is notable is how the citation draws on the second part of Psalm 22, that portion known as the vindicatory part (or what Amy Peeler terms the 'exuberant section'),[26] rather than the one in which the sufferer's isolation or abandonment is recorded. Hebrews use of the psalm therefore testifies to the post-mortem – or post-suffering? – vindication of Jesus, a vindication that is divinely enabled and for which the vindicated one's praise is occasioned. At the key point of the psalm, when lament turns to vindication, we have the quotation: 'God has delivered. As Jesus cried out in dereliction, so he now announces his triumph at the exaltation.'[27] This might suggest, therefore, that the early Church was utilizing the full extent of the psalmic text rather than merely the first 'suffering' part, and this might add weight – by extension – to the notion that Mark had the full gamut of the psalm in view.[28] Peeler seems to concur, and concludes in respect of the suffering alluded to in Psalm 22.1: 'Jesus' suffering remains on the minds of the audience even if Jesus does not articulate it here.'[29]

Such a conclusion becomes more likely in view of the wider context of the quotations. The citations in 2.12–13 are preceded by explicit discussion of Jesus' death, his actual 'tasting' of it (2.9) and the suffering he so endured (2.9–10). It thus seems probable that, for biblically literate hearers, familiar with the wider scope of Psalm 22, they might be encouraged make the connections with Jesus' sufferings (2.9–10) and the suffering of the righteous figure of Psalm 22.1–21, particularly through the reference to Psalm 22.15 and its explicit claim that *'you led me down into the dust of death.'* Likewise the scriptural citations are immediately followed by Hebrews' appeal to the *achievements* of Jesus' death, namely that, through death, Jesus might beat the one who holds power over death – the Devil (2.14). That is, the appeal to Psalm 22 is appropriately juxtaposed with an explication of Jesus' death, partly to articulate its reality (2.9, 14), partly to explicate it efficacy (2.14–15) and partly to demonstrate the need for Jesus to be like his fellow sisters and brothers so as to make the atonement 'successful' (2.17) – the same sisters and brothers, one assumes, announced in Psalm 22.22. Hebrews 2.8–18 might therefore be said to capture the full contours of Psalm 22, its articulation of both suffering *and* vindication. And if Hebrews 5.7 does have in mind the Markan cry of dereliction, as suggested above, then there is further association with the first half of Psalm 22, albeit not explicitly named as such by the letter.

By contrast, Gert Steyn, commenting on the quotation in Hebrews 2.12 of Psalm 22.22, argues that 'there is no indication that the author of Hebrews used it here in the same sense' as the gospel writers.[30] While such interpretative caution is normally appropriate, and while it remains true that Hebrews does specifically cite the 'other' part of the psalm (i.e. that exhibiting the 'forsaken' imagery) found within the Gospels, the continuity argued above remains significant. And as a minimum, there is continuity with the psalm being placed on Jesus' lips and therefore associated *with Jesus*; in both Hebrews and Mark the psalm is spoken by him, broadly in relation to his death, and the cry is addressed to God. It seems legitimate, therefore, to argue that Hebrews is reading the psalm in full, as attesting to both the real suffering that ensued but also the divine vindication it ultimately promised. Johnson arrives at the same conclusion, proposing in respect of 2.12: 'Hebrews is . . . using scriptural passages that would be recognized within the Christian community as messianic in the broad sense, and as touching on the paradox that one rejected by humans is vindicated by God.'[31]

Bearing in mind Hebrews' characterization of Jesus as *faithful* high priest (2.17), one might suggest that Hebrews construes Psalm

22 as portraying a faithful sufferer rather than a righteous one. The appeal to Psalm 22 – and thus to Christ as a 'faithful sufferer' – might also be in service of showing Christ's empathy with the readers' suffering (cf. 2.18; 12.3–4) and hence, by implication, that their suffering would receive divine vindication and was thus not in vain. They should remain faithful as he remained faithful. This would also invest Jesus' death with an exemplary aspect (akin to what we have seen in Paul and will also see in 1 Peter), particularly in terms of solidarity with his sisters and brothers.

In view of the reading of Psalm 22, we might ponder whether the same interpretation might be made of Psalm 118, another text we have seen the Gospels use extensively to unpack the significance and nature of Jesus' death. Hebrews explicitly quotes Psalm 118.6 in Hebrews 13.6, though not in an overtly mortal context, and one wonders whether the psalm's use within the Passion Narrative has significance here. Any such connection is only implicit, as Hebrews gives no formal signal to take the wider (Passion) usage of Psalm 118 into account, but bearing in mind the subsequent exemplary appeal to Jesus (Heb. 13.8, 12–15), some form of association with Jesus' death is not unfeasible. As we have noted, the psalm sees the vindication of the one who was opposed and rejected, and the context of Hebrews 13.12–13 would seem to echo the dual sense of rejection and triumph that the psalm embodies, and which Mark's Passion, in particular, seems to embrace. At the very least one might venture that the psalm's flavour fits well with Hebrews' own portrayal of the royal Son par excellence (1.2), who is obedient and made perfect through suffering (cf. 5.8–9). It might, then, form part of what it could mean for Hebrews for Jesus Christ to die *kata tas graphas*.

Hebrews 10.5–9 – Psalm 40.6–8

The second incidence of OT Scripture being placed on Jesus' lips is an extended quotation of Psalm 40 in Hebrews 10.5–7 (and repeated in 10.8–9). The citation is utilized to demonstrate, from Scripture, the inefficacy of the old sacrificial system (10.5–6) and its incapacity to take away sin (10.1–4). Whereas the annual repetition of the old system served only to underscore the inefficacy of taking away sins, and as a reminder of its incapacity to do so (10.3), Hebrews finds in Psalm 40 both the scriptural testimony to such inefficacy and the christological voice of an obedient *bodily* offering that would be welcomed by God (10.4–10). In the eyes of Hebrews, the psalmist depicts Christ's sacrifice of his body as effective in a way that the sacrifices of the old covenant could not be. Throughout the epistle, Hebrews understands Jesus' death in sacrificial terms and, with the citation of Psalm 40.6–8, it appeals to the Scriptures to underscore or explicate the essential inefficacy of the old system. Or to put it in the terms of Martin Karrer: 'LXX Psalm 39 [i.e. Ps. 40] condenses the Christological point of Hebrews.'[32]

Core, though, to Hebrews' use of the psalm is the given LXX textual form. The Masoretic text of Psalm 40.6 reads *'but you have given me an open ear'* rather than a prepared body, and thus would not enable the particular offering Hebrews seeks to exploit. Only the LXX reading of 'body' offers that option, and hence Hebrews' use of that particular textual form is crucial. The reason for the textual variance is not clear – perhaps 'ear' is seen as representing the whole – or it may be that Hebrews knew of both readings, and thought 'body' was the one that fully brought out the ethos of the psalm at this point (i.e. rather than being a textual variant, Hebrews considered it the true essence of the text). But either way, if Hebrews wishes to articulate a view on Christ's death that involves the sacrifice of his *body* as high priest, and for this to be the 'once for all' sacrifice, it can only do so because of the particular text form available to it. Or at least, it can do so in terms of priestly offering, but not necessarily of a *high* priest, as the psalm text does not include a reference to the high priest.[33]

Jesus' Death and Paraenetic sections of Hebrews

The Letter to the Hebrews broadly divides into two streams or sections of material: one that might be termed 'doctrinal' and one that might be viewed as 'hortatory' or 'paraenetic'. These streams are intertwined in the structure of the letter, and Hebrews switches between them as it progresses.[34] Whereas much of the explication of Jesus' death, and hence the OT attestation to it, occurs within the doctrinal streams (as we have seen), one might surmise that the impact of Jesus' death, and the readers' response to it, are still integrally 'associated' with the paraenetic material. OT imagery is prevalent here too, as the audience is compared to – portrayed even – as the wilderness generation, and particularly their rejection of God at Kadsesh Barnea at the point of entry to the land (Deut. 1.19–40). Hebrews cites Psalm 95 in this regard, a text that presents the reader with the implications of the wilderness generation's rejection of God's offer of rest (3.7–12). As David wrote the psalm after Israel had entered the promised land, Hebrews interprets it as setting forth a new (sabbath) rest (4.8–11), one that remains open to those who embrace Christ's once and for all sacrifice (4.1–2).

Broadly speaking, Christ's obedience as a faithful sufferer (3.1–6; 12.1–3) is juxtaposed with Israel's disobedience as faithless sufferers (3.16–19; 10.26–31). Scriptural citation is offered to exhort the readers to faithful suffering (Hab. 2.4; Heb. 10.37–38), and we see, as with Paul, the OT being used to sustain an exemplary response to Jesus' death. Particularly pertinent to our concerns, perhaps, is Hebrews 6.4–8. Here the author interprets apostasy as not just rejecting Jesus but crucifying him again (6.6). This not only explicitly foregrounds Jesus' death in the hortatory material, it contextualizes the response to his death against the backdrop of the Old Testament and its associated imagery; that is, Hebrews uses the Deuteronomic categories of blessing and curse (cf. Deut. 11.26–28) to articulate the outcome of the response to Jesus. To stay faithful to Jesus' sacrifice is 'blessing' (6.7) whereas to reject it, and 'crucify' Jesus again, is to be cursed (6.8).

Conclusion

Jesus' high-priestly, Day of Atonement self-offering is central to Hebrews' overall presentation. Likewise the Jewish Scriptures are core to the epistle's theologizing and doctrinal formulation. Both of these aspects – the importance both of Jesus' death and of the Old Testament – were found to be similarly so for Paul, yet we noted that there was surprisingly little direct correlation between them with his epistolary corpus. Hebrews swings the pendulum in the other direction. Jesus' death and its use of the Jewish Scriptures are integrally intertwined, and one cannot properly disentangle one aspect from the other. Hebrews takes several OT texts already associated with Jesus' death (Pss. 22; 110; Isa. 53; Jer. 31; perhaps Ps. 118) and recasts them within a particular Yom Kippur tapestry. But in so doing, it also adds to the corpus of Scriptures that might be used in relation to Jesus' death, both for authenticating its efficacy (Ps. 40) and also for articulating a faithful response to it (Ps. 95). If any NT text were to claim the *kata tas graphas* mantle for itself, then it would surely be Hebrews.

8

The Old Testament in the 'Passion' of the Other New Testament Epistles

We finally turn to those epistolary texts at the end of the New Testament, those ones that are neither Pauline nor from the hand of Hebrews (James; 1/2 Peter; 1/2/3 John and Jude). These epistolary documents are often known corporately as the 'General' or 'Catholic Epistles' and are seen as having a wider audience than just one destination; that is, they look beyond a specific or particular matter of activity. In recent years they have garnered attention for how they might be considered as a corpus of texts rather than as separate epistles,[1] but we will consider them in more individual rather than corporate fashion. This is for several reasons. As we have already observed, the Johannine epistles are normally found to sit better with the Johannine corpus; we have already given them due consideration, if only to comment that there is relatively little to say in terms of their use of the OT to formulate understanding of Jesus' death. Indeed, that itself is a key finding, namely that not *every* NT text is exploring the significance of a crucified Messiah and/or discerning how such understanding might be shaped by the use of the OT. Second, the individual texts within the corpus have remarkably different assessments of our topic question. The Letter of James, for example, famously makes no mention of Jesus' death and resurrection (and indeed relatively little mention of Jesus at all).[2] It does, though, quote and allude to the OT in a number of ways, particularly by using OT characters in exemplary fashion (2.21–26; 5.11, 17),[3] and is clearly versed in OT language and imagery (cf. the citation of Lev. 19.18 in James 2.8). Yet it has no 'need' to unpack such OT imagery in relation to Jesus' death, in stark contrast, say, to Luke and its dominant, fulfilment hermeneutic. Even when Jesus' suffering might have proved an appropriate exemplar, for example in terms of the need for endurance, James turns to Job, rather than Jesus, for heuristic and exhortatory purposes (5.10–11). Similarly, James makes appeal to Abraham's 'offering' of Isaac (2.21–24) but draws no christological significance from the event, whether in respect of the cross or the resurrection (cf. the contrasting approach of Heb. 11.17–19).[4] This may be for a number of reasons, of course. It may testify to a later dating for the epistle, when the offence or shame of the cross had waned, and hence did not necessitate the apologetic use of the OT. Or it might also confirm that scriptural formulation permeated other aspects of life, and not just demonstrating the crucifixion as fulfilment; other ways of responding to and remembering Jesus were equally *kata tas graphas*.

1 Peter

The primary Catholic Epistle text for our topic is 1 Peter, a text replete with OT imagery and one that focuses on the achievements of Christ's sufferings. It has a particular dependence on Psalm 34, formally quoted in 3.10–12 (Ps. 34.13–17), and the psalm is thought to be 'key to understanding the whole letter'.[5] Technically speaking, such dependence does not explicitly inform 1 Peter's articulation of the *death* of Jesus, and reminds us once more that not all OT links necessarily pertain to the implications of the crucified Messiah. However, Psalm 34 can rightly be characterized as a psalm of righteous suffering, at least in terms of YHWH's attention to the prayers of the (righteous) sufferer (34.4, 6) and his vindication of them accordingly (34.7, 17). And the centrality of Psalm 34 for 1 Peter likewise testifies to the importance of suffering within the epistolary text, and the way Christ's – righteous – suffering is exemplary for those who suffer as Christians. John's Gospel has probably quoted Psalm 34.20 in respect of Jesus' bones not being broken (John 19.36), and it seems that the psalm's righteous sufferer character has caused it to become associated with Jesus' death and the wider Passion tradition.[6]

While it is a critical text for the interpretation of 1 Peter, Psalm 34 is not the epistle's sole scriptural resource. On the contrary – the epistle is riddled with OT references and imagery, and unpacks both the christological and ethical implications of Jesus' salvific sufferings, which Peter avers were testified in advance by the prophets (1.10–12).[7] That is to say, for Peter, Christ's suffering death was prophesied within the Scriptures, due to the influence of the Spirit of Christ within them (1.11). The sufferings Jesus experienced are therefore not unexpected; indeed, they are scripturally anticipated. Bearing in mind the subsequent citations of Isaiah (1 Pet. 2.22–25), it seems plausible that Peter thinks that the Spirit specifically indwells him, and that it is the Isaianic testimony that particularly prophesied Christ's suffering and glory.[8]

And while Peter focuses on both Jesus' suffering and that of his readers, the primary locus for such suffering is surely Jesus' death (2.18–25). The portrayal of Jesus as a rejected stone (2.7) suggests a familiarity with the Passion Narrative and its associated imagery, especially as other NT writers also use the texts cited within the 2.6–8 unit (cf. Acts 4.11). But Jesus' death is particularly central for Peter because of its imitatory or exemplary value. Peter can speak of Christ's suffering because he experienced it first hand (5.1), but he also depicts it as the experience his (Christian) readers might aspire to model (3.14, 17). Those who bear the name of Christ – Peter explicitly labels his audience as 'Christians' (4.16) – share in the sufferings of Christ (4.12–14), and their response to that suffering is to be modelled on that of Jesus (2.21). As such, Peter 'does not call his audience to imitate specific details of Jesus' teachings or works but rather to the general arc of his life, specifically his suffering and his death'.[9] Or as Jobes surmises: 'the Christian life is very much the way of the cross.'[10]

The text is probably pseudonymous but nonetheless still associated with the figure of Peter, who is, in the tradition at least, connected with the Markan Gospel (cf. 1 Pet. 5.13). Peter writes the letter from Babylon (5.13), surely coded imagery for Rome and traditionally the provenance of Mark's Gospel, and the author explicitly identifies '*my son Mark*' (5.13). Setting the historical-critical questions to one side, textually at least, there is good reason to conceive of some kind of family resemblance between 1 Peter and Mark – their frequent use of Isaiah (1 Pet. 1.24–25; 2.6, 8, 22–25; 3.14; cf. Mark 1.3; 4.12; 7.6–7) or the emphasis on the suffering Christ (1 Pet. 2.22–25; cf. Mark 8.31; 10.45) being two characteristic shared features. 1 Peter is potentially also a relatively late NT text, and its use of the OT may therefore reflect established tradition rather than Petrine formulation; the appeal to Isaiah 53 in 1 Peter 2.22–25 may, for example, derive from a pre-existent creedal formula or hymn rather than from Peter's hand. But even if it is not Peter's 'own' work, it still represents a heavy dependence on OT formulation and is worthy of comment in that regard.

With its abundant use of the Jewish Scriptures, 1 Peter is somewhat like Hebrews, especially with its application of a *christological* hermeneutic to scriptural texts, reading them as pointing to Christ and fulfilled in/by him. 1 Peter 1.10–12 seems determinative in this regard.[11] Horrell summarizes 1 Peter's hermeneutic as:

> a claim that the true subject of biblical prophecy – and, by extension, of the Jewish Scriptures as a whole – is Christ, and that the fulfilment of what is said by the prophets is found in the Christian gospel and is appropriated by Christian believers.[12]

However, it does not preach, or expound the texts sermonically in the same way that Hebrews characteristically does. Instead 1 Peter offers plenty of OT quotation, which functions to bolster the strength of the argument being made. This means, for example, that the Christian community addressed by Peter are to understand themselves in terms of the Scriptures. The readers are described as strangers and exiles (1.1; 2.11), drawing, one surmises, on OT diaspora or exile language. They are identified as beneficiaries of Christ's death, specifically having been sprinkled with Christ's blood (1.2). While this is not a formal quotation, and neither is the subsequent 'blood' reference (1.19), 1 Peter 1.2 immediately locates the readers' world view in terms of Jesus' death, and does so in the light of the OT imagery. The language of the sprinkling of blood (1.2) is evocative of Exodus 24.6–8, thus contextualizing Jesus' death in sacrificial and covenantal terms (akin one might say to that of Hebrews – cf. Heb. 9.19–21). 1 Peter 1.19 is probably a reference to the Passover Lamb (cf. *'without blemish'* – Exod. 12.5), bearing in mind the letter's frequent appeal to exile and aliens,[13] but it may also allude to Isaiah 53.7, particularly in view of the explicit, later use of the fourth Servant Song (1 Pet. 2.22–25, esp. 2.23). Peter's unblemished lamb (i.e. Christ – 1.19) gives up its precious blood, and this has significant echoes of Isaiah's lamb being led to the slaughter for some form of self-offering (Isa. 53.7).[14] As such, we may have here in 1 Peter an amalgam of two traditions in respect of Christ's death, with the motif of Isaiah 53 'developed in a Passover setting'.[15]

1 Peter 2 – living stones

Having issued an affirmation that the audience have tasted that the Lord is good (2.3), itself an allusion to Psalm 34.8, Peter turns to a series of expositions pertaining to the implications of Jesus' death (2.4–10), each of which draws on OT imagery to formulate its argument. The bridge to the exhortations of 2.4–5 probably derive from a further allusion to Psalm 34, this time to 34.4–5 and the invitation therein to seek and come to the Lord.[16] Either way, 2.4–5 departs from the maternal vocabulary of 2.1–2 and instead establishes *stone* imagery as the binding motif or catchword of 2.4–8, intertwining the 'rejected' living stone (2.4) and those other living stones (2.5) who have benefitted from his sacrificial offering. 1 Peter 2.6–8 then offers the proof or evidence for the characterization of 2.4 (the rejected stone), while 2.9–10 picks up 2.5 (the elect people as stones).

The designation of the rejected/living stone (2.4) is surely Christ, but at least in 2.4–5 this is merely asserted rather than proved. This might suggest that the designation of Jesus in such 'stone' terms had already become established within early Christian tradition, and that the terminology therefore no longer needed further explanation. We have seen several examples of stone language already being used (Acts 4.11; Rom. 9.32–33), and it is the particular image, using Psalm 118, that the Synoptics utilize for Jesus' own indication of his future death (Matt. 21.42; Mark 12.10; Luke 20.17). Indeed, of all seven NT passages that speak of a 'rejected stone', Jesus is the consistent designee,[17] and this perhaps attests to the existence of *testimonia* that portrayed Christ in such terms and on which Peter is drawing. Peter's readers are to come to this living stone (2.4) and model such 'stone-ness', that they too might become living stones (2.5). From the outset of the epistolary narrative, therefore, we see Peter portray Jesus' death as having exemplary or imitatory function, and with the OT used to inform and sustain such mimesis.

The Old Testament 'proof' for the rejected-now-living stone of 1 Peter 2.4 is found in a composite citation of texts (2.6–8) we have previously encountered in relation to Jesus' death. Where Romans 9.33 combined Isaiah 28.16 and 8.14, and where Acts 4.11 cited Psalm 118.22, Peter juxtaposes all three texts together, with 'stone' functioning as the binding catchword, and the full force of scriptural warrant is applied (Isa. 28.16, cf. 1 Pet. 2.6; Ps. 118.22, cf. 1 Pet. 2.7; Isa. 8.14, cf. 1 Pet. 2.8).[18] The two Isaianic citations attest to the implications of Jesus' death; just as in their Pauline usage (Rom. 9.32–33), they outline the essential scandal or stumbling block that Christ's death represents (2.8). Again as with Romans 9.32–33, the citations are able to do dual diligence: Christ is the precious, living/life-giving cornerstone (2.6) but simultaneously the very thing that occasions (non-believing) humans to fall (2.8). The Psalm 118.22 citation performs a similar task, stipulating that the rejected stone is nonetheless the one that is the head or cornerstone (2.7). Hence the cumulative effect of the 2.6–8 composite citation is not so much that the prophets anticipated Jesus' suffering/death (cf. 1.11) but that they predicted the human *rejection* of that death. Prophetic testimony is marshalled not just for outworking the actuality of the Passion (see 2.22–25 below) but also to set forth the implications of the Passion for those who would or would not believe.

1 Peter 2.18–25 – Isaiah 53

Whereas we have previously found NT references to Isaiah 53 tending to be allusive or contested, 1 Peter 2.22–25 offers a direct citation of parts of the Servant Song, and is regarded within NT scholarship as a (the?) definitive comparison with the Servant's work. Peter may not have been the first NT author to make the connection with Isaiah 53 but he is the one that does so most explicitly. The common vocabulary, the preservation of the parallelism of the poetry and the Isaianic exodus language all suggest that Isaiah 53 lies at the heart of the pericope, and forms a core ingredient therefore of Peter's Christology. It is possible that a christological hymn, based on the Isaianic language, formed the basis of the unit – and the repeated '*hos*' clauses and the paragraph's wider rhythm would support such a view – but regardless of its origins, the Isaiah 53 reference points remain most prominent, as follows:

1 Peter	Isaiah 53
'*He committed no sin, and no deceit was found in his mouth*' (2.22)	'*Although he had done no violence, and there was no deceit in his mouth*' (53.9)
'*When he was abused, he did not return abuse*' (2.23)	'*Like a sheep that before its shearers is silent, so he did not open his mouth*' (53.7)[19]
'*He himself bore our sins in his body on the cross*' (2.24)	'*Surely he has borne our infirmities and carried our diseases*' (53.4) '*Yet he bore the sin of many, and made intercession for the transgressors*' (53.12)
'*By his wounds you have been healed*' (2.24)	'*And by his bruises we are healed*' (53.5)
'*For you were going astray like sheep*' (2.25)	'*All we like sheep have gone astray; we have all turned to our own way*' (53.6)

Several features of Peter's use of the Song warrant further comment. First, Peter re-sequences the citations according to the pattern of the Passion chronology (trial, insults, crucifixion), rather than replicates the flow of the Isaiah text. The Servant Song is 're-ordered' to fit the Passion trajectory. This would suggest that

Isaiah 53 functions as the lens for Peter's exegesis of Jesus' death, rather than Peter starting with or from the Servant Song. Second, the Petrine account has several points of connection or 'echoes' of the Gospels' Passion Narrative. That there was no deceit in Jesus' mouth (1 Pet. 2.23) potentially alludes to the Lucan claim of *'Father, forgive them'* (Luke 23.34) and/or Jesus' non-response to the mockery that he receives from afar. Matthew 27.27–31 or Mark 15.16–20 might also form potential parallels, although technically the Synoptic accounts only mention the soldiers' actions rather than Jesus' (non-)response. Peter's emphasis that Jesus committed no sin (2.22) is also commensurate with Luke's prevailing portrayal of Jesus as *dikaios*, and innocent of all the charges levied against him. There are also some points of difference or comparison, particularly with OT Passion source texts. The righteous sufferer of Psalm 22, a focal template for the Markan Passion, rails against his oppressors (cf. Ps. 22.12–13, 16–18). Peter's Isaianic lamb, however, does not retaliate, and is closer to the (Lucan) sufferer figure of Psalm 31 (though see below regarding 1 Peter 5.8).[20]

Third, the number of Petrine links and points of connection with Isaiah 53 is significant, far more than we have identified in other mooted allusions or quotations, and thus the 'volume' of the Petrine use of the Servant Song is comparatively high. The deliberate nature of the Isaiah 53 allusion here perhaps raises questions as to why the other NT writers do not make their – alleged – Suffering Servant connections so explicitly. Fourth, several – minor – lexical changes or additions to the LXX *Vorlage* serve to reinforce the efficacious aspect of the Servant's work. Peter stresses that it was Christ *himself* who physically bore sins, and the *'sins of many'* (Isa. 53.12) becomes *'our sins'* (2.24), partly for pastoral reasons, one surmises, but partly also to underscore the vicarious aspect of the Christ's suffering. Fifth, the purpose of Christ's sufferings – and hence those of the Servant – is twofold: they have atoning significance (2.24–25), in that they 'achieve' something, namely healing and the restoration of souls; but they also have exemplary value (2.22–23) and function as a model for Peter's readers (2.21). If anything, the latter aspect is the primary one; it is the suffering

Jesus endures *during* his death and his response to it – rather than the death per se – that forms the epistle's *imitatio* paraenesis (cf. also 4.1; 5.1).

Hence just as with Paul in Romans, we find the Servant's sufferings given christological interpretation, but such interpretation has both ethical *and* soteriological purpose. As with Paul's use of Psalm 69 in Romans 15.3, so here with the Isaiah 53 citations, Jesus' death is shown to be 'according to the Scriptures'; but in both cases the appeal *kata tas graphas* has an exemplary as well as an apologetic function. The Jewish Scriptures are used to endorse both aspects. It is perhaps no surprise, then, that Peter uses the OT elsewhere to evidence or support the way believers are to embrace or model Jesus' death. For example, Peter's addressees are to be aware of the devil, prowling like a roaring lion, seeking their destruction (5.8). Such leonine imagery may be a counterpoint to the prior picture of the readers as sheep (2.25), but it is more probably an allusion to Psalm 22.13 and the lion figure that threatens the righteous sufferer. If so it would exemplify a psalm used in respect of *Jesus'* sufferings being similarly used in respect of those of his followers (and in light of the Psalm 22 provenance, would also offer further evidence of a quasi-Markan flavour to the Petrine account).

Two further points may be made in respect of 1 Peter 2.22–25. First, embedded into the Isaianic imagery are other points of OT reference. As with other examples we have identified, 1 Peter 2.24 more literally reads '*on the tree*' rather than '*on the cross*'. The absence of *stauros* may be an apologetic desire to remove any offensive reference to the cross but, more probably, it is a further NT reference to Deuteronomy 21.22–23 and the cursed implications of being hung from a tree/cross (cf. Acts 5.30; 10.39; 13.29). Likewise 1 Peter 2.25b, building on the Isaiah 53 sheep allusion, extends it to incorporate the broad shepherd imagery of Ezekiel 34.1–31 and YHWH's declaration to shepherd the sheep of Israel (cf. Ezek. 34.15). While the Servant acts of his own volition, his work achieves YHWH's plan to restore his sheep.[21] The allusion may even pick up Isaiah 6.10 and the imagery of healing found there, particularly as that text is so formative for Mark's portrayal of Jesus' ministry.[22]

Second, in view of the dependence on Isaiah 53 (2.21–25), and bearing in mind its similarity to Mark's Gospel, it seems possible that Peter has a wider Isaianic spectrum in in mind. If the 'story' of 1 Peter is a narrative of those in exile (1.1; 2.11) moving to the 'heavenly' destination (1.4), then Isaiah 40–55 might be the template on which Peter unpacks its Passion story. Just as with Mark's potential Isaianic New Exodus,[23] 1 Peter offers a similar framework of the move from exile to freedom, specifically a move occasioned by the kind of suffering exhibited by the Isaianic servant. Isaiah 54 celebrates the completion of the exodus, the end of the exile: Jerusalem's glory is to be extended (54.2), the overthrow of foreign nations completed (54.3) and YHWH the Redeemer (54.7) will be God over all the earth (54.5). Isaiah 53 is the means by which the 'journey' or the end of exile is achieved; the Servant's suffering is the 'process' by which the exodus will be completed.

1 Peter 3.19 and 4.6

One further aspect of 1 Peter's portrayal of Jesus' death is its potential reference to a 'descent to the dead' or to the realm of Hades. The incident is attested in certain forms of the Apostles' Creed and was thought to have taken place on Holy Saturday, between Good Friday and Easter Sunday. While technically outside of the Passion Narrative, it is equally not part of the resurrection narrative either and, for our purposes, still falls under the general umbrella term of 'Jesus' death'.

Two Petrine texts have been cited in support of the descent tradition: 1 Peter 3.19 and 4.6. The first of these has a particular OT contextualization to it, as Peter appeals to the salvific imagery of the Flood narrative and the salvation of eight figures through that episode (3.20). Peter connects the episode with the rite of baptism (3.21), and this has contributed to the perception that 1 Peter has its origins within baptismal liturgy, but the discourse is also notable for its potential allusion to Christ's 'descent'. In 'former times', potentially those of Noah, Christ is said to have made proclamation to imprisoned spirits (3.19), probably the – dead – spirits of those who had been unfaithful and had not believed God/Noah. Such a reading of 3.19–20 would be commensurate with a descent to the dead. However, this interpretation has become less persuasive now, particularly in the light of William Dalton's work on the passage,[24] and generally speaking, 1 Peter 3.19 is thought to address Jesus' *exaltation* rather than his descent. The imprisoned spirits addressed those fallen angels, and specifically the disobedient angels of Genesis 6.2–3, but viewed through the lens of the 1 Enoch tradition.[25] Hence while there is a wider 'scriptural' framework to the passage, it cannot be said to pertain to Jesus' death, and thus is outside of our concerns.

The contribution of 1 Peter 4.6, however, is more relevant. Its claim to address a descent to the dead is more likely, and is one of only a handful of passages that might possibly be said to manifest that tradition (cf. perhaps also Eph. 4.9). Peter notes that the gospel is *'proclaimed to the dead'* (4.6), but does not explicitly identify who the dead are. It is possible that they are those who have recently died, and who would – worryingly – miss out on Christ's return, the scenario found most prominently in 1 Thessalonians 4.13–18. However, such anxiety does not seem to be important prevalent for Peter's audience, and more probably the text does speak of Jesus addressing – most probably on Holy Saturday – the dead, and offering them some form of 'good news'.[26] The difficulty for our purposes is that 1 Peter 4.6 has no obvious OT citation linked with it, and while it would seem to relate to Jesus' death, there is little evidence of the purported descent being specified as *kata tas graphas*. Conversely, the text that probably does not speak of Jesus' death (3.19) is the one that does have scriptural association or evidence. It is interesting, therefore, that if 4.6 is within the scope of Jesus' death, Peter offers no scriptural warrant to validate the 'descent'. And for a text that is so indebted to OT citation, the lack of scriptural appeal to what could be such a significant issue is notable. It may just be that the epistle's focus on Christ's suffering is the primary driver for Peter's appeal to the OT, and the scope/reference of 4.6 falls outside such concerns.

Conclusion

Green summarizes Peter's use of the Old Testament as follows:

> Peter's task is not to read the Scriptures christologically but to show how a christological reading of Scripture guides the church in its identity and in the pursuit of its mission. . . . Peter reads the situation of Christian audience from the perspective of the career of Jesus Christ, and the career of Jesus Christ from the perspective of the Scriptures – specifically, from the scriptural plot line concerned with the vindication and glory of the rejected and suffering righteous.[27]

Green's analysis would seem particularly appropriate for Peter's use of the Old Testament in respect of Jesus' death. Jesus' sufferings are read through the lens of Scripture as the sufferings of a righteous figure, rejected by humans but ultimately vindicated by God (whether through Isaiah 53 or Psalm 34 or the amalgam of 'rock' citations). These texts, read in the light of Christ the vindicated sufferer, then become the 'example' for Peter's audience for how they might respond to similar suffering and rejection by the world around them. Just as Christ followed the steps laid down by Isaiah 53, so the audience are to follow in Christ's steps.

9

Conclusion

What have we learnt of the NT writers' use of the Old Testament in respect of their refection on Jesus' death? We began with the Pauline assertion, inherited from early Church tradition, that Jesus Christ died *kata tas graphas* (1 Cor. 15.3), and have considered the way the NT writings might evidence or manifest such a claim. We have looked at the various texts deployed in this regard, and the different interpretative strategies so adopted, and have identified points of both commonality and contrast. Similarly, we have tried to tease out the flavour or approach to how the different writers go about contextualizing or speaking of Jesus' death, their different Passion Narratives (or equivalent), in an attempt to see how the Jewish Scriptures might be said to inform or shape those discourses. What might we conclude in this regard?

1 The vast majority of the NT writers utilize the Jewish Scriptures to speak of Jesus' death

As a general rule of thumb, it is hard for the NT writers to talk about Jesus' death without in some way invoking the Old Testament. All four evangelists root their analysis in the OT when narrating Christ's Passion, and each draws regularly on the Jewish Scriptures to formulate their retelling. For Hebrews and 1 Peter, when they come to speaking of Jesus' death, scriptural citation is key, whether it be through explicit appeal to the fourth Servant Song (1 Pet. 2.21–25) or via the amalgam of texts on which Hebrews calls (Pss. 40 and 110 in particular). Paul likewise reflects the *kata tas graphas* tradition, and there are several epistolary instances that evidence it (e.g. 1 Cor. 2.9 or Rom. 15.3);

but there is surprisingly little direct application in this regard. In his written epistles at least, there are relatively few examples on Paul's part of demonstrating the *kata tas graphas* principle, and the examples we identified were at best implicit (inter alia Rom. 4.25; Phil. 2.6–11).

But not *every* NT writer defaults to scripturalizing Jesus' death and its implications. 1 John can reflect fairly extensively on Jesus' death, but without any obvious appeal to the Old Testament. And likewise, some NT writers just do not say very much – if anything – about the Passion, but can still demonstrate use of the Jewish Scriptures. The Epistle of James is the primary example of this, but it is also notable how 2 Peter and Jude, texts well-versed in the Jewish Scriptures, equally don't deploy that knowledge in respect of Jesus' death.

The scriptural mandate remains central, however, and almost every aspect of the Passion Narrative may be seen as manifesting an OT background, from leaving the upper room through to Jesus' arrest, from the trial narratives through to the burial scene. Such centrality is manifest in a number of ways beyond mere textual citation. It may derive from the broad Day of Atonement template on which Hebrews explores Jesus' high-priestly self-offering. It may relate to the NT writer's particular hermeneutic, whether through Luke's prophetic promise–fulfilment lens, or in John's perspective that the Scriptures speak directly about Jesus (cf. John 5.46). Or it may be evident from the structure of the Passion Narratives themselves. We have noted that the Markan and Matthean narratives both begin with scriptural citation (Mark 14.27; Matt. 26.31), and Scripture thereby might be seen as offering a programmatic statement on the ensuing events. Luke probably also uses the Isaiah 53.12 citation as a blueprint for the outworking of the subsequent Passion (Luke 22.37). Or it might be the *mode* of scriptural interpretation that gives an OT citation gravitas or significance. It is notable, for example, how often Scripture is placed on Jesus' lips in the gospel Passion Narratives; that is, when Jesus speaks he invariably speaks – or even quotes – Scripture, be it in the Gethsemane scene, during his arrest and trial(s), on the way to Golgotha and most notably from the cross. This might come through Jesus voicing explicit Old Testament quotations, it might come via allusive references in his speech or it might be an amalgam of both. Indeed, one could make a case that almost everything the Markan Jesus says within the Passion retelling could be construed as having a scriptural background or resonance:

- Jesus' quotation of Zechariah 13.7 (14.27) at the outset of the Passion Narrative;
- Jesus' Gethsemane prayer, drawing on righteous sufferer testimony (Ps. 42.6, 11, 43.5);
- Jesus' declaration that the Scripture be fulfilled (14.49);
- Jesus' reply to the high priest (14.62, alluding to Dan. 7.13 and Ps. 110.1);
- Jesus' cry of dereliction (15.34, citing Ps. 22.1).

This is akin to what we in find in Hebrews too, where Jesus only speaks twice, but in each instance he directly quotes from the Scriptures (Heb. 2.12, cf. Ps. 22.22; Heb. 10.5–7, cf. Ps. 40). And this is particularly significant for Jesus' *final* words. Brown notes how, in contemporary dramas, a character's last speech was normally their most important, and in the Passion accounts, those final words – of the most important character in the narrative – are scriptural citations.[1] It seems to matter, then, that Jesus' final words are Scripture. Scripture 'has the last word', one might say (just as it also has the first).

2   There is a particular corpus of texts used to speak of Jesus' death

In his volume on the use of the Old Testament in the Passion Narratives, Moo locates four groups or collections of texts that would seem to shape the evangelistic Passion accounts: Zechariah 9–14, the Isaianic Servant Songs, the lament psalms and what he terms 'Old Testament Sacrificial Imagery'. We have not really had cause to dissent from Moo's conclusion. In the non-gospel material, these texts (perhaps with the exception of Zech. 9–14) continue to be the primary ones so employed, and suggest that the pre-canonical Passion Narrative was impacting on how/what texts were being used for talking about Jesus' death.

Sacrificial imagery, for example, pervades Hebrews' artic-ulation of the Passion, especially in its association with the covenant-making moment, and Revelation likewise has a number of points of reference with sacrifice- or blood-related terminology. We might also note, perhaps to nuance Moo's category rather than add a fifth one, that Passover imagery is also a frequent locus or source in this regard.[2] Moo does include Paschal imagery under the broader Sacrifice theme, but in light of its extensive use across the NT, it might warrant being more foregrounded in this regard. The Passover Lamb is a prominent figure within John's Gospel, but we have also seen it alluded to within 1 Peter (1 Pet. 1.19) and Revelation (Rev. 5.6), and Paul specifically describes Jesus as a Paschal lamb (1 Cor. 5.7). From time to time the Passover motif can also be fused together with the Isaiah 53 tradition (in 1 Peter, Revelation, John), creating an amalgam of scriptural images on which the NT authors might draw.

Of Moo's other categories, it is fair to say that the Zechariah 9—14 discourse is less prominent outside of the Gospels and, indeed, is only minimally cited in Luke. It does not receive the same range of citation that the Servant Songs and the lament psalms attract. The use of Isaiah 53 is reasonably consistent across the NT, but in a frustrating way. While its citation in 1 Peter 2.22–25 is explicitly signalled, its usage elsewhere, par-ticularly in Paul, remains somewhat allusive. One can make a case that all the texts we have considered utilize it to support the vicarious nature of Jesus' death (e.g. Luke 22.37; Acts 8.32–33; Rom. 4.25), but equally, in none of those instances is it explicitly so, and in most the evidence still remains essentially ambiguous. One can easily overstate the use of Isaiah 53 in the NT, and the proverbial jury is still out in terms of the Song's overall contribu-tion to understanding Jesus' death.

Yet one might still suggest that the epistolary reflection on Jesus' death – and the scriptural texts so used – broadly equate with those texts the evangelists use, and that have been associated with an inherited Passion Narrative or tradition. As such, this may further the case for the existence of an – early? – non-canonical Passion tradition, one framed by and replete with scriptural attestation, and on which is predicated Paul's appeal of 1 Corinthians 15.3.

It is also striking, though, that the range of cited OT texts is itself quite limited, and testifies to just how *few* passages are used to frame ideas around Jesus' death.[3] It is also noticeable that it is not the 'obvious' messianic passages that are so used. If there are 'messianic psalms' (Psalm 2 perhaps), while they are not completely absent from the Passion tradition (cf. Acts 4.25–26; 13.33; Heb. 5.5), they are only very loosely associated with Jesus' death and are certainly not the primary contributors to narrating it or evaluating its significance. Even the contribution of Isaiah 53, for example, derives from *later* reflection on it (i.e. in the light of Jesus' death), and the more 'christological' reading of the Fourth Servant Song does not seem to equate to any pre-Passion interpretation of that text. As Hofius surmises, it is a *Christian* reading of the passage that makes sense of it in relation to 1 Corinthians 15.3–4.[4] Texts like Isaiah 53, or Psalms 22 or 69, become 'messianic' in the light of Christ, as they provide the template against which Jesus' Passion is interpreted. Hence although we have suggested in various places that *kata tas graphas* was an appeal to the full scope of the scriptural record (cf. Mark 14.49; Rom. 1.2), and that, as with the Lucan testimony, the full gamut of the Scriptures pointed to Jesus (Luke 24.27), it remains the case that *in practice* the range of cited texts remains remarkably small. We might have expected a greater correspondence with, or use of, Genesis 22, for example, particularly bearing in mind its familiarity elsewhere in Second Temple Judaism,[5] but that is far from the textual testimony. The NT text that makes the most use of the *Aqedah* (James 2.21–24) is famously the one that makes no mention of Jesus' death at all. And even if there are allusions to Genesis 22 in parts of John's Gospel (e.g. 3.16), they are barely signalled, and one would still expect further explicit reference.

3 Certain texts have prominence with the Passion retelling

Even within the relatively small 'canon' of texts used in Passion matters, there is something of a further canon within the canon – or pecking order – in this regard. While some might surmise that Isaiah 53 assumes a certain prominence in this regard, we have found that its use across the NT corpus is far from consistent and hardly explicit. Whereas one can moot a number of potential allusions to, or echoes of the Song in all the texts we have discussed, the lack of *explicit* citation, and what might be seen as the hesitancy to quote it directly, is a telling datum.

By contrast, the degree to which the righteous sufferer (RS) or lament psalms are integral to the Passion Narrative is striking. We have seen consistent use of a number of such psalms, but with particular prominence given to Psalms 22, 31, 42 and 69. The way they are used may vary from author to author, and different NT writers will opt for one particular RS psalm over another, dependent on their particular focus or interests. Mark's Passion, for example, is framed around and more suited to the spirit of Psalm 22, whereas Luke finds an appropriate conversation partner in Psalm 31. 1 Peter looks primarily to Psalm 34, a different type of RS psalm but one that befits its focus on exemplary suffering. Psalmic texts are particularly useful or appropriate because they are commonly first-person direct speech, and they manifest the capacity for the 'speaker' of the psalm to be 'relocated' or recast, particularly for christological purposes. Paul, by virtue of such 'christological ventriloquism', can portray Christ praying Psalm 69 (Rom. 15.3), or Hebrews can hear the exalted Jesus proclaiming Psalm 22 as an expression of his vindication (Heb. 2.12). Even John, who offers several, third-party editorial comments as to the fulfilment of Scripture, still places RS citation on Jesus' lips to inculcate the righteous sufferer characterization (e.g. Ps. 69.9 in John 19.28–29). And the RS remit arguably extends even to those events more on the periphery of the Passion account. Luke's scriptural warrant for Judas' betrayal draws on Psalm 69, demonstrative that the experience of duplicity is an expected one for a righteous sufferer.

Hence it is difficult to dissent from Green's thesis statement: 'throughout the Passion account – from its opening to its finale – by means of conceptual allusions, linguistic agreements, and explicit citations, the Suffering Righteous stands in the background of the portrayal of Jesus' death.'[6] Or at least it is difficult except perhaps to query whether the Righteous Sufferer stands in the *background* of the Passion portrayal. In view of the volume and frequency of the citation, one might assert instead that the Righteous Sufferer Jesus stands at the *foreground* of the Passion account. If one were to remove the RS material from the Passion tradition, if one were to 'disrobe' Jesus of that characterization, then one would be left with comparatively little 'Passion'. Or to put it another way, the RS characterization is able to bridge – unite? – the various different Passion portrayals we find across the NT corpus, evangelistic and epistolary. Where the character of the individual Passion accounts can significantly vary, often in quite significant ways, the appeal to the RS texts establishes some intra-biblical continuity and constancy. Indeed, if *kata tas graphas* really is a consistent theme across the Passion tradition and in the various NT writers' use of it, then the RS or lament psalms bear particular responsibility for engendering it.

We should enter one caveat here, however. To recognize the foregrounding of the RS psalms within the Passion tradition is not to say that Jesus died as a paradigmatic righteous sufferer. Second Temple Judaism offered many examples of righteous sufferer narratives (*Wisdom of Solomon* 2–5 is often mentioned in this regard, or parts of the Maccabean texts), and it is conceivable, one supposes, that the early Church might have availed itself of them.[7] But that is not the verdict of the NT writers. The Pauline testimony is that Jesus died *as Christ* and as king (John 19.19–22), and with full messianic status or credentials. The presenting problem with which we opened our discussion – that is, the fundamental difficulty or contradiction of a crucified Christ – still remains the case; it has not been superseded by another (non-messianic) narrative. We are merely noting that the crucified christological 'skeleton' is enfleshed with scriptural imagery characterized by and drawn from the righteous sufferer psalms, and this serves to make sense of the crucified Messiah incongruity. °

Alongside this reasonably small corpus of OT Texts, or perhaps materializing out of it, certain key texts emerge as having a particular resonance or significance for Jesus' death. Dodd proposed that such *testimonia* arose within the life and practice of the early Church, and there seems good reason to broadly concur with his proposal. For example, both Paul and Peter utilize rock imagery – and its associated stumbling block (*skandalon*) – to depict the response

---

° The psalms were trad. 178 ascribed to David, Israel's ideal king & ~~and~~ ~~ancestor~~ of the anticipated royal Messiah. Thus, David's laments in individual psalms could be understood as prophetic anticipation of Messianic laments. (So Ps. 22:1) The reality of a suffering Messiah needed to be

to Jesus' death (Rom. 9.33; 1 Pet. 2.6–8), and this would seem to correspond to the similar use of the rejected stone image of Psalm 118 when the Synoptic Jesus predicts his Passion (Mark 12.10–11; Luke 20.17–18). It is interesting, then, that Paul does not use the same rock or *skandalon* expression in 1 Corinthians 1–2, when it might have been appropriate to do so (assuming there was a *testimonium* or familiar confessional formula available to him).

At the same time, there still remains a broad category of 'Scripture' that seems to be pertinent for the NT writers. While they do speak occasionally of the Prophets corpus, as opposed to the Law and/or the Psalms, and invest that with general fulfilment capacity, that tends to be the most specific the NT writers get. There seems to be a general reluctance to specify or identify texts, and only rarely is the source of a citation explicitly named. Sometimes, though, the origin or source of the text does seem to matter. It is important for Luke, for example, that David wrote Psalm 16 (Acts 2.25–32); likewise, it matters for John to explicitly name Isaiah as the source of the quotations in John 12.38–40, as he intimates that, in speaking the prophecy, Isaiah saw Jesus. Yet equally, sometimes the *Vorlage* ascription is given erroneously. As we have seen, Matthew 27.9–10 owes more to Zechariah than to the accredited Jeremiah, and thus the – mistaken? – attribution to the latter would seem to imply some impact or significance. And sometimes we are not sure of the source, or whether it even exists; Paul's citation in 1 Corinthians 2.9 has the force and significance of a scriptural quotation, but its actual origin remains contested. But generally speaking it is the *scriptural* categorization of the text that matters rather than the actual source. Indeed, in the case of John's Gospel, even the actual text itself being fulfilled becomes ambiguous (cf. John 19.28–29), let alone its source. What matters is that Scripture is fulfilled; that is, that God has 'willed' the event in question.

4 The Passion accounts and the choice of scriptural texts are mutually informing

For the gospel writers, the tenor or shape of their Passion Narrative is inextricably linked to the choice of, and use of the Old

accounted for, preferably as fulfillment of prophetic Divine Scripture — [179] even if such fulfillment didn't clearly explain the purpose(s) of such suffering. (cf. p. 71)

Testament. 'According to the Scriptures' is an integral component of the Passion discourse, but it is also shaped by the overall redactional interests of the writer concerned. This may explain something of the ambiguity – or potential diversity? – found within 1 Corinthians 15.3; that is, it is possible that Paul's non-designation of the specific scriptural texts to which the *kata tas graphas* alludes was because there was already a plurality of ways 'according to the Scriptures' might be operative. For example, for Luke it matters that Jesus is *dikaios* (innocent), so the choice of Scriptures serves to shape that characterization (e.g. Luke 22.37; cf. Isa. 53.12). John has far less use of Psalm 22 than does Matthew, as the Matthean cry of desolation (Matt. 27.46) is incompatible with John's portrayal of Jesus as being in command of the Passion situation and fulfilling his Father's – and his own – purposes. Instead John's crucifixion scene places greater emphasis on the explicit fulfilment of Scripture and Jesus' capacity to be the agent and focus of such fulfilment. As Borg and Crossan rightly point out, there is 'no uninterpreted account of the death of Jesus in the New Testament'.[8]

We might draw two implications from this. First, Scripture is therefore not incidental to the Passion accounts. It is also more than a mere ingredient whose essence or flavour gets lost in its new evangelistic or epistolary form. Rather, the OT is an intrinsic, core element in the way the respective accounts are portrayed, and its status qua Scripture is not removed or absolved once integrated into the – new – Passion setting. On the contrary, it would seem that the scriptural 'status' or 'character' of the text is even more important in the New Testament context, as it is that very scriptural 'essence' that demonstrates the divine 'approval' of the crucified messiah.

Second, the NT writers will tend to read the – same – scriptural texts in different ways. Take David's association with the Psalms corpus, for example. In several instances David's authorship of the psalm is paramount, and the NT writer understands David reading prophetically, beyond his own experience. This is particularly the case in the Petrine speeches of Acts, where Peter can cite Psalm 16 and conclude that David 'prophesies' a messianic figure who would not be abandoned to Hades (Acts 2.29–32).

One might effectively call this a 'predictive' or 'prophetic' reading of a psalmic text, and one with a particularly messianic bent. Alternatively, we might encounter the NT writers' reading backwards, or setting Jesus' experience against the broader narrative of David. Ahearne-Kroll proposes, for example, that Mark's use of Psalm 22 knowingly has David in mind, as it makes sense of Jesus' royal status but also portrays Jesus in terms of the 'suffering David of the Psalms [lament psalms]'.[9] For John, Zechariah 12.10 can shed light on the soldiers' post-mortem piercing of Jesus (John 19.37), whereas for Revelation it becomes a more eschatologically orientated text, juxtaposed with Jesus' coming (Rev. 1.7). The same author can even read the same text with different lenses and implications. For example, in the same Romans text, Paul can ascribe the voicing of the Psalm to both David (Rom. 11.9–10) and Jesus (Rom. 15.3), and draw different implications accordingly. The NT writers' scripturalizing of Jesus' death is a far from monochrome process.

5 The need to demonstrate scriptural fulfilment for Christ's death was paramount

At the outset of our discussion we noted that the 'crucified Christ' is the problem that needed to be resolved, and that the apologetic task of the early Church was to find scriptural warrant for what was so scandalous a premise. We have encountered a number of instances in which that fulfilment aspect is manifest and the 'drive' to find fulfilment somewhat pressing. The need to prove such fulfilment occasioned some rather odd readings of scriptural texts, however. Whether it is Matthew's misreading of Zechariah and the resulting two animals (Matt. 21.4–7), or whether it is John's awkward explanation of the fulfilment of the division of clothing (John 19.23–24), the burden of scriptural fulfilment has occasionally been at the expense of – historical – reality. Similarly, the particular *event* that is witnessing the fulfilment can look somewhat strange or peripheral to the focal Passion event. It is not clear, for example, why the division of Jesus' clothing particularly warranted scriptural confirmation, yet all four gospel writers endeavour to ascribe it such. This can mean that the text being cited as fulfilled may be equally ambiguous (this is certainly the case with John), and again, what seems to matter is that Scripture per se is fulfilled rather than individual or particular passages/ texts.

This has therefore generated some 'surprises' within the evangelistic testimony. Whereas Mark and particularly Luke both see Jesus' death within a scriptural fulfilment framework (Mark 14.49; Luke 24.44), they don't evidence that principle through explicit, evidential fulfilment quotations (Luke 22.37 aside, perhaps). The reader is left to make the connection. Matthew and John's accounts do make more of the formal fulfilment aspect but in differing ways. John has a number of fulfilment quotations in its Passion discourse but applies them in more ambiguous fashion, sometimes without clear demarcation of the actual text being fulfilled. Matthew, for all its initial attention to fulfilment, has no OT quotation to demonstrate that fulfilment in respect of Jesus' death. Instead, it is the demise of *Judas* for which Matthew offers scriptural testimony (Matt. 27.9–10), this appeal being the only incidence of a fulfilment quotation in the Matthean Passion. In the opening chapter of this book we remarked that the NT writers seem to have given particular attention to both Jesus' birth and his death, specifically as to how those events might be seen to have had scriptural warrant or attestation. For Matthew, however, such attention tends far more towards Jesus' birth than towards his death.

6   Use of Scripture is more than just fulfilment

In particular, the Old Testament is used to underscore the exemplary aspect of Jesus' death. While the Corinthian *kata tas graphas* designation was primarily soteriological (i.e. '*Christ died* for our sins'), the phrase's wider referent in the NT also extends to include a mimetic or model dimension. Christ's death as a righteous sufferer has an exemplary character, and the Jewish Scriptures, and particularly – but not exclusively – the RS psalms, provide resource or framework for this. It is notable how all the non-gospel texts we have considered make this connection. For Hebrews, the paraenetic [*] material is both infused with scriptural quotation and allusion, but pertains likewise to the response to Jesus' death, and particularly the suggestion that to apostatize is to crucify Jesus again (Heb. 6.4–6). For Paul, Christ's sufferings have a significant mimetic or exemplary dimension (Phil. 3.8–11), and the OT is used to calibrate or inform that mimesis, particularly in Romans 15.3 and 2 Corinthians 4.7–14. And most explicitly, 1 Peter's prevailing theme is the exemplary aspect of Christ's suffering (1 Pet. 2.21–25), with Christ setting a pattern for Peter's readers (2.21; 4.1).

A further comment might be made on this. One might surmise that a number of NT writers, the gospel writers included, assume that Christ's suffering – and even his suffering unto death – is the path his disciples should follow. The way to the cross is to be followed by Jesus' followers. Mark's Jesus invites its readers to take up their 'cross' and follow Jesus (8.34), or Luke characteristically patterns the destiny of Stephen or Paul going to their martyrs' deaths. Hebrews urges its audience to go to Jesus outside the camp and bear the abuse he bore (Heb. 13.13). We have also suggested that for many of the NT writers the sufferings/death of Jesus are in some way exemplary, and that the Jewish Scriptures are used to demonstrate the case for this. Both Jesus' death and its exemplary nature are warranted via scriptural testimony. At the same time, it is notable that the appeal to follow after Jesus and to embrace his suffering is *not* itself directly attributed to Scripture. It is implicit or secondary perhaps – one thinks of 1 Peter 2.22–25 in this regard – but generally speaking there is no explicit prophetic appeal to attest the fact that the one who is faithful to Jesus will experience suffering unto death. Indeed, the Markan Passion Narrative goes in the other direction, finding scriptural warrant for the disciples' desertion (Mark 14.27), rather than for their active embrace of suffering.

The model is generally thus:

- Scripture *warrants* Jesus' suffering warrants followers' suffering.
  <u>NOT</u>
- Scripture *warrants* followers' suffering.

Hebrews 10.36–38 may come close to echoing the latter, but even that quotation is more of a scriptural warning to 'keep going'

[*] of or relating to 183 moral, ethical instruction or paraenesis

rather than a prophetic declaration that the disciple will 'suffer'. To put it another way, the NT writers' ascription of 'righteous suffering' to Jesus' followers is made through (first) portraying Jesus as the RS, and then extending his model or pattern – through scriptural appeal – to the disciples/followers.[10]

Conclusion

In sum, we might surmise that we have seen a two-way process in operation: the Scriptures shed light on Jesus' death but Jesus' death also shed – new? – light on the Jewish Scriptures.[11] The exegetical approaches of the NT writers are not necessarily new, and indeed show a number of parallels with contemporary Second Temple interpreters. What is new, however, is the focus on a crucified Christ, and the interpretative implications of what was so counter-intuitive. And what emerges is an 'interpretative quilt'[12] of quotations, allusions, echoes, images and examples, all contributing to the foundational notion that Christ died 'according to the Scriptures'. The *kata tas graphas* designation is thus critical, and gets to the very essence of how the early Church thought about the significance and implications of Jesus' death.

Bibliography

Ahearne-Kroll, Stephen P., 'Challenging the Divine: LXX Psalm 21 in the Passion Narrative of the Gospel of Mark', pages 119–48 in *The Trial and Death of Jesus: Essays on the Passion Narrative in Mark*. Edited by Geert van Oyen and Tom Shepherd. Leuven: Peeters, 2006.

Ahearne-Kroll, Stephen P., *The Psalms of Lament in Mark's Passion: Jesus' Davidic Suffering*, Society for New Testament Studies Monograph Series 142. Cambridge: Cambridge University Press, 2007.

Aitken, Ellen Bradshaw, 'Ta drōmena kai ta legomena: The Eucharistic Memory of Jesus' Words in First Corinthians', *Harvard Theological Review* 90:4 (1997): 359–70.

Aitken, Ellen Bradshaw, *Jesus' Death in Early Christian Memory: The Poetics of the Passion*. Novum Testamentum et orbis antiquus 53. Göttingen: Vandenhoeck & Ruprecht, 2004.

Aitken, Ellen Bradshaw, 'Tradition in the Mouth of the Hero: Jesus as an Interpreter of Scripture', pages 97–103 in *Performing the Gospel: Orality, Memory, and Mark*. Edited by Richard A. Horsley, Jonathan A. Draper and John Miles Foley. Minneapolis, MN: Fortress Press, 2006.

Allen, David M., *Deuteronomy and Exhortation in Hebrews: An Exercise in Narrative Re-presentation*. Wissenschaftliche Untersuchungen zum Neuen Testament 2/238. Tübingen: Mohr Siebeck, 2008.

Allen, David M., 'Secret Disciples: Nicodemus and Joseph of Arimathea', pages 149–69 in *Jesus Amongst Friends and Enemies: A Historical and Literary Introduction to Jesus in the Gospels*. Edited by Chris Keith and Larry W. Hurtado. Grand Rapids, MI: Baker, 2011.

Allen, David M., 'Genesis in James, 1 and 2 Peter and Jude', pages 147–65 in *Genesis in the New Testament*. Edited by Steve Moyise and Maarten J. J. Menken. London: T. & T. Clark, 2012.

Allen, David M., *The Historical Character of Jesus: Canonical Insights from Outside the Gospels*. London: SPCK, 2013.

Allen, David M., 'Why Bother Going Outside?: The Use of the Old Testament in Heb. 13:10–16', pages 239–52 in *The Scriptures of Israel in Jewish and Christian Tradition: Essays in Honour of Maarten J. J. Menken*. Edited by Bart J. Koet, Steve Moyise and Joseph Verheyden. Leiden: Brill, 2013.

Allen, David M., 'Introduction: The Study of the Use of the Old Testament in the New', *Journal for the Study of the New Testament* 38:1 (2015): 3–16.

Allison, Dale C., *The New Moses: A Matthean Typology*. Minneapolis, MN: Fortress Press, 1993.

Allison, Dale C., *Constructing Jesus: Memory, Imagination, and History*. London: SPCK, 2010.

Attridge, Harold W., *The Epistle to the Hebrews*. Hermeneia. Philadelphia, PA: Fortress Press, 1989.

Attridge, Harold W., 'Giving Voice to Jesus: Use of the Psalms in the New Testament', pages 101–12 in *Psalms in Community: Jewish and Christian Textual, Liturgical, and Artistic Traditions*. Edited by Harold W. Attridge and Margot E. Fassler. Society of Biblical Literature Symposium Series 25. Atlanta, GA: SBL, 2003.

Barbarick, Clifford A., 'Milk to Grow On: The Example of Christ in 1 Peter', pages 216–39 in *Getting 'Saved': The Whole Story of Salvation in the New Testament*. Edited by Charles H. Talbert, Jason A. Whitlark and Andrew E. Arterbury. Grand Rapids, MI: Eerdmans, 2011.

Barclay, John M. G., *Pauline Churches and Diaspora Jews*. Grand Rapids, MI: Eerdmans, 2016.

Barrett, C. K., *The Gospel According to St John: An Introduction with Commentary and Notes on the Greek Text*. 2nd edn. London: SPCK, 1978.

Barrett, C. K., 'Luke/Acts', pages 231–44 in *It is Written: Scripture citing Scripture: Essays in Honour of Barnabas Lindars, SSF*. Edited by D. A. Carson and H. G. M. Williamson. Cambridge: Cambridge University Press, 1988.

Bauckham, Richard, 'James, 1 and 2 Peter, Jude', pages 303–17 in *It is Written: Scripture citing Scripture: Essays in Honour of Barnabas Lindars, SSF*. Edited by D. A. Carson and H. G. M. Williamson. Cambridge: Cambridge University Press, 1988.

Bauckham, Richard, *The Climax of Prophecy: Studies on the Book of Revelation*. Edinburgh: T. & T. Clark, 1993.

Bauckham, Richard, *Jesus and the God of Israel: God Crucified and other Studies on the New Testament's Christology of Divine Identity*. Grand Rapids, MI: Eerdmans, 2009.

Beale, G. K., *The Right Doctrine from the Wrong Texts?: Essays on the Use of the Old Testament in the New*. Grand Rapids, MI: Baker, 1994.

Beale, G. K., *Handbook on the New Testament Use of the Old Testament: Exegesis and Interpretation*. Grand Rapids, MI: Baker Academic, 2012.

Beale, G. K., *John's Use of the Old Testament in Revelation*. Library of New Testament Studies. London: Bloomsbury, 2014.

Beale, G. K. and D. A. Carson, *Commentary on the New Testament Use of the Old Testament*. Grand Rapids, MI: Baker Academic, 2007.

Beale, G. K. and Sean M. McDonough, 'Revelation', pages 1081–1161 in *Commentary on the New Testament Use of the Old Testament.* Edited by G. K. Beale and D. A. Carson. Grand Rapids, MI: Apollos, 2007.

Beale, Greg, 'Revelation', pages 318–36 in *It is Written: Scripture citing Scripture: Essays in Honour of Barnabas Lindars, SSF.* Edited by D. A. Carson and H. G. M. Williamson. Cambridge: Cambridge University Press, 1988.

Beavis, Mary Ann, *Mark*. Paideia Commentaries. Grand Rapids, MI: Baker Academic, 2011.

Beers, Holly, *The Followers of Jesus as the 'Servant': Luke's Model from Isaiah for the Disciples in Luke–Acts.* Library of New Testament Studies 535. London: Bloomsbury, 2015.

Beilby, James K., Paul R. Eddy, Robert M. Price, John Dominic Crossan, Luke Timothy Johnson, James D. G. Dunn and Darrell L. Bock, *The Historical Jesus: Five Views.* Downers Grove, IL: IVP Academic, 2009.

Berding, Kenneth and Jonathan Lunde, *Three Views on the New Testament Use of the Old Testament.* Counterpoints Series: Bible and Theology. Grand Rapids, MI: Zondervan, 2008.

Betz, Otto, 'Jesus and Isaiah 53', pages 70–87 in *Jesus and the Suffering Servant: Isaiah 53 and Christian origins.* Edited by W. H. Bellinger and William R. Farmer. Harrisburg, PA: Trinity Press, 1998.

Beutler, Johannes, 'The Use of "Scripture" in the Gospel of John', pages 147–58 in *Exploring the Gospel of John: In Honor of D. Moody Smith.* Edited by R. Alan Culpepper and C. Clifton Black. Louisville, KY: Westminster John Knox, 1996.

Blomberg, Craig L., *From Pentecost to Patmos: An Introduction to Acts through Revelation.* Nashville, TN: Broadman & Holman, 2006.

Bock, Darrell, 'Scripture and the Realisation of God's Promises', pages 41–62 in *Witness to the Gospel: The Theology of Acts.* Edited by I. Howard Marshall and David Peterson. Grand Rapids, MI: Eerdmans, 1998.

Bock, Darrell, 'Isaiah 53 in Acts 8', pages 133–44 in *The Gospel according to Isaiah 53: Encountering the Suffering Servant in Jewish and Christian Theology.* Edited by Darrell L. Bock and Mitch Glaser. Grand Rapids, MI: Kregel, 2012.

Bond, Helen K., *The Historical Jesus: A Guide for the Perplexed.* London: T. & T. Clark, 2012.

Borg, Marcus J. and John Dominic Crossan, *The Last Week: What the Gospels Really Teach about Jesus's Final Days in Jerusalem.* London: SPCK, 2008.

Boring, M. Eugene, *Mark: A Commentary.* New Testament Library. Louisville, KY: Westminster John Knox, 2006.

Boxall, Ian, *Discovering Matthew: Content, Interpretation, Reception.* London: SPCK, 2014.

Breytenbach, Cilliers, 'The Septuagint Version of Isaiah 53 and the early Christian Formula "He was Delivered for Our Trespasses"', *Novum Testamentum* 51:4 (2009): 339–51.

Breytenbach, Cilliers, 'Narrating the Death of Jesus in Mark: Utterances of the Main Character, Jesus.' *Zeitschrift für die neutestamentliche Wissenschaft und die Kunde der älteren Kirche* 105:2 (2014): 153–68.

Brown, Raymond E., *A Crucified Christ in Holy Week: Essays on the Four Gospel Passion Narratives.* Collegeville, MN: Liturgical Press, 1986.

Brown, Raymond E., *The Death of the Messiah: From Gethsemane to the Grave – A Commentary on the Passion Narratives in the Four Gospels.* The Anchor Yale Bible Reference Library. New Haven, CT: Yale University Press, 2008.

Bryan, Christopher. *A Preface to Mark: Notes on the Gospel in its Literary and Cultural Settings.* Oxford: Oxford University Press, 1993.

Buchanan, George Wesley, *To the Hebrews: Translation, Comment and Conclusions.* Anchor Bible 36. Garden City, NY: Doubleday, 1972.

Bynum, Wiliam Randulph, 'Quotations of Zechariah in the Fourth Gospel', pages 47–74 in *Abiding Words: the Use of Scripture in the Gospel of John.* Edited by Alicia D. Myers and Bruce G. Schuchard. Society of Biblical Literature Resources for Biblical Study 81. Atlanta, GA: SBL, 2015.

Caird, George B., 'Exegetical method of the Epistle to the Hebrews'. *Canadian Journal of Theology* 5:1 (1959): 44–51.

Campbell, Douglas A., 'The Story of Jesus in Romans and Galatians', pages 97–124 in *Narrative Dynamics in Paul: A Critical Assessment.* Edited by Bruce W. Longenecker. Louisville, KY: Westminster John Knox, 2002.

Campbell, William Sanger, '"Why did you abandon me?": Abandonment Christology in Mark's Gospel', pages 99–117 in *The Trial and Death of Jesus: Essays on the Passion Narrative in Mark.* Edited by Geert van Oyen and Tom Shepherd. Leuven: Peeters, 2006.

Cane, Anthony, *The Place of Judas Iscariot in Christology.* Aldershot: Ashgate, 2004.

Carey, Holly J., *Jesus' Cry from the Cross: Towards a First-Century Understanding of the Intertextual Relationship between Psalm 22 and the Narrative of Mark's Gospel.* Library of New Testament Studies 398. London: T. & T. Clark, 2009.

Carroll, John T. and Joel B. Green, *The Death of Jesus in Early Christianity.* Peabody, MA: Hendrickson, 1995.

Carson, D. A., 'John and the Johannine Epistles', pages 245–64 in *It is Written: Scripture citing Scripture: Essays in Honour of Barnabas Lindars, SSF.* Edited by D. A. Carson and H. G. M. Williamson. Cambridge: Cambridge University Press, 1988.

Clark-Soles, Jaime, 'Scripture Cannot be Broken: The Social Function of the Use of Scripture in the Fourth Gospel', pages 95–117 in *Abiding Words: The Use of Scripture in the Gospel of John*. Edited by Alicia D. Myers and Bruce G. Schuchard. Society of Biblical Literature Resources for Biblical Study 81. Atlanta, GA: SBL, 2015.

Clivaz, Claire and Sara Schulthess, 'On the source and rewriting of 1 Corinthians 2.9 in Christian, Jewish and Islamic traditions (1 Clem 34.8; GosJud 47.10–13; a ḥadīth qudsī)', *New Testament Studies* 61:2 (2015): 183–200.

Cockerill, Gareth Lee, *The Epistle to the Hebrews*. The New International Commentary on the New Testament. Grand Rapids, MI: Eerdmans, 2012.

Collins, Adela Yarbro, *Mark: A Commentary*. Hermeneia. Minneapolis, MN: Fortress Press, 2007.

Compton, Jared, *Psalm 110 and the Logic of Hebrews*. Library of New Testament Studies 537. London: Bloomsbury T. & T. Clark, 2015.

Conzelmann, Hans, *The Theology of St. Luke*. London: Faber & Faber, 1960.

Crossan, John Dominic, *The Cross that Spoke: The Origins of the Passion Narrative*. San Francisco, CA: Harper & Row, 1988.

Crossan, John Dominic, *The Birth of Christianity: Discovering what Happened in the Years Immediately after the Execution of Jesus*. Edinburgh: T. & T. Clark, 1999.

Dahl, Nils Alstrup and Donald Juel, *Jesus the Christ: The Historical Origins of Christological Doctrine*. Minneapolis, MN: Fortress Press, 1991.

Dalton, William J., *Christ's Proclamation to the Spirits: A Study of 1 Peter 3:18–4:6*. Analecta Biblica 23. Rome: Pontifical Biblical Institute, 1965.

Daly-Denton, Margaret, *David in the Fourth Gospel: The Johannine Reception of the Psalms*. Arbeiten zur Geschichte des antiken Judentums und des Urchristentums 47. Leiden: Brill, 2000.

Daly-Denton, Margaret, 'The Psalms in John's Gospel', pages 119–37 in *The Psalms in the New Testament*. Edited by Steve Moyise and M. J. J. Menken. London: T. & T. Clark, 2004.

Davids, Peter H., *The First Epistle of Peter*. The New International Commentary on the New Testament. Grand Rapids, MI: Eerdmans, 1990.

Davies, W. D. and Dale C. Allison, *A Critical and Exegetical Commentary on the Gospel According to Saint Matthew*. The International Critical Commentary. Edinburgh: T. & T. Clark, 1997.

Davis, Ellen F., 'Exploding the Limits: Form and Function in Psalm 22', *Journal for the Study of the Old Testament* 17:53 (1992): 93–105.

deSilva, David A., *Despising Shame: Honor Discourse and Community Maintenance in the Epistle to the Hebrews*. Society of Biblical Literature Dissertation Series 152. Atlanta, GA: Scholars Press, 1995.

deSilva, David A., *Perseverance in Gratitude: A Socio-Rhetorical Commentary on the Epistle 'to the Hebrews'*. Grand Rapids, MI: Eerdmans, 2000.

Dibelius, Martin, *From Tradition to Gospel*. New York: Charles Scribner, 1934.

Doble, Peter, *The Paradox of Salvation: Luke's Theology of the Cross*. Society for New Testament Studies Monograph Series 87. Cambridge: Cambridge University Press, 1996.

Doble, Peter, 'The Psalms in Luke–Acts', pages 83–117 in *The Psalms in the New Testament*. Edited by Steve Moyise and M. J. J. Menken. London: T. & T. Clark, 2004.

Docherty, Susan, 'New Testament Scriptural Interpretation in its Early Jewish Context'. *Novum Testamentum* 57:1 (2015): 1–19.

Docherty, Susan E., *The Use of the Old Testament in Hebrews: A Case Study in Early Jewish Bible Interpretation*. Wissenschaftliche Untersuchungen zum Neuen Testament 2/260. Tübingen: Mohr Siebeck, 2009.

Dodd, C. H., *According to the Scriptures: The Sub-Structure of New Testament Theology*. London: Nisbet, 1952.

Donahue, John R., 'Introduction: From Passion Traditions to Passion Narrative', pages 1–20 in *The Passion in Mark: Studies on Mark 14—16*. Edited by Werner H. Kelber. Philadelphia, PA: Fortress Press, 1976.

Edwards, J. Christopher, *The Ransom Logion in Mark and Matthew: Its Reception and its Significance for the Study of the Gospels*. Wissenschaftliche Untersuchungen zum Neuen Testament 2/327. Tübingen: Mohr Siebeck, 2012.

Eklund, Rebekah, *Jesus Wept: The Significance of Jesus' Laments in the New Testament*. Library of New Testament Studies 515. London: Bloomsbury, 2015.

Ellis, E. Earle, *Paul's Use of the Old Testament*. Grand Rapids, MI: Baker, 1957.

Eubank, Nathan, 'A Disconcerting Prayer: On the Originality of Luke 23:34a', *Journal of Biblical Literature* 129:3 (2010): 521–36.

Evans, Craig, 'How Mark Writes', pages 135–48 in *The Written Gospel*. Edited by Markus N. A. Bockmuehl and Donald Alfred Hagner. Cambridge: Cambridge University Press, 2005.

Evans, Craig A., *Word and Glory: On the Exegetical and Theological Background of John's Prologue*. Journal for the Study of the New Testament Supplement Series 89. Sheffield: JSOT Press, 1993.

Evans, Craig A., *Jesus and his Contemporaries: Comparative Studies*. Arbeiten zur Geschichte des antiken Judentums und des Urchristentums 25. Leiden: Brill, 1995.

Evans, Craig A., 'The Old Testament in the New', pages 130–45 in *The Face of New Testament Studies: A Survey of Recent Research*. Edited by Scot McKnight and Grant R. Osborne. Grand Rapids, MI: Baker Academic, 2004.

Evans, Craig A., 'Isaiah 53 in the Letters of Peter, Paul, Hebrews and John', pages 145–70 in *The Gospel according to Isaiah 53: Encountering the Suffering Servant in Jewish and Christian Theology*. Edited by Darrell L. Bock and Mitch Glaser. Grand Rapids, MI: Kregel, 2012.

Evans, Craig A., 'Why Did the New Testament Writers Appeal to the Old Testament?' *Journal for the Study of the New Testament* 38:1 (2015): 36–48.

Fee, Gordon D., *The First Epistle to the Corinthians*. New International Commentary on the New Testament. Grand Rapids, MI: Eerdmans, 1987.

Fee, Gordon D., *Paul's Letter to the Philippians*. New International Commentary on the New Testament. Grand Rapids, MI: Eerdmans, 1995.

Foster, Paul, 'Echoes without Resonance: Critiquing Certain Aspects of Recent Scholarly Trends in the Study of the Jewish Scriptures in the New Testament'. *Journal for the Study of the New Testament* 38:1 (2015): 96–111.

Foster, Robert J., *The Significance of Exemplars for the Interpretation of the Letter of James*. Wissenschaftliche Untersuchungen zum Neuen Testament 2/376. Tübingen: Mohr Siebeck, 2014.

Fowl, Stephen E., *Philippians*. The Two Horizons New Testament Commentary. Grand Rapids, MI: Eerdmans, 2005.

France, R. T., *Jesus and the Old Testament: His Application of Old Testament Passages to Himself and his Mission*. London: Tyndale Press, 1971.

France, R. T., 'The Formula-Quotations of Matthew 2 and the Problem of Communication', pages 114–34 in *The Right Doctrine from the Wrong Texts?: Essays on the Use of the Old Testament in the New*. Edited by G. K. Beale. Grand Rapids, MI: Baker, 1994.

France, R. T., 'The Writer of Hebrews as a Biblical Expositor'. *Tyndale Bulletin* 47:2 (1996): 245–76.

Gathercole, Simon J., *Defending Substitution: An Essay on Atonement in Paul*. Grand Rapids, MI: Baker Academic, 2015.

Gheorgita, Radu, *The Role of the Septuagint in Hebrews*. Wissenschaftliche Untersuchungen zum Neuen Testament 2/160. Tübingen: Mohr Siebeck, 2003.

Gibson, Jeffrey B., 'The Function of the Charge of Blasphemy in Mark 14.64', pages 171–87 in *The Trial and Death of Jesus: Essays on the Passion Narrative in Mark*. Edited by Geert van Oyen and Tom Shepherd. Leuven: Peeters, 2006.

Goldingay, John, *Reading Jesus' Bible: How the New Testament Helps us Understand the Old Testament*. Grand Rapids, MI: Eerdmans, 2017.

Goodacre, Mark, 'Scripturalization in Mark's Crucifixion Narrative', pages 33–47 in *The Trial and Death of Jesus: Essays on the Passion Narrative in Mark*. Edited by Geert van Oyen and Tom Shepherd. Leuven: Peeters, 2006.

Gorman, Heather, *Interweaving Innocence: A Rhetorical Analysis of Luke's Passion Narrative Luke 22:66—23:49*. Cambridge: James Clarke, 2016.

Green, Joel B., *The Death of Jesus: Tradition and Interpretation in the Passion Narrative*. Wissenschaftliche Untersuchungen zum Neuen Testament 2/33. Tübingen: Mohr, 1988.

Green, Joel B., *1 Peter*. The Two Horizons New Testament Commentary. Grand Rapids, MI: Eerdmans, 2007.

Green, Joel B. and Mark D. Baker, *Recovering the Scandal of the Cross: Atonement in New Testament and Contemporary Contexts*. Carlisle: Paternoster Press, 2003.

Guthrie, George H., *The Structure of Hebrews: A Text-Linguistic Analysis*. Supplements to Novum Testamentum 73. Leiden: Brill, 1994.

Guthrie, George H., 'Hebrews' Use of the Old Testament: Recent Trends in Research'. *Currents in Biblical Research* 1:2 (2003): 271–94.

Hafemann, Scott J., 'Paul's Use of the Old Testament in 2 Corinthians', *Interpretation* 52:3 (1998): 246–57.

Hanson, A. T., 'Hebrews', pages 292–302 in *It is Written: Scripture citing Scripture: Essays in Honour of Barnabas Lindars, SSF*. Edited by D. A. Carson and H. G. M. Williamson. Cambridge: Cambridge University Press, 1988.

Hanson, Anthony Tyrrell, *The Living Utterances of God: The New Testament Exegesis of the Old*. London: Darton, Longman & Todd, 1983.

Hanson, Anthony Tyrrell, *The Prophetic Gospel: A Study of John and the Old Testament*. Edinburgh: T. & T. Clark, 1991.

Harrington, Jay M., *The Lukan Passion Narrative – the Markan material in Luke 22,54—23,25: A Historical Survey, 1891–1997*. Leiden: Brill, 2000.

Hays, Richard, *Echoes of Scripture in the Letters of Paul*. New Haven, CT: Yale University Press, 1989.

Hays, Richard B., 'Who has Believed our Message: Paul's Reading of Isaiah', pages 46–70 in *New Testament Writers and the Old Testament: An Introduction*. Edited by John Court. London: SPCK, 2002.

Hays, Richard B., 'Is Paul's Gospel Narratable?' *Journal for the Study of the New Testament* 27:2 (2004): 217–40.

Hays, Richard B., *The Conversion of the Imagination: Paul as Interpreter of Israel's Scripture*. Grand Rapids, MI: Eerdmans, 2005.

Hays, Richard B., 'The Story of God's Son: The Identity of Jesus in the Letters of Paul', pages 180–99 in *Seeking the identity of Jesus: A Pilgrimage*. Edited by Beverly Roberts Gaventa and Richard B. Hays. Grand Rapids, MI: Eerdmans, 2008.

Hays, Richard B., *Reading Backwards: Figural Christology and the Fourfold Gospel Witness*. London: SPCK, 2015.

Hays, Richard B., *Echoes of Scripture in the Gospels*. Waco, TX: Baylor University Press, 2016.

Hays, Richard B. and Joel B. Green, 'The Use of the Old Testament by the New Testament Writers', pages 122–39 in *Hearing the New Testament: Strategies for Interpretation*. Edited by Joel B. Green. Grand Rapids, MI: Eerdmans, 2010.

Hengel, Martin, *The Atonement: A Study of the Origins of the Doctrine in the New Testament*. London: SCM Press, 1981.

Hera, Marianus Pale, *Christology and Discipleship in John 17*. Wissenschaftliche Untersuchungen zum Neuen Testament 2/342. Tübingen: Mohr Siebeck, 2013.

Hofius, Otfried, 'The Fourth Servant Song in the New Testament Letters', pages 163–88 in *The Suffering Servant: Isaiah 53 in Jewish and Christian Sources*. Edited by Bernd Janowski and Peter Stuhlmacher. Grand Rapids, MI: Eerdmans, 2004.

Hooker, Morna, *Not Ashamed of the Gospel: New Testament Interpretations of the Death of Christ*. Carlisle: Paternoster Press, 1994.

Hooker, Morna, 'Isaiah in Mark', pages 35–49 in *Isaiah in the New Testament*. Edited by Steve Moyise and M. J. J. Menken. London: T. & T. Clark, 2005.

Hooker, Morna D., 'Christ, the "End" of the Cult', pages 189–212 in *The Epistle to the Hebrews and Christian Theology*. Edited by Richard Bauckham, Daniel R. Driver, Trevor A. Hart and Nathan MacDonald. Grand Rapids, MI: Eerdmans, 2009.

Hooker, Morna D., *Jesus and the Servant: The Influence of the Servant Concept of Deutero-Isaiah in the New Testament*. London: SPCK, 1959.

Horrell, David, 'Who are "the Dead" and when was the Gospel Preached to them? The Interpretation of 1 Pet. 4.6'. *New Testament Studies* 49:1 (2003): 70–89.

Horrell, David G., *1 Peter*. London: T. & T. Clark, 2008.

Horrell, David G., *Becoming Christian: Essays on 1 Peter and the Making of Christian Identity*. Library of New Testament Studies 394. London: Bloomsbury, 2013.

Hughes, Graham, *Hebrews and Hermeneutics*. Society for New Testament Studies Monograph Series 36. Cambridge: Cambridge University Press, 1979.

Huizenga, Leroy Andrew, *The New Isaac: Tradition and Intertextuality in the Gospel of Matthew*. Supplements to Novum Testamentum 131. Leiden: Brill, 2009.

Hurtado, Larry W., *Lord Jesus Christ: Devotion to Jesus in Earliest Christianity*. Grand Rapids, MI: Eerdmans, 2003.

Janowski, Bernd and Peter Stuhlmacher (eds), *The Suffering Servant: Isaiah 53 in Jewish and Christian Sources*. Grand Rapids, MI: Eerdmans, 2004.

Jobes, Karen H., *1 Peter*. Baker Exegetical Commentary on the New Testament. Grand Rapids, MI: Baker Academic, 2005.

Johnson, Luke Timothy, *The Gospel of Luke*. Sacra Pagina 3. Collegeville, MN: Liturgical Press, 1991.

Johnson, Luke Timothy, *Hebrews: A Commentary*. The New Testament Library. Louisville, KY: Westminster/John Knox, 2006.

Jordaan, Gert J. C. and Pieter Nel, 'From King-Priest to Priest-King: Psalm 110 and the Basic Structure of Hebrews', pages 229–40 in *Psalms and Hebrews: Studies in Reception*. Edited by Dirk J. Human and Gert Jacobus Steyn. Library of Hebrew Bible/Old Testament Studies 527. New York: T. & T. Clark, 2010.

Juel, Donald, *Messianic Exegesis: Christological Interpretation of the Old Testament in Early Christianity*. Philadelphia, PA: Fortress Press, 1988.

Kahler, Martin, *The So-called Historical Jesus and the Historic and Biblical Christ*. Philadelphia, PA: Fortress Press, 1964.

Karrer, Martin, 'LXX Psalm 39.7–10 in Hebrews 10.5–7', pages 126–46 in *Psalms and Hebrews: Studies in Reception*. Edited by Dirk J. Human and Gert Jacobus Steyn. Library of Hebrew Bible/Old Testament Studies 527. New York: T. & T. Clark, 2010.

Keesmaat, Sylvia C., 'The Psalms in Romans and Galatians', pages 139–61 in *The Psalms in the New Testament*. Edited by Steve Moyise and M. J. J. Menken. London: T. & T. Clark, 2004.

Kimball, Charles A., *Jesus' Exposition of the Old Testament in Luke's Gospel*. Journal for the Study of the New Testament Supplement Series 94. Sheffield: JSOT Press, 1994.

Koch, Dietrich-Alex, 'The Quotations of Isaiah 8,14 and 28,16 in Romans 9,33 and 1 Peter 2,6.8 as Test Case for Old Testament Quotations in the New Testament', *Zeitschrift für die neutestamentliche Wissenschaft und die Kunde der älteren Kirche* 101:2 (2010): 223–40.

Kovacs, Judith, 'The Archons, the Spirit and the Death of Christ: Do We Need the Hypothesis of Gnostic Opponents to Explain 1 Corinthians 2.6–16?,' pages 217–36 in *Apocalyptic and the New Testament: Essays in Honor of J. Louis Martyn*. Edited by Joel Marcus and Marion Soards. Sheffield: JSOT Press, 1989.

Laws, Sophie, 'Hebrews, Letter to the', pages 328–31 in *Jesus: The Complete Guide*. Edited by Leslie Houlden. London: Continuum, 2005.

Lee, Gregory W., *Today When You Hear His Voice: Scripture, the Covenants and the People of God*. Grand Rapids, MI: Eerdmans, 2016.

Lee, Yongbom, *The Son of Man as the Last Adam: The Early Church Tradition as a Source of Paul's Adam Christology*. Eugene, OR: Pickwick, 2012.

Licona, Michael R., *Why are there Differences in the Gospels? What we can Learn from Ancient Biography*. New York: Oxford University Press, 2017.

Lim, Kar Yong, 'The Sufferings of Christ are Abundant in Us' (2 Corinthians 1.5): A Narrative Dynamics Investigation of Paul's Sufferings in 2 Corinthians. Library of New Testament Studies 399. London: T. & T. Clark, 2009.

Lim, Timothy H., The Formation of the Jewish Canon. The Anchor Yale Bible Reference Library. New Haven, CT: Yale University Press, 2013.

Lincoln, Andrew T., Truth on Trial: The Lawsuit Motif in the Fourth Gospel. Peabody, MA: Hendrickson, 2000.

Lincoln, Andrew T., The Gospel According to Saint John. Black's New Testament Commentaries. Peabody, MA: Hendrickson, 2005.

Lincoln, Andrew T., Born of a Virgin?: Reconceiving Jesus in the Bible, Tradition, and Theology. Grand Rapids, MI: Eerdmans, 2013.

Lindars, Barnabas, New Testament Apologetic. London: SCM Press, 1961.

Litwak, Kenneth D., Echoes of Scripture in Luke–Acts: Telling the History of God's People Intertextually. Journal for the Study of the New Testament Supplement Series 282. London: T. & T. Clark, 2005.

Marcus, Joel, The Way of the Lord: Christological Exegesis of the Old Testament in the Gospel of Mark. Louisville, KY: Westminster/John Knox, 1992.

Marcus, Joel, 'The Old Testament and the Death of Jesus: The Role of Scripture in the Gospel Passion Narratives', pages 205–33 in The Death of Jesus in Early Christianity. Edited by John T. Carroll and Joel B. Green. Peabody, MA: Hendrickson, 1995.

Marcus, Joel, 'Crucifixion as Parodic Exaltation', Journal of Biblical Literature 125:1 (2006): 73–87.

Marcus, Joel, Mark 8–16: A New Translation with Introduction and Commentary. The Anchor Yale Bible 27A. New Haven, CT: Yale University Press, 2009.

Martin, Ralph P. and Brian J. Dodd, Where Christology Began: Essays on Philippians 2. Louisville, KY: Westminster John Knox, 1998.

Matera, Frank J., The Kingship of Jesus: Composition and Theology in Mark 15. SBL Dissertation Series 66. Chico, CA: Scholars Press, 1982.

Matera, Frank J., 'The Death of Jesus according to Luke: A Question of Sources', Catholic Biblical Quarterly 47:3 (1985): 469–85.

Matera, Frank J., Passion Narratives and Gospel Theologies: Interpreting the Synoptics through their Passion stories. New York: Wipf & Stock, 2001.

Mathewson, David, 'Isaiah in Revelation', pages 189–210 in Isaiah in the New Testament. Edited by Steve Moyise and M. J. J. Menken. London: T. & T. Clark, 2005.

McKnight, Scot, 'Covenant and Spirit: The Origins of New Covenant Hermeneutic', pages 41–54 in The Holy Spirit and Christian Origins: Essays in Honor of James D. G. Dunn. Edited by Graham Stanton, Bruce W. Longenecker and Stephen C. Barton. Grand Rapids, MI: Eerdmans, 2004.

McKnight, Scot, *Jesus and his Death: Historiography, the Historical Jesus, and Atonement Theory*. Waco, TX: Baylor University Press, 2005.

McKnight, Scot, *A Community called Atonement*. Nashville, TN: Abingdon, 2007.

McWhirter, Jocelyn, 'Messianic Exegesis in Mark's Passion Narrative', pages 69–97 in *The Trial and Death of Jesus: Essays on the Passion Narrative in Mark*. Edited by Geert van Oyen and Tom Shepherd. Leuven: Peeters, 2006.

Menken, M. J. J., *Matthew's Bible: The Old Testament Text of the Evangelist*. Bibliotheca Ephemeridum theologicarum Lovaniensium 173. Leuven: University Press; Dudley, MA: Peeters, 2004.

Menken, M. J. J. and Steve Moyise (eds), *The Psalms in the New Testament*. London: T. & T. Clark, 2004.

Menken, M. J. J. and Steve Moyise (eds), *Isaiah in the New Testament*. London: T. & T. Clark, 2005.

Menken, M. J. J. and Steve Moyise (eds), *Deuteronomy in the New Testament*. Library of New Testament Studies 358. London: T. & T. Clark, 2007.

Menken, M. J. J. and Steve Moyise (eds), *The Minor Prophets in the New Testament*. Library of New Testament Studies 377. London: T. & T. Clark, 2009.

Menken, M. J. J. and Steve Moyise (eds), *Genesis in the New Testament*. Library of New Testament Studies 466. London: T. & T. Clark, 2012.

Menken, Marteen J. J., 'Old Testament Quotations in the Gospel of John', pages 29–45 in *New Testament writers and the Old Testament: An Introduction*. Edited by John Court. London: SPCK, 2002.

Menken, Maarten J. J., 'The Minor Prophets in John's Gospel', pages 79–96 in *The Minor Prophets in the New Testament*. Edited by M. J. J. Menken and Steve Moyise. Library of New Testament Studies 377. London: T. & T. Clark, 2009.

Miller, Paul, '"They Saw His Glory and Spoke of Him": The Gospel of John and the Old Testament', pages 127–51 in *Hearing the Old Testament in the New Testament*. Edited by Stanley E. Porter. Grand Rapids, MI: Eerdmans, 2006.

Moffitt, David M., *Atonement and the Logic of Resurrection in the Epistle to the Hebrews*. Supplements to Novum Testamentum 141. Leiden: Brill, 2011.

Moffitt, David M., 'The Interpretation of Scripture in the Epistle to the Hebrews', pages 77–97 in *Reading the Epistle to the Hebrews: A Resource for Students*. Edited by Eric Farrel Mason and Kevin B. McCruden. Society of Biblical Literature Resources for Biblical Study 66. Leiden: Brill, 2011.

Moo, Douglas J., *The Old Testament in the Gospel Passion Narratives*. Sheffield: Almond Press, 1983.

Moyise, Steve, 'The Psalms in Revelation', pages 231–46 in *The Psalms in the New Testament*. Edited by Steve Moyise and M. J. J. Menken. London: T. & T. Clark, 2004.

Moyise, Steve, 'Isaiah in 1 Peter', pages 175–88 in *Isaiah in the New Testament*. Edited by Steve Moyise and M. J. J. Menken. London: T. & T. Clark, 2005.

Moyise, Steve, *Paul and Scripture*. London: SPCK, 2010.

Moyise, Steve, *The Later New Testament Writers and Scripture*. London: SPCK, 2012.

Moyise, Steve, *Was the Birth of Jesus According to Scripture?* London: SPCK, 2013.

Moyise, Steve, *The Old Testament in the New: An Introduction*. 2nd edn. London: Bloomsbury, 2015.

Moyise, Steve, 'Wright's Understanding of Paul's Use of Scripture', pages 165–80 in *God and the Faithfulness of Paul: A Critical Examination of the Pauline Theology of N. T. Wright*. Edited by Christoph Heilig, Michael F. Bird and J. Thomas Hewitt. Tübingen: Mohr Siebeck, 2016.

Myers, Alicia D., *Characterizing Jesus: A Rhetorical Analysis on the Fourth Gospel's Use of Scripture in its Presentation of Jesus*. Library of New Testament Studies 458. London: T. & T. Clark, 2012.

Newman, Judith H., *Praying by the Book: The Scripturalization of Prayer in Second Temple Judaism*. Early Judaism and its Literature 14. Atlanta, GA: Scholars Press, 1999.

Nienhuis, David R., *Not by Paul Alone: The Formation of the Catholic Epistle Collection and the Christian Canon*. Waco, TX: Baylor University Press, 2007.

Nienhuis, David R. and Robert W. Wall, *Reading the Epistles of James, Peter, John, and Jude as Scripture: The Shaping and Shape of a Canonical Collection*. Grand Rapids, MI: Eerdmans, 2013.

North, Wendy E. S., *A Journey round John: Tradition, Interpretation and Context in the Fourth Gospel*. Library of New Testament Studies 534. London: T. & T. Clark.

Novakovic, Lidija, *Raised from the Dead According to Scripture: The Role of Israel's Scripture in the Early Christian Interpretations of Jesus' Resurrection*. Jewish and Christian Texts Series 12. London and New York: Bloomsbury/T. & T. Clark, 2012.

Novakovic, Lidija, *Resurrection: A Guide for the Perplexed*. London: T. & T. Clark, 2016.

O'Brien, Kelli S., 'Innocence and Guilt: Apologetic, Martyr Stories, and Allusion in the Markan Trial Narratives', pages 205–28 in *The Trial and Death of Jesus: Essays on the Passion Narrative in Mark*. Edited by Geert van Oyen and Tom Shepherd. Leuven: Peeters, 2006.

O'Brien, Kelli S., *The Use of Scripture in the Markan Passion Narrative*. Library of New Testament Studies 384. London: T. & T. Clark, 2010.

Ortlund, Dane, 'The Insanity of Faith: Paul's Theological Use of Isaiah in Romans 9:33', *Trinity Journal* 30:2 (2009): 269–88.

Pao, David W., *Acts and the Isaianic New Exodus*. Wissenschaftliche Untersuchungen zum Neuen Testament 2/130. Tübingen: Mohr Siebeck, 2000.

Pao, David W. and Eckhard J. Schnabel, 'Luke', pages 251–414 in *Commentary on the New Testament Use of the Old Testament*. Edited by G. K. Beale and D. A. Carson. Grand Rapids, MI: Apollos, 2007.

Parsons, Mikeal C., 'Isaiah 53 in Acts 8: A Reply to Professor Morna Hooker', pages 104–19 in *Jesus and the Suffering Servant: Isaiah 53 and Christian Origins*. Edited by W. H. Bellinger and William R. Farmer. Harrisburg, PA: Trinity Press, 1998.

Peeler, Amy L. B., *You are my Son: The Family of God in the Epistle to the Hebrews*. Library of New Testament Studies 486. London: Bloomsbury, 2014.

Perrin, Norman, 'The High Priest's Question and Jesus' Answer', pages 80–95 in *The Passion in Mark: Studies on Mark 14–16*. Edited by Werner H. Kelber. Philadelphia, PA: Fortress Press, 1976.

Pervo, Richard I., *Acts: A Commentary*. Hermeneia. Minneapolis, MN: Fortress Press Press, 2009.

Porter, Stanley E., 'The Use of the Old Testament in the New Testament: A Brief Comment on Method and Terminology', pages 79–96 in *Early Christian Interpretation of the Scriptures of Israel: Investigations and Proposals*. Edited by Craig A. Evans and James A. Sanders. Sheffield: Sheffield Academic Press, 1997.

Porter, Stanley E., 'Scripture Justifies Mission: The Use of the Old Testament in Luke–Acts', pages 104–26 in *Hearing the Old Testament in the New Testament*. Edited by Stanley E. Porter. Grand Rapids, MI: Eerdmans, 2006.

Porter, Stanley E., *Sacred Tradition in the New Testament: Tracing Old Testament Themes in the Gospels and Epistles*. Grand Rapids, MI: Baker Academic, 2016.

Porter, Stanley E., *The Synoptic Problem: Four Views*. Grand Rapids, MI: Baker Academic, 2016.

Porter, Stanley E. and Christopher D. Stanley (eds), *As it is Written: Studying Paul's use of Scripture*. Society of Biblical Literature Symposium Series 50. Leiden: Brill, 2008.

Richardson, Christopher, 'The Passion: Reconsidering Hebrews 5.7–8', pages 51–67 in *A Cloud of Witnesses: The Theology of Hebrews in its Ancient Contexts*. Edited by Richard Bauckham, Trevor Hart, Nathan MacDonald and Daniel Driver. London: T. & T. Clark, 2008.

Richardson, Neil, *Paul for Today: New Perspectives on a Controversial Apostle*. London: Epworth, 2008.

Rindge, Matthew S., 'Reconfiguring the Akedah and Recasting God: Lament and Divine Abandonment in Mark', *Journal of Biblical Literature* 131:4 (2011): 755–74.

Robbins, Vernon K., 'The Reversed Contxtualisation of Psalm 22 in the Markan Crucifixion: A Socio-Rhetorical Analysis', pages 1161–83 in *The Four Gospels 1992: Festschrift Frans Neirynck*. Edited by Frans van Segbroeck. Leuven: Peeters, 1992.

Rulmu, Callia, 'The Use of Psalm LXIX, 9 in Romans XV, 3: Shame as Sacrifice', *Biblical Theology Bulletin* 40:4 (2010): 227–33.

Schutter, William L., *Hermeneutic and Composition in I Peter*. Wissenschaftliche Untersuchungen zum Neuen Testament 2/30. Tübingen: Mohr 1989.

Scott, Ian W., *Paul's Way of Knowing: Story, Experience and the Spirit*. Grand Rapids, MI: Baker Academic, 2009.

Scott, Matthew, *The Hermeneutics of Christological Psalmody in Paul: An Intertextual Enquiry*. Society for New Testament Studies Monograph Series 158. Cambridge: Cambridge University Press, 2014.

Senior, Donald, *The Passion of Jesus in the Gospel of Luke*. Wilmington, DE: M. Glazier, 1989.

Senior, Donald, *The Passion of Jesus in the Gospel of Matthew*. Collegeville, MN: M. Glazier, 1990.

Senior, Donald, *The Passion of Jesus in the Gospel of John*. Collegeville, MN: Liturgical Press, 1991.

Shum, Shiu-Lun, *Paul's Use of Isaiah in Romans: A Comparative Study of Paul's Letter to the Romans and the Sibylline and Qumran Sectarian Texts*. Wissenschaftliche Untersuchungen zum Neuen Testament 2/156. Tübingen: Mohr Siebeck, 2002.

Smith, Barry D., *The Meaning of Jesus' Death: Reviewing the New Testament's Interpretations*. London: Bloomsbury, 2017.

Smith Jr., D. Moody, 'The Use of the Old Testament in the New', pages 3–65 in *The Use of the Old Testament in the New and other Essays: Studies in Honor of William Franklin Stinespring*. Edited by William F. Stinespring and James M. Efird. Durham, NC: Duke University Press, 1972.

Stanley, Christopher D., *Arguing With Scripture: The Rhetoric of Quotations in the Letters of Paul*. London: T. & T. Clark, 2004.

Stanley, Christopher D. (ed.), *Paul and Scripture: Extending the Conversation*. Atlanta, GA: Society of Biblical Literature, 2012.

Stanton, Graham, 'Matthew', pages 205–19 in *It is Written: Scripture citing Scripture: Essays in Honour of Barnabas Lindars, SSF*. Edited by D. A. Carson and H. G. M. Williamson. Cambridge: Cambridge University Press, 1988.

Steyn, Gert J., 'Jesus Sayings in Hebrews', *Ephemerides Theologicae Lovanienses* 77:4 (2001): 433–40.

Still, Todd D. (ed.), *Jesus and Paul Reconnected: Fresh Pathways into an Old Debate*. Grand Rapids, MI: Eerdmans, 2007.

Stuhlmacher, Peter, 'Isaiah 53 in the Gospels and Acts', pages 147–62 in *The Suffering Servant: Isaiah 53 in Jewish and Christian Sources*. Edited by Bernd Janowski and Peter Stuhlmacher. Grand Rapids, MI: Eerdmans, 2004.

Taylor, Vincent, *The Passion Narrative of St. Luke: A Critical and Historical Investigation*. Society for New Testament Studies Monograph Series 19. Cambridge: Cambridge University Press, 1972.

Theissen, Gerd, *The Gospels in Context: Social and Political History in the Synoptic Tradition*. Edinburgh: T. & T. Clark, 1992.

Thiselton, Anthony C., *The First Epistle to the Corinthians: A Commentary on the Greek Text*. New international Greek Testament Commentary. Grand Rapids, MI: Eerdmans, 2000.

Thompson, Marianne Meye, '"They Bear Witness to Me": The Psalms in the Passion Narrative in the Gospel of John', pages 267–83 in *The Word Leaps the Gap: Essays on Scripture and Theology in Honor of Richard B. Hays*. Edited by J. Ross Wagner, Christopher Kavin Rowe and A. Katherine Grieb. Grand Rapids, MI: Eerdmans, 2008.

Thompson, Marianne Meye, *John: A Commentary*. New Testament Library. Louisville, KY: Westminster John Knox, 2015.

Vanhoye, Albert, *La Structure Littéraire de 'L'Epitre aux Hébreux'*. 2nd rev. edn. Paris: Desclée De Brouwer, 1976.

Vermes, Geza, *Scripture and Tradition in Judaism: Haggadic Studies*. Studia post-Biblica 4. Leiden: Brill, 1961.

Wagner, J. Ross, *Heralds of the Good News: Isaiah and Paul 'In Concert' in the Letter to the Romans*. Supplements to Novum Testamentum 101. Leiden: Brill, 2002.

Wagner, J. Ross, 'Isaiah in Romans and Galatians', pages 117–32 in *Isaiah in the New Testament*. Edited by Steve Moyise and M. J. J. Menken. London: T. & T. Clark, 2005.

Watson, Francis, *Paul and the Hermeneutics of Faith*. London: T. & T. Clark, 2004.

Watts, Rikk, 'The Psalms in Mark's Gospel', pages 25–45 in *The Psalms in the New Testament*. Edited by Steve Moyise and M. J. J. Menken. London: T. & T. Clark, 2004.

Watts, Rikki E., *Isaiah's New Exodus and Mark*. Wissenschaftliche Untersuchungen zum Neuen Testament 2/88. Tübingen: Mohr Siebeck, 1997.

Watts, Rikki E., 'Jesus' Death, Isaiah 53, and Mark 10:45: A Crux Revisited', pages 125–51 in *Jesus and the Suffering Servant: Isaiah 53 and Christian Origins*. Edited by W. H. Bellinger and William R. Farmer. Harrisburg, PA: Trinity Press, 1998.

Watts, Rikki E., 'Messianic servant or the end of Israel's Exilic Curses?: Isaiah 53.4 in Matthew 8.17'. *Journal for the Study of the New Testament* 38:1 (2015): 81–95.

Weatherly, Jon A., *Jewish Responsibility for the Death of Jesus in Luke–Acts*. Sheffield: Sheffield Academic Press, 1994.

Wedderburn, A. J. M., *The Death of Jesus: Some Reflections on Jesus-traditions and Paul*. Wissenschaftliche Untersuchungen zum Neuen Testament 299. Tübingen: Mohr Siebeck, 2013.

Wenham, David, *Paul and Jesus: The True Story*. Grand Rapids, MI: Eerdmans, 2002.

Whitlark, Jason A., *Resisting Empire: Rethinking the Purpose of the Letter to 'the Hebrews'*. Library of New Testament Studies 484. London: Bloomsbury, 2014.

Wilson, Benjamin R., *The Saving Cross of the Suffering Christ: The Death of Jesus in Lukan Soteriology*. Beihefte zur Zeitschrift für die neutestamentliche Wissenschaft 223. Walter de Gruyter, 2016.

Woan, Sue, 'The Psalms in 1 Peter', pages 213–29 in *The Psalms in the New Testament*. Edited by Steve Moyise and M. J. J. Menken. London: T. & T. Clark, 2004.

Wright, N. T., *Paul and the Faithfulness of God*. Christian Origins and the Question of God 4. London: SPCK.

Wright, N. T., *The Climax of the Covenant: Christ and the Law in Pauline Theology*. Edinburgh: T. & T. Clark, 1991.

Wright, N. T., 'The Letter to the Romans', pages 393–770 in *The New Interpreter's Bible Vol. 10*. Edited by Leander Keck. Nashville, TN: Abingdon, 2002.

Endnotes

1 Introduction

1 Tracing the precise origin of the quotation is not a straightforward task, however, and it is thus best to speak of the quotation as 'apocryphal'- (or even Deutero- !) Hengel.

2 Evans, 'The Old Testament in the New', 130.

3 For background on the 'Quest for the Historical Jesus' and the so-called four stages or phases it traditionally comprises, see Beilby et al., *The Historical Jesus: Five Views*; Bond, *The Historical Jesus: A Guide for the Perplexed*.

4 See Kahler, *The So-Called Historical Jesus and the Historic and Biblical Christ*, 80, n. 11. Technically, Kahler is speaking of the gospel genre as a whole, but his point is essentially made in respect of Mark.

5 Finding an appropriate term or nomenclature to describe this focus is not easy: *thanatology* is too scientific a term, whereas *soteriology* or *martyrology* assume too narrow a focus for the type of engagement in which are participating. O'Brien, 'Innocence and Guilt: Apologetic, Martyr Stories, and Allusion in the Markan Trial Narratives', argues that the Markan Passion Narrative has a martyrological character, and that may be the case, but one hesitates to apply that categorization to the other Passion accounts, at least at this stage in our discussion.

6 Hooker, 'Christ, the "End" of the Cult', 208-9.

7 Moo, *The Old Testament in the Gospel Passion Narratives*, 397.

8 Edwards, *The Ransom Logion in Mark and Matthew* uses this nomenclature for the saying.

9 Gathercole, *Defending Substitution: An Essay on Atonement in Paul*, 58.

10 See inter alia Campbell, 'The Story of Jesus in Romans and Galatians'; Hays, 'Is Paul's Gospel Narratable?'; Hays, 'The Story of God's Son: The Identity of Jesus in the Letters of Paul'.

11 Marcus, 'The Old Testament and the Death of Jesus: The Role of Scripture in the Gospel Passion Narratives', 206.

12 Moyise, *Was the Birth of Jesus According to Scripture?*

13 For a strong argument for the existence of a pre-canonical Passion Narrative, see Green, *The Death of Jesus: Tradition and Interpretation in the Passion Narrative*, passim.

14 Cf. Donahue, 'Introduction: From Passion Traditions to Passion Narrative', 1–8, for example.

15 See Carroll and Green, *The Death of Jesus in Early Christianity*, 3–22, for an extensive review of the question.

16 Donahue, 'Introduction', 1–8, for example, locates it within the context of early Christian preaching and worship. See also Green, *Death of Jesus*.

17 See Aitken, 'Ta drōmena kai ta legomena: The Eucharistic Memory of Jesus' Words in First Corinthians', 359–70, and more expansively, Aitken, *Jesus' Death in Early Christian Memory: The Poetics of the Passion*.

18 On the origins and sources of Luke's Passion Narrative, see Gorman, *Interweaving Innocence: A Rhetorical Analysis of Luke's Passion Narrative (Lk 22:66 — 23:49)*.

19 Crossan, *The Cross That Spoke: The Origins of the Passion Narrative*.

20 As this is a NT volume, we do not include the Gospel of Peter. That is not to say that the text does not have much to say about the portrayal of Jesus' death (its resurrection account is somewhat creative!), but rather that it is a question of scope.

21 Dibelius, *From Tradition to Gospel*, 179. Dibelius was also one of the earliest scholarly voices to explore the way the OT was used to structure and shape the Passion Narrative.

22 The testimony of Deuteronomy 21.22–23 is that the one who hangs on the tree is cursed. Technically, the 'hanging' is post-mortem, and the curse pertains to the *hanging* rather than to the death, but contemporary evidence (e.g. the Temple Scroll at Qumran, as well as the NT itself) suggests that hanging on a tree had become synonymous with crucifixion and therefore the crucified one would indeed bear the Deuteronomic curse. See Matera, *Passion Narratives and Gospel Theologies: Interpreting the Synoptics through their Passion Stories*, 3–4.

23 See Evans, *Word and Glory: On the Exegetical and Theological Background of John's Prologue*, 176.

24 Smith, *The Meaning of Jesus' Death: Reviewing the New Testament's Interpretations*.

25 Green, *Death of Jesus*, 318. 'Excluding' or 'minimizing' the manner of Jesus' death, and thereby the associated offence or *skandalon*, it was presumably an 'option' for the early Church. Hence their focal attention to its scandal warrants the kind of questions we are asking.

26 Hooker, *Not Ashamed of the Gospel: New Testament Interpretations of the Death of Christ*, 48. Earlier in the same volume she avers of Paul: 'It is important to understand that Paul's argument starts from the fact of

the cross. The death of Christ has to be explained – and in the process of explanation, it becomes that which explains everything else' (31).

27 Goodacre, 'Scripturalization in Mark's Crucifixion Narrative', 37–8. He further surmises: 'Scholars still seldom appreciate just what an extraordinary undertaking it is to have tried to write a narrative about a hero who was crucified' (46).

28 Hays, *The Conversion of the Imagination: Paul as Interpreter of Israel's Scripture*, 27.

29 Or at least that is how it is presented by Justin.

30 Moo, *Old Testament in the Gospel Passion Narratives*, 171, also 162–71.

31 Stuhlmacher, 'Isaiah 53 in the Gospels and Acts', 147–62. Stuhlmacher concludes: 'Given Jesus' own understanding, the Easter witnesses were able for the first time to relate the whole Suffering Servant text to an individual historical figure and to interpret Jesus's sufferings soteriologically from this text' (161). See further Janowski and Stuhlmacher, *The Suffering Servant: Isaiah 53 in Jewish and Christian Sources*. Porter, *Sacred Tradition in the New Testament: Tracing Old Testament Themes in the Gospels and Epistles*, 93–6 also advocates that Jesus himself understood his ministry in terms of the Suffering Servant.

32 Marcus, *The Way of the Lord: Christological Exegesis of the Old Testament in the Gospel of Mark*, 186.

33 Evans, 'Isaiah 53 in the Letters of Peter, Paul, Hebrews and John', 153.

34 Porter, *Sacred Tradition in the New Testament*, 82–3, offers a number of possibilities for the implied identity of the Servant figure, recognizing that the 'relatively vague language' used in respect of the Servant serves to generate such a variety of interpretative possibilities.

35 Juel, *Messianic Exegesis: Christological Interpretation of the Old Testament in Early Christianity*, 132.

36 Hooker, *Jesus and the Servant: The Influence of the Servant Concept of Deutero-Isaiah in the New Testament*.

37 Watts, *Isaiah's New Exodus and Mark*; Pao, *Acts and the Isaianic New Exodus*.

38 Jobes, *1 Peter*.

39 Watts, 'Messianic Servant or the End of Israel's Exilic Curses?: Isaiah 53.4 in Matthew 8.17', 81–95.

40 The epistle to the Hebrews is striking in this regard. As a text permeated with OT reference to Jesus' death, scholars have still appealed either to honour/shame (deSilva, *Despising Shame: Honor Discourse and Community Maintenance in the Epistle to the Hebrews*) or Roman imperial imagery (Whitlark, *Resisting Empire: Rethinking the Purpose of the Letter to 'the Hebrews'*) as its primary interpretative key.

41 See Gorman, *Interweaving Innocence*.

42 Huizenga, *The New Isaac: Tradition and Intertextuality in the Gospel of Matthew*, 61.

43 Foster, 'Echoes without Resonance: Critiquing Certain Aspects of Recent Scholarly Trends in the Study of the Jewish Scriptures in the New Testament'.

44 For example, Goldingay, *Reading Jesus's Bible: How the New Testament Helps us Understand the Old Testament*, 1–4.

45 For example: Beale and Carson, *Commentary on the New Testament Use of the Old Testament*; Beale, *Handbook on the New Testament Use of the Old Testament: Exegesis and Interpretation*; Berding and Lunde, *Three Views on the New Testament Use of the Old Testament*; Moyise, *The Old Testament in the New: An Introduction*.

46 This is the term used by Goodacre, 'Scripturalization'.

47 On the emergence of the Hebrew canon, see Lim, *The Formation of the Jewish Canon*.

48 Porter, 'The Use of the Old Testament in the New Testament: A Brief Comment on Method and Terminology', 79–96; see also Porter, *Sacred Tradition in the New Testament*.

49 Hays, *Echoes of Scripture in the Letters of Paul*; these are similarly applied to the Gospels in Hays, *Echoes of Scripture in the Gospels*. See also Beale, *Handbook*.

50 See review of the subdiscipline in Allen, 'Introduction: The Study of the Use of the Old Testament in the New', 3–16, for example, or Docherty, 'New Testament Scriptural Interpretation in its Early Jewish Context', 1–19. For an excellent bibliography of various literature on the topic, see Hays and Green, 'The Use of the Old Testament by the New Testament Writers', 122–39.

51 Dodd, *According to the Scriptures: The Sub-Structure of New Testament Theology*. This 'sub-structure' aspect was important enough for it to become the subtitle of Dodd's work.

52 Lindars, *New Testament Apologetic*.

53 For example, Lindars, *New Testament Apologetic*, 90, described Psalm 22 as 'a quarry for pictorial details in writing the story of the Passion'.

54 Moyise, *Old Testament in the New*, 211–12.

55 Juel, *Messianic Exegesis*.

56 Juel, *Messianic Exegesis*, 109.

57 Hays, *Conversion of the Imagination*, 110. There are a number of potential allusions to Psalm 89 in the NT, and some may be construed as relating to Jesus' death. John 12.34, for example, may allude to Psalm 89.36, and that may incorporate a wider Passion/resurrection tradition; likewise Revelation 1.5 may offer a resurrection perspective on Psalm 89.27. For a more vigorous defence of Juel's work and its application to the Markan Passion, see McWhirter, 'Messianic Exegesis in Mark's Passion Narrative', 69–97.

58 Though note that Lindars still argues against the Passion Narrative's dependence on a worked out, established atonement theory: 'Atonement theology and Passion apologetic are worked out together, and naturally the same scriptures are useful for both' (134).

59 See inter alia Moyise, *Paul and Scripture*; Moyise, *The Later New Testament Writers and Scripture*; Moyise, *Old Testament in the New*.

60 Hays, *Echoes (Gospels)*.

61 Beale, *Handbook*.

62 Menken, *Matthew's Bible: The Old Testament Text of the Evangelist*.

63 Menken and Moyise (eds), *The Psalms in the New Testament*; Menken and Moyise (eds), *Isaiah in the New Testament*; Menken and Moyise (eds), *Deuteronomy in the New Testament*; Menken and Moyise (eds), *The Minor Prophets in the New Testament*; Menken and Moyise (eds), *Genesis in the New Testament*.

64 Moo, *Old Testament in the Gospel Passion Narratives*.

65 Hooker, 'Christ, the "End" of the Cult', 208; emphasis in original.

66 Brown, *The Death of the Messiah: From Gethsemane to the Grave – A Commentary on the Passion Narratives in the Four Gospels*.

67 Brown, *Death of the Messiah*.

68 See for example Novakovic, *Raised from the Dead According to Scripture: The Role of Israel's Scripture in the Early Christian Interpretations of Jesus' Resurrection*; also Novakovic, *Resurrection: A Guide for the Perplexed*.

69 Though see Allen, *The Historical Character of Jesus: Canonical Insights from Outside the Gospels* for a wider discussion on such matters.

70 On Jesus' self-understanding in relation to his death, see for example McKnight, *Jesus and His Death: Historiography, the Historical Jesus, and Atonement Theory*.

71 On Jesus' own use of the Scriptures, see Evans, 'Why Did the New Testament Writers Appeal to the Old Testament?'.

72 Crossan, *The Birth of Christianity: Discovering what Happened in the Years Immediately after the Execution of Jesus*, 520–5; Borg and Crossan, *The Last Week: What the Gospels Really Teach About Jesus's Final Days in Jerusalem*, 155–9. The scriptural/prophetic text is given a historical basis when incorporated into the Passion retelling.

73 Goodacre, 'Scripturalization', 33–47. He draws on the approach of Newman, *Praying by the Book: The Scripturalization of Prayer in Second Temple Judaism* in this regard.

74 On the Crossan–Brown–Goodacre discussion, see further Allison, *Constructing Jesus: Memory, Imagination, and History*, 387–92. He quips: 'A memory can be told in many languages, including the language of Scripture' (389).

2   The Old Testament in Mark's Passion

1 Hooker, 'Isaiah in Mark', 35.

2 Bryan, *A Preface to Mark: Notes on the Gospel in its Literary and Cultural Settings*, 149.

3 Boring, *Mark: A Commentary*, 405.

4 See Dodd, *According to the Scriptures*.

5 Watts, *Isaiah's New Exodus*.

6 Hooker, 'Isaiah in Mark', 37.

7 Watts, 'The Psalms in Mark's Gospel', 25–45.

8 Mark is well known for its threefold structure and preference for working in blocks of threes: the three Passion predictions or the three temporal episodes into which the day of death is divided (the nine, twelfth and third hour, each of which also have threefold connections). On the threefold style, see Evans, 'How Mark Writes', 138–44. This often involves an A-B-A type structure, in which Mark 'sandwiches' one narrative within another, a process often described as intercalation.

9 There may be some Hebraic wordplay operative here (*ben* – son; *eben* – stone).

10 The 'Hallel psalms' are a designation – that is, of 'praise' – normally given to Psalms 113–118. It is possible, though Mark does not specify it as such, that the hymn sung prior to leaving the upper room (Mark 14.26) is a Hallel psalm. Psalm 118 is also part of the Passover liturgy, sung at the time of sacrifice of the paschal lambs (so Jobes, *1 Peter*, 153), and thus may have formed part of the preceding upper-room celebrations.

11 Watts, 'Psalms in Mark's Gospel', 32.

12 Watts, 'Jesus' Death, Isaiah 53, and Mark 10:45: A Crux Revisited', 125–51.

13 On this matter, and the Isaiah 53–Mark 10.45 association, see Edwards, *The Ransom Logion in Mark and Matthew: Its Reception and its Significance for the Study of the Gospels*, 7–8.

14 See Bryan, *Preface to Mark*.

15 Cited in Bryan, *Preface to Mark*. He further notes that the references, even the quotations, are not precise ones, and this may reflect the Gospel's oral traditions and means of citation.

16 O'Brien, *The Use of Scripture in the Markan Passion Narrative*, 4.

17 Marcus, *Way of the Lord*, 152.

18 Beavis, *Mark*. So also Hooker, *Not Ashamed of the Gospel*, 57; Matera, *Passion Narratives*.

19 Brown, *A Crucified Christ in Holy Week: Essays on the Four Gospel Passion Narratives*, 23.

20 Some have surmised that Mark 15.40 is an echo of Psalm 38.10–11 and the righteous sufferer's experience of 'nearest ones' standing far away – cf. Marcus, *Mark 8–16: A New Translation with Introduction and Commentary*, 1068–9. See also Goodacre, 'Scripturalization', 33–47.

21 Matera, 'The Death of Jesus According to Luke: A Question of Sources', 476.

22 Campbell, '"Why Did You Abandon Me?": Abandonment Christology in Mark's Gospel', 117.

23 Lindars, *New Testament Apologetic*, 81, surmises that Mark 9.12 might reflect Isaiah 53.3 and the common language of rejection.

24 Marcus, 'Old Testament and the Death of Jesus', 212; so also Marcus, *Mark 8—16*, 1068–9.

25 Goodacre, 'Scripturalization', 33–47. Goodacre effectively notes this in terms of his critique of those who see the Passion Narrative as merely 'prophecy historicized'.

26 Underscoring the potentially tragic aspect to this, Wedderburn, *The Death of Jesus: Some Reflections on Jesus-Traditions and Paul*, 89–95, proposes that the Gethsemane scene gives no indication that Jesus' impending death will 'bring redemption or atonement, or even that it will somehow benefit others' (90).

27 Lindars, *New Testament Apologetic*.

28 John is described as attired in Elijah-style clothing. This might not count as a formal 'lexical' allusion but it is central to Mark's evangelistic use of the OT.

29 Evans, 'Why Did the New Testament Writers Appeal to the Old Testament?', 45.

30 Betz, 'Jesus and Isaiah 53', 86–7, emphasis in original.

31 In light of such 'misapplication' it may be that Zechariah 13.7 is not a 'Christian' proof text, and therefore not offer evidence of Zechariah 9—14 being the repository of imagery for understanding Jesus' death. It is not an 'obvious' candidate in this regard. Instead, and to explain its strange introduction here, it may reflect Jesus' own view of his imminent Passion.

32 See also Moo, *Old Testament in the Gospel Passion Narratives* in this regard.

33 But note there is perhaps still some parallelism here, as Zechariah 13.7d LXX continues with a divine declaration of action against the shepherds.

34 France, *Jesus and the Old Testament: His Application of Old Testament Passages to Himself and His Mission*, 108.

35 Docherty, 'New Testament Scriptural Interpretation', 15.

36 Collins, *Mark: A Commentary*, 670.

37 Boring, *Mark*, 393.

38 France, *Jesus and the Old Testament*, 108.

39 On the wider Zechariah 9—14 backdrop, see Marcus, *Way of the Lord*, 154–64.

40 These may stem from one original psalm.

41 Boring, *Mark*, 397.

42 Collins, *Mark*, 676.

43 Evans, *Jesus and His Contemporaries: Comparative Studies*, 411–12, is sceptical about the divine nominal reference, and it is true that the high priest does not explicitly pick up the allusion. However, in 'glass half full' fashion, one still needs to account for why this particular form of response is used (with all its resonant implications).

44 See Watts, 'Psalms in Mark's Gospel', 25–45.

45 O'Brien, 'Innocence and Guilt', 221.

46 Evans, *Jesus and His Contemporaries*, 407–23.

47 On the subject of the 'blasphemy' conclusion, see Gibson, 'The Function of the Charge of Blasphemy in Mark 14.64', 171–89.

48 Perrin, 'The High Priest's Question and Jesus' Answer', 80–95.

49 See Attridge, 'Giving Voice to Jesus: Use of the Psalms in the New Testament', 101–12. He locates the origins of such association within the liturgical life of the early Church.

50 Matera, *The Kingship of Jesus: Composition and Theology in Mark 15*, 127–131. He surmises that there is sufficient scholarship to suggest 'that the whole of Psalm 22 gave shape to early traditions concerning the Passion. The early community was intensely conscious of the entire psalm and its parallels with the Passion of Jesus' (129).

51 Robbins, 'The Reversed Contxtualisation of Psalm 22 in the Markan Crucifixion: A Socio-Rhetorical Analysis', 1161–83.

52 Marcus, *Mark 8 – 16*, 1051.

53 Eklund, *Jesus Wept: The Significance of Jesus' Laments in the New Testament*, 40.

54 Breytenbach, 'Narrating the Death of Jesus in Mark: Utterances of the Main Character, Jesus', 167.

55 Rindge, 'Reconfiguring the Akedah and Recasting God: Lament and Divine Abandonment in Mark', 762.

56 See the wider discussion in Davis, 'Exploding the Limits: Form and Function in Psalm 22', 93–105.

57 Such practice is given particular attention in Watts, 'Psalms in Mark's Gospel', 25–45.

58 See for example Marcus, 'Crucifixion as Parodic Exaltation', 73–87.

59 What one calls/labels the psalms significantly affects how one characterizes their usage. Lindars, *New Testament Apologetic*, 88–110, for example, describes them as 'Passion Psalms', bearing in mind – in his construal – their 'apologetic' usage within the Passion Narrative.

60 Ahearne-Kroll, 'Challenging the Divine: LXX Psalm 21 in the Passion Narrative of the Gospel of Mark', 127, n. 26. He argues that the psalms of lament discourse is core to the Markan Passion portrayal, and their *lament* character must be preserved and embraced when discussing Mark's account of Jesus' death. He also argues for the presence of Psalms 22, 41, 42, 43 and 69 in the Passion account.

61 Ahearne-Kroll, *The Psalms of Lament in Mark's Passion: Jesus' Davidic Suffering*, 218–9.

62 Brown, *Death of the Messiah*, 1043–51. He strongly resists the application of the whole psalm to Mark 15.34, contending that it would effectively entail the contrary to what Jesus cried out on the cross.

63 Carey, *Jesus' Cry from the Cross: Towards a First-Century Understanding of the Intertextual Relationship between Psalm 22 and the Narrative of Mark's Gospel*, 5.

64 Carey, *Jesus' Cry*, passim.

65 Eklund, *Jesus Wept*, 43–5. So likewise Goldingay, *Reading Jesus's Bible*, 182: 'The anticipatory praise of Psalm 22.22–31 can thus be imagined on the lips of Jesus, as was the present lament of the opening part of the psalm.'

66 Matera, *Passion Narratives*, 45–7, takes a more *via media* approach, advocating that the interpreter should take seriously both the vindication aspect of the dimension, while giving full cognizance to the suffering/desertion it entails.

67 Borg and Crossan, *The Last Week*.

68 O'Brien, *Use of Scripture*; see also O'Brien, 'Innocence and Guilt', 205–28.

3 The Old Testament in Matthew's Passion

1 Boxall, *Discovering Matthew: Content, Interpretation, Reception*, 1–4.

2 See Moyise, *Was the Birth of Jesus According to Scripture?*. For a further discussion on the respective merits of Matthew's exegetical method, and whether it fulfils or rather 'twists' the Scriptures, see the various essays in Beale, *The Right Doctrine from the Wrong Texts?: Essays on the Use of the Old Testament in the New*.

3 Of course, one might venture that the citation of Isaiah 7.14 in Matthew 1.22–23 is similarly 'infamous', for its wider theological implications around the virgin birth. On this, see Lincoln, *Born of a Virgin?: Reconceiving Jesus in the Bible, Tradition, and Theology*.

4 See France, 'The Formula-Quotations of Matthew 2 and the Problem of Communication'.

5 Goldingay, *Reading Jesus's Bible*, 61–74, speaks of Matthew 1–2 showing how 'Jesus fills out promises' made in the First (Old) Testament.

6 Davies and Allison, *A Critical and Exegetical Commentary on the Gospel According to Saint Matthew*, 574.

7 Attridge, 'Giving Voice to Jesus', 101.

8 Cf. the discussion in Allison, *The New Moses: A Matthean Typology*.

9 For consideration on various ways of resolving the Synoptic Questions, see inter alia Porter, *The Synoptic Problem: Four Views*.

10 Gorman, *Interweaving Innocence* reviews the wider discourse around Luke's potential 'other' Passion source material, but argues that the Lucan variations do not necessitate another non-canonical written source. Instead, the changes to Mark derive from Luke's own preferences and perspective.

11 Senior, *The Passion of Jesus in the Gospel of Matthew*, 48.

12 Matthew's 'enhancement' of the allusion to Psalm 22.8 – and likewise Luke's emendation – confirms that 'Matthew and Luke recognized an allusion to Psalm 22.8–9 in Mark 15.29–30' – cf. O'Brien, *Use of Scripture*, 110.

13 Marcus, 'Old Testament and the Death of Jesus'.

14 So Lindars, *New Testament Apologetic*, 110.

15 Cane, *The Place of Judas Iscariot in Christology*, 50.

16 Matera, *Passion Narratives*, 90.

17 So Evans, 'Old Testament in the New', 137. He does, though, also recognize the links to Jeremiah 18.1–3, 19.11 and 32.6–15.

18 Matera, *Passion Narratives*, 107.

19 Evans, 'Old Testament in the New', 137.

20 This may well be the kind of resignifying move Matthew makes in 2.17–18, and the scriptural fulfilment evidenced there.

21 There may be a further ironic twist to the use of the OT in Matthew's portrayal of the royal entry. In the Matthean account, Jesus enters Jerusalem – David's city – as a royal figure, the Son of David, and mounted on a donkey and a colt (21.4–9). This may be a (reverse?) allusion to David fleeing Jerusalem (and Absalom), and his encounter with Ziba, who offers him two donkeys on which to ride (2 Samuel 16.1–4). See further Menken, *Matthew's Bible*, 110–11.

22 Senior, *Passion of Jesus in the Gospel of Matthew*, 114.

23 Allen, 'Secret Disciples: Nicodemus and Joseph of Arimathea'.

4 The Old Testament in Luke–Acts' Passion

1 Hooker, *Not Ashamed of the Gospel*, 78.

2 Conzelmann, *The Theology of St. Luke*, 201.

3 Doble, *The Paradox of Salvation: Luke's Theology of the Cross*; Wilson, *The Saving Cross of the Suffering Christ: The Death of Jesus in Lukan Soteriology*. Though Wilson still acknowledges that 'the preaching of Paul in Acts seems to lack the sort of soteriological interpretation of Jesus' death that is so conspicuous in Paul's own account of his gospel (cf. 1 Cor. 15.3–5).' Acts 20.28 is perhaps one exception to Wilson's classification, but it may equally be the exception that proves the rule.

4 They may point to other aspects of Luke's account too; that is, attention to Luke's use of the OT does not just inform assessments of his soteriology. It might also impact on how we assess, say, Lucan missiology. It is notable, for example, how recent work on Luke's use of Isaiah servant imagery has stressed that the reader/disciple – as much as Jesus – takes on the role/mission of the Servant, and responds accordingly. See Beers, *The Followers of Jesus as the 'Servant': Luke's Model from Isaiah for the Disciples in Luke–Acts.*

5 Green and Baker, *Recovering the Scandal of the Cross: Atonement in New Testament & Contemporary Contexts*, 74.

6 Beers, *Followers of Jesus as the 'Servant'*, 177, surmises that the limited Lucan *theologia crucis* also derives from the wider understanding of 'salvation' in Isaiah; that is, it goes beyond Christ's atoning work and incorporates societal justice and peace. Hence 'Luke's lack of atonement emphasis also suggests he was reading Isaiah well.'

7 Our assumption is that Luke is responsible for both the Gospel and Acts, and the two texts may be treated as one 'whole'.

8 Doble, *Paradox of Salvation*, 6–7. For a view advocating the core soteriological or salvific aspect of the Lucan passion, see Senior, *The Passion of Jesus in the Gospel of Luke*. Such salvific evidence 'explode[s] in to view in the Passion account' (137).

9 Barrett, 'Luke/Acts', 231.

10 See Hays, *Reading Backwards: Figural Christology and the Fourfold Gospel Witness*. A similar argument is made in Litwak, *Echoes of Scripture in Luke–Acts: Telling the History of God's People Intertextually*, esp. 201–8.

11 Litwak, *Echoes of Scripture in Luke–Acts*, 203, emphasis added. He notes further: 'The necessity for Jesus to suffer may be seen in Scripture not by finding specific texts that point to the Messiah suffering, dying and rising, but by seeing the general pattern of suffering, death and vindication of the righteous, especially of prophets.'

12 See Aitken, 'Tradition in the Mouth of the Hero: Jesus as an Interpreter of Scripture', 97–103.

13 Hooker, *Not Ashamed of the Gospel*, 78.

14 Cf. Kimball, *Jesus' Exposition of the Old Testament in Luke's Gospel*. Though cf. Litwak, *Echoes of Scripture in Luke–Acts* and his concern to nuance and/or define these terms with more specificity. Porter's summary is probably apposite: 'the idea of prophetic fulfilment of the Old Testament passages of Luke and Acts is a useful hypothesis to utilize in Lukan studies' – Porter, 'Scripture Justifies Mission: The Use of the Old Testament in Luke–Acts', 107.

15 See Gorman, *Interweaving Innocence*.

16 Pao and Schnabel, 'Luke', 389. The difference between Mark 14.36 and Luke 22.42 is thus subtle. While in both instances Jesus prays that God might 'remove the cup', Luke prefaces it with the caveat 'if you are willing'.

17 Marcus, 'Old Testament and the Death of Jesus', 228.

18 Barrett, 'Luke/Acts', 231–6.

19 See the excellent survey of the options in Moyise, *Old Testament in the New*.

20 Luke's appeal is more 'correct' than that of Mark. Not only does it expand the Isaiah ascription to 'in the words of the book of the prophet Isaiah' (3.4), it also removes the additional putative Malachi material of Mark 1.2.

21 Moyise, *Old Testament in the New*, 65–89.

22 Johnson, *The Gospel of Luke*, 300.

23 The imagery of the falling stone may also be an allusion to Daniel 2.34.

24 Doble, 'The Psalms in Luke–Acts', 113: 'Luke characteristically appropriates to Jesus psalms of David's autobiography'.

25 Hooker, *Not Ashamed of the Gospel* speaks of Satan being 'in retreat' in Luke 4 – 22.

26 For a comprehensive review of research and writing on Luke's use of the Markan Passion Narrative, see Harrington, *The Lukan Passion Narrative – the Markan Material in Luke 22,54 – 23,25: A Historical Survey, 1891–1997*.

27 Vincent Taylor, *The Passion Narrative of St. Luke: A Critical and Historical Investigation*.

28 Gorman, *Interweaving Innocence*.

29 Luke 23.45 also implies the curtain was torn in the middle rather than in two, from top to bottom (Mark 15.38). The implication of this difference is not entirely clear.

30 Neither Luke nor John identify the location as Gethsemane, but leave it nameless.

31 Luke 22.43–44 might be said to depict Jesus in pre-crucifixion anguish, but these verses are probably a late addition to the Lucan account.

32 As such variation seems explanatorily significant, it is surprising that Porter, *Sacred Tradition in the New Testament*, 71–2, surmises that the three Synoptic accounts of Jesus' reply (Mark 14.62; Matt. 26.64; Luke 22.69) are 'sufficiently similar' for Mark's alone to be considered. The variation between the three accounts seems to be greater than Porter allows.

33 It is notable that Luke uses Markan tradition here (cf. Mark 15.40), but takes Mark's more negative assessment of the women's onlooking 'from afar' and recalibrates in a positive sense, to emphasize the 'presence' with Jesus. Mark's use of Ps. 38.11 is the more consistent one in respect of the psalm's own tenor. See Marcus, *Mark 8 – 16*, 1068–9.

34 Attridge, 'Giving Voice to Jesus', 102. Attridge avers that this portrayal is shaped or conditioned by Luke's predominantly Gentile audience.

35 Gorman, *Interweaving Innocence*.

36 Marcus, 'Old Testament and the Death of Jesus', 209. As we shall subsequently see, there is not dissimilar use of Psalm 34 in 1 Peter.

37 Doble, 'Psalms in Luke–Acts', 112.

38 Pao and Schnabel, 'Luke', 381–3. They conclude: 'Jesus explains that his mission, soon to be accomplished in his death, inaugurates the new covenant by drawing on Isa. 53; Exod. 24.8; Jer. 31.31–34. This mission can be achieved only by fulfilling the role of the Isaianic servant of Yahweh in his vicarious death' (383).

39 Hays, *Echoes (Gospels)*.

40 See Wilson, *Saving Cross of the Suffering Christ*, 98–101.

41 Pao and Schnabel, 'Luke', 385. France, *Jesus and the Old Testament*, 114–16, makes a similar argument, but with the added element that the use of the Servant language derives from Jesus himself, and from Jesus' *own* understanding of his mission in Isaianic Servant terms.

42 Luke might also have the imagery of Isaiah 53.12d operative here, namely Jesus' making intercession for the transgressors (cf. 23.39–43), but that is not explicitly named.

43 Johnson, *Gospel of Luke*. Isaiah 53.12d, of course, is not cited, however.

44 Moo, *Old Testament in the Gospel Passion Narratives*, 361.

45 Hence Marcus' assertion that 'many of the less dignified aspects of . . . the Suffering Servant of Isaiah are eliminated' may be an over-statement (Marcus, 'Old Testament and the Death of Jesus', 208). Luke explicitly cites from Isaiah 53, and in a way that associates Jesus directly with criminals.

46 Luke does not use *zulos* for the cross, it is true, but that may be to avoid the ramifications of the innocent one being seen to be cursed by hanging from a tree (cf. Deut. 21.22–23).

47 Moo, *Old Testament in the Gospel Passion Narratives*, 360.

48 Eklund, *Jesus Wept*, 45.

49 Doble, *Paradox of Salvation*, 166.

50 The mockery is also informed by allusion to Psalm 69.21 and the offer of *oxos* wine (23.36); Luke has combined the offer of the wine and the soldiers' mockery into one point of reference.

51 See Eubank, 'A Disconcerting Prayer: On the Originality of Luke 23:34a', 521–36, for a review of the manuscript tradition evidence, and the proposal for it to be in some sense genuine or original. He considers the way anti-Jewish sentiment may have occasioned the absence of the prayer (i.e. to reinforce the sense that Jewish people were responsible for Jesus' death), or equally that Jesus' intercession (23.34a) was removed because God had seemed not to have 'answered' it; that is, with the fall of the city, God was not 'forgiving' Jerusalem, rather judging it.

52 For further discussion of Luke's removal of the cry of desolation, see Doble, *Paradox of Salvation*, 165–73. Psalm 22.1 is incompatible with Luke's depiction of the *dikaios* figure's absolute commitment to God.

53 Wilson, *Saving Cross of the Suffering Christ*, 115–17.

54 All three texts are ascribed to David and, in their LXX form, share, for example, the opening phrase *eis to telos*; that is, 'regarding completion' (NETS).

55 Dodd, *According to the Scriptures*, 96, avers that Psalm 31 has a similar 'plot' to that of Psalm 22. In both texts, 'the hero suffers shame ignominy, torment, disaster, and then by the sheer grace of God is delivered, raised up, glorified' (102).

56 Gorman, *Interweaving Innocence*, 151. Matera, 'The Death of Jesus', 469–85 also draws attention the filial obedience of Jesus – cf. 2.49; 4.43; 9.22; 13.33; 17.25; 19.5; 22.7, 37.

57 Eklund, *Jesus Wept*, 47.

58 Matera, 'Death of Jesus'.

59 Foster, 'Echoes without Resonance', 101.

60 Barrett, 'Luke/Acts', 238.

61 See further Cane, *Place of Judas Iscariot in Christology*, 47–54.

62 Such analysis of this and other speeches within Acts leads Bock, 'Scripture and the Realisation of God's Promises', to conclude: 'a suffering, but raised Messiah, has rich roots in scripture' (55).

63 Pervo, *Acts: A Commentary*, 107.

64 The application of the 'prophet like Moses' to Jesus is not exact, that is true, but it would seem to be implied within the wider context of Peter's speech.

65 Bock, 'Isaiah 53 in Acts 8', 133. Bock seeks to import understanding of *why* Jesus died – not just that he did so.

66 Parsons, 'Isaiah 53 in Acts 8: A Reply to Professor Morna Hooker', 104–19, argues that Isaiah 53 represents the kind of text Luke refers to in chapter 24 of the gospel account. The cited elements of the Servant Song relate to their pertinence for the eunuch, and his perception of shared marginalization and social ostracization.

67 For example, Hooker argues that Acts 8/Isaiah 53 offers evidence that the Messiah must suffer/die, but it does not extend to the fact that the servant dies *for the sins of others*; there is no vicarious element cited here and the quotation is thus somewhat limited. Beers, *Followers of Jesus as the 'Servant'*, 147, takes an opposite view, setting the Isaianic parameters more widely: 'the Isaianic NE is . . . apparently the larger context for Philip's work'.

68 Blomberg, *From Pentecost to Patmos: An Introduction to Acts through Revelation*, 39, emphasis added. Blomberg's phrasing effectively renders Acts 8.32–33 as an explicit fulfilment proposal. However, while there is some correlation between Jesus and the Isaiah text, such fulfilment categorization cannot be justified from the rather parsimonious account Luke offers here (particularly when compared to the expansive fulfilment claims made in respect of the psalmic material earlier on in Luke–Acts).

69 For an argument that Acts 8 offers 'explicit prophetic fulfilment' of the Isaiah 53 text, see Bock, 'Isaiah 53 in Acts 8', 133–44.

70 Porter, *Sacred Tradition in the New Testament*, 82–5.

5   The Old Testament in John's Passion

1 Moyise, *Old Testament in the New*.

2 North, *A Journey Round John: Tradition, Interpretation and Context in the Fourth Gospel*, 54–5.

3 Miller, '"They Saw His Glory and Spoke of Him": The Gospel of John and the Old Testament', 128–33. He avers that Christology dictates John's use of Scripture, with the Prologue determinative in this regard.

4 Myers, *Characterizing Jesus: A Rhetorical Analysis on the Fourth Gospel's Use of Scripture in Its Presentation of Jesus*, 1.

5 Stanton, 'Matthew', 217.

6 This is reflected in the name and extent of this second group of material within the Fourth Gospel. Is it termed the Book of Passion (so Dodd) or the Book of Glory (so Brown)? The nomenclature one gives it impacts on how one views the context of the material.

7 See the discussion of the respective merits of the John 17–Gethsemane relationship in Hera, *Christology and Discipleship in John 17*, 9–11.

8 Attridge, 'Giving Voice to Jesus', 106 ventures that John was 'struggling with an unwelcome bit of tradition' in this regard.

9 Wedderburn, *Death of Jesus*, 91.

10 Carroll and Green, *Death of Jesus in Early Christianity*, 82.

11 Lincoln, *The Gospel According to Saint John*, 37–8. See also Lincoln, *Truth on Trial: The Lawsuit Motif in the Fourth Gospel*.

12 Carroll and Green, *Death of Jesus in Early Christianity*.

13 Moyise, *Old Testament in the New*.

14 Marianne Meye Thompson, '"They Bear Witness to Me": The Psalms in the Passion Narrative in the Gospel of John', 267.

15 Miller, 'They Saw His Glory', 131, emphasis added.

16 Beutler, 'The Use of "Scripture" in the Gospel of John', 157.

17 North, *Journey Round John*, 54–6, however, argues that as Jesus' word(s) become equivalent to, or counted as, Scripture, the reference in 17.12 may be to a Jesus logion, as is the case in 18.9.

18 Hanson, *The Prophetic Gospel: A Study of John and the Old Testament*, 186.

19 Moyise, *Old Testament in the New*, 100.

20 Daly-Denton, *David in the Fourth Gospel: The Johannine Reception of the Psalms*, 201–8.

21 Clark-Soles, 'Scripture Cannot Be Broken: The Social Function of the Use of Scripture in the Fourth Gospel', 113.

22 Cf. Daly-Denton, 'The Psalms in John's Gospel', 125. She cites 1 Corinthians 14.21 and Romans 3.19 as equivalent scenarios.

23 So Meye Thompson, *John: A Commentary*, 334.

24 Marcus, 'Old Testament and the Death of Jesus', 229.

25 Daly-Denton, 'The Psalms in John's Gospel', 133.

26 Technically John uses the language of completion rather than fulfilment in terms of the scriptural association, but this probably occasioned by the similar use of completion/finished language earlier in the verse and in 19.30.

27 Barrett, *The Gospel According to St John: An Introduction with Commentary and Notes on the Greek Text*, 553.

28 Daly-Denton, 'The Psalms in John's Gospel', 135.

29 Attridge, 'Giving Voice to Jesus', 105, suggests that 'the citation [of Ps. 69] in John 2 obviously retains a reference to the Passion'.

30 Brown, *Death of the Messiah*, 1077, surmises that this may form a 'lamb of God' *inclusio* with John the Baptist utterance of 1.29.

31 Porter, *Sacred Tradition in the New Testament*, 127–51, argues for the pervasive influence of Exodus 12/Passover imagery across John's account.

32 Barrett, *Gospel According to St John*, 558. So also Menken, 'Old Testament Quotations in the Gospel of John', 41–3: John's Jesus is both righteous sufferer and the Passover lamb.

33 Hanson, *Prophetic Gospel: A Study of John and the Old Testament*, 223.

34 So Myers, *Characterizing Jesus*, 69.

35 Bynum, 'Quotations of Zechariah in the Fourth Gospel', 47.

36 See Bynum, 'Quotations of Zechariah', 47–8.

37 Menken, 'The Minor Prophets in John's Gospel', 87, concludes therefore that 'John's quotation . . . represents an independent early Christian translation into Greek of the Hebrew text.'

38 Thompson, 'They Bear Witness to Me', 269–70.

39 Scott, *The Hermeneutics of Christological Psalmody in Paul: An Intertextual Enquiry*, 64.

40 See further Thompson, 'They Bear Witness to Me', 267–83.

41 Licona, *Why Are There Differences in the Gospels? What We Can Learn from Ancient Biography*, 166. Senior, *The Passion of Jesus in the Gospel of John*, 116–17, reads this in similar fashion; that is, that it is active thirst for deeper relationship with God.

42 Licona, *Why Are There Differences in the Gospels?*.

43 Eklund, *Jesus Wept*, 40.

44 Green and Baker, *Recovering the Scandal of the Cross* draw more Day of Atonement significance from these potential allusions, but the interpretation is more asserted than proved.

45 Carson, 'John and the Johannine Epistles', 257: 'John's quarrel with his opponents has less to do with their treatment of the OT than with their treatment of the FG.'

46 Beale, *John's Use of the Old Testament in Revelation*, 61. He further notes the 'general acknowledgement that The Apocalypse contains more Old Testament references than any other New Testament book' (60).

47 Cf. Hooker, *Not Ashamed of the Gospel*, 135: 'John presents Jesus as the one who through death has become king.'

48 Moyise, 'The Psalms in Revelation', 236–7.

49 Beale, *John's Use of the Old Testament in Revelation*, sets a very wide remit. He opines: 'John's intention may be to indicate that Jesus' death, resurrection and gathered church is the inaugurated fulfilment of Daniel' (115).

50 Beale and McDonough, 'Revelation', 1098–1102, argue that Revelation 4 – 5 is shaped by the structure and narrative of Daniel 7.

51 Mathewson, 'Isaiah in Revelation', 191–2.

52 Bauckham, *The Climax of Prophecy: Studies on the Book of Revelation*, 231–2, also notes the influence of Isaiah 53.9 on Revelation 14.5: 'there was no deceit in his/their mouth.'

53 Beale and McDonough, 'Revelation', 1101.

54 Goldingay, *Reading Jesus's Bible*.

55 Smith, 'The Use of the Old Testament in the New', 57. He notes, though, that John still 'sets up the sharpest antithesis between the Old and the New that is found in the New Testament'.

56 Evans, 'Old Testament in the New', 141.

6   The Old Testament in Paul's Depiction of Jesus' Death

1 Richard Hays has been a leading voice for such an approach – see for example Hays, 'Story of God's Son'; Hays, 'Is Paul's Gospel Narratable?'.

2 Wedderburn, *Death of Jesus*, 129, notes: 'A theology of the cross, a *theologia crucis*, is synonymous with Paul's theology.'

3 Ellis, *Paul's Use of the Old Testament* lists 93 citations, but issues around classification and precision necessitate the general 'around 100' designation.

4 Hooker, 'Isaiah in Mark', 35.

5 Aitken, *Jesus' Death in Early Christian Memory*.

6 Moyise, *Old Testament in the New*, 146.

7 On Paul as a reader of Scripture, see Watson, *Paul and the Hermeneutics of Faith*.

8 See for example Allen, *Historical Character of Jesus*; Wenham, *Paul and Jesus: The True Story*; Still (ed.), *Jesus and Paul Reconnected: Fresh Pathways into an Old Debate*.

9 See inter alia Stanley (ed.), *Paul and Scripture: Extending the Conversation*; Porter and Stanley (eds), *As It Is Written: Studying Paul's use of Scripture*; Ellis, *Paul's Use of the Old Testament*; Moyise, *Paul and Scripture*.

10 Hays, *Echoes (Paul)*.

11 Stanley, *Arguing with Scripture: The Rhetoric of Quotations in the Letters of Paul*.

12 Watson, *Paul and the Hermeneutics of Faith*.

13 Wright, *Paul and the Faithfulness of God*. See the evaluation of this in Moyise, 'Wright's Understanding of Paul's Use of Scripture', 165–80.

14 Watson, *Paul and the Hermeneutics of Faith*.

15 Stanley, *Arguing with Scripture*.

16 For the purposes of this volume, we are considering the usage of the OT in all the epistles attributed to Paul. This is essentially for heuristic and practical reasons, and makes no claim as to the purported Pauline authorship.

17 Hanson, *The Living Utterances of God: The New Testament Exegesis of the Old*, 93–6.

18 UBS4 lists potential allusions to Numbers 25.1–2 (Rev. 2.14, 20) and Numbers 25.1, 9 (1 Cor. 10.8), but neither instance pertains to Jesus' death.

19 Wedderburn, *Death of Jesus*, 110.

20 See the essays in Martin and Dodd (eds), *Where Christology Began: Essays on Philippians 2*.

21 Allison, *Constructing Jesus*, 422, suggests one might have been extant by the 40s. See also Theissen, *The Gospels in Context: Social and Political History in the Synoptic Tradition*, 166–99.

22 Allison, *Constructing Jesus*, 392–405. A similar assessment is made in Porter, *Sacred Tradition in the New Testament*, 231.

23 And there is real and evident diversity here. For example, Romans is awash with Isaiah citation, particularly in respect of Romans 9–11, where Paul grapples with tough questions of Jew–Gentile inclusion, but in Galatians (so often thought of as Romans-lite or Romans *in nuce*), there is comparatively little use of Isaiah at all.

24 Moyise, *Old Testament in the New*, 126; emphasis added.

25 Hays, *Echoes (Paul)*; see also Hays, *Conversion of the Imagination*, 101.

26 Hays, *Conversion of the Imagination*, 101; emphasis in original.

27 Aitken, *Jesus' Death in Early Christian Memory*, 29–32. Paul only uses 'sins' in the plural elsewhere in 1 Corinthians 15.15, Galatians 1.4 and Romans 4.7. For an alternative view, see Fee, *The First Epistle to the Corinthians*, 724, n. 54.

28 Gathercole, *Defending Substitution*, 57.

29 Cf. Aitken, *Jesus' Death in Early Christian Memory*, 29: on 1 Corinthians 15.3: 'there is little doubt that Paul has recourse here to a summary statement, which he knows as the gospel.'

30 See Stanley, *Arguing with Scripture*, 75–96.

31 Barclay, *Pauline Churches and Diaspora Jews*, 96.

32 Hurtado, *Lord Jesus Christ: Devotion to Jesus in Earliest Christianity*, 99.

33 Scott, *Paul's Way of Knowing: Story, Experience and the Spirit*, 215.

34 See Wright, *The Climax of the Covenant: Christ and the Law in Pauline Theology*, 137–56.

35 Marcus, 'Old Testament and the Death of Jesus', 233.

36 Weatherly, *Jewish Responsibility for the Death of Jesus in Luke–Acts*, 179.

37 Gathercole, *Defending Substitution*. For a different construal of Pauline atonement, notably around 1 Thessalonians 5, see Hooker, *Not Ashamed of the Gospel*.

38 Hofius, 'The Fourth Servant Song in the New Testamen Letters', 177. So also Edwards, *Ransom Logion in Mark and Matthew*, 40: 'Where Paul may have had several scriptures in mind, one of them was almost certainly Isaiah 53.'

39 Hofius, 'Fourth Servant Song', 188.

40 Shum, *Paul's Use of Isaiah in Romans: A Comparative Study of Paul's Letter to the Romans and the Sibylline and Qumran Sectarian Texts*, 190, emphasis added.

41 Breytenbach, 'The Septuagint Version of Isaiah 53 and the Early Christian Formula "He Was Delivered for Our Trespasses"', 340–1.

42 Hays, 'Who Has Believed Our Message: Paul's Reading of Isaiah', 47.

43 Horrell, *Becoming Christian: Essays on 1 Peter and the Making of Christian Identity*, 22.

44 Though Betz, 'Jesus and Isaiah 53', 75–6, instead advocates for a holistic, non-atomistic reading of the passage, and brings in the wider concerns of Isaiah 53.

45 Wagner, 'Isaiah in Romans and Galatians', 128.

46 The NRSV adds 'to death' to Romans 4.25 (i.e. handed over *to death* for our trespasses), which reinforces the suggested Isaiah 53.12 allusion.

47 Edwards, *Ransom Logion in Mark and Matthew*.

48 Edwards, *Ransom Logion in Mark and Matthew* thinks Galatians 1.4 is a combination of Isaiah 53 and the ransom logion.

49 See the discussion in Dahl, *Jesus the Christ: The Historical Origins of Christological Doctrine*, 137–51.

50 This pertains, of course, to the question of how Jesus himself thought of his impending suffering and death. Such questions are beyond our scope, but see for example McKnight, *Jesus and His Death*.

51 Lim, '*The Sufferings of Christ Are Abundant in Us' (2 Corinthians 1.5): A Narrative Dynamics Investigation of Paul's Sufferings in 2 Corinthians*, 125, n. 9.

52 Hooker, *Jesus and the Servant*. Lee, *The Son of Man as the Last Adam: The Early Church Tradition as a Source of Paul's Adam Christology*, 36–7 offers a response to Hooker's concerns.

53 Fowl, *Philippians*, 117.

54 Bauckham, *Jesus and the God of Israel: God Crucified and Other Studies on the New Testament's Christology of Divine Identity*, 42–5.

He concludes: 'Can the Lord also be the Servant? The passage [i.e. Phil. 2.6–11], inspired by Deutero-Isaiah and by the Christ-event, answers: only the Servant can also be the Lord' (45).

55 Fee, *Paul's Letter to the Philippians*, 212.

56 See Clivaz and Schulthess, 'On the Source and Rewriting of 1 Corinthians 2.9 in Christian, Jewish and Islamic Traditions (1 Clem 34.8; Gosjud 47.10–13; a Ḥadīth Qudsī)', 183–200; Kovacs, "The Archons, the Spirit and the Death of Christ: Do We Need the Hypothesis of Gnostic Opponents to Explain 1 Corinthians 2.6–16?', 217–36.

57 For example, Menken and Moyise (eds), *Isaiah in the New Testament*, makes no mention of 1 Corinthians 2.9 as an Isaianic citation, indicative perhaps of the agnosticism as to the quotation's *Vorlage*.

58 Thiselton, *The First Epistle to the Corinthians: A Commentary on the Greek Text*, 224.

59 Hays, *Echoes (Paul)*, 64.

60 Wagner, 'Isaiah in Romans and Galatians', 122. Elsewhere Wagner, *Heralds of the Good News: Isaiah and Paul 'in Concert' in the Letter to the Romans*, 145–51, proposes that Isaiah 28.16 is an intratextual development of 8.14.

61 On this citation, see the section on 1 Peter 2.4–8.

62 For the finer textual discussion, see Koch, 'The Quotations of Isaiah 8,14 and 28,16 in Romans 9,33 and 1 Peter 2,6.8 as Test Case for Old Testament Quotations in the New Testament', 223–40.

63 Ortlund, 'The Insanity of Faith: Paul's Theological Use of Isaiah in Romans 9:33', 282–3.

64 See Dodd, *According to the Scriptures*, on the existence of an early *testimonia* collection.

65 Take for example Richardson, *Paul for Today: New Perspectives on a Controversial Apostle*, 80–2.

66 Green and Baker, *Recovering the Scandal of the Cross*, 47.

67 McKnight, *A Community Called Atonement*, 63.

68 Hurtado, *Lord Jesus Christ*, 133–4.

69 Hays, *Conversion of the Imagination*, 108.

70 Hafemann, 'Paul's Use of the Old Testament in 2 Corinthians', 250, emphasis added. He continues: 'Psalm 116 provides an interpretive lens through which Paul sees the significance of his experience in Christ, the suffering righteous one' (251). Hays, *Conversion of the Imagination*, 109, concludes similarly that 2 Corinthians 4.13 offers a further instance of Paul reading the psalm text as if Christ himself is praying it.

71 Hays, *Echoes (Paul)*.

72 See Attridge, 'Giving Voice to Jesus', 111–12.

73 See Rulmu, 'The Use of Psalm LXIX, 9 in Romans XV, 3: Shame as Sacrifice', 227–33; Hays, *Conversion of the Imagination*, 101–18.

74 'Paul does not install Christ explicitly as speaker in his quotation, but Christ is the best candidate for the role': Scott, *Hermeneutics of Christological Psalmody*, 65.

75 Rulmu, 'The Use of Psalm LXIX, 9 in Romans XV, 3', 231. And previously: 'Paul does read the Psalm typologically, that is, referring to Christ, but also as a paradigm of his own experience and that of his church' (229).

76 See Scott, *Hermeneutics of Christological Psalmody*, 64–5.

77 Hays, *Conversion of the Imagination*, 104.

78 Wright, 'The Letter to the Romans', 745.

79 Allison, *Constructing Jesus*, 408, concurs, venturing that 'when Paul penned Romans 15:3, he had in mind what most of his subsequent readers have had in mind, namely, something like the tableau in Mark 15 and parallels.'

80 Hays, *Conversion of the Imagination*, 118. On this note, it is interesting, then, that Romans 8.19–30 and its language of suffering and anticipated redemption does not obviously utilize the righteous sufferer imagery. One might have expected some echo of or allusion to it.

81 Keesmaat, 'The Psalms in Romans and Galatians', 156.

7 The Old Testament in Hebrews' Passion

1 There is an extensive discourse on Hebrews' use of the Old Testament. See, inter alia, Caird, 'Exegetical Method of the Epistle to the Hebrews'; France, 'The Writer of Hebrews as a Biblical Expositor'; Guthrie, 'Hebrews' Use of the Old Testament: Recent Trends in Research'; Hanson, 'Hebrews'; Gheorgita, *The Role of the Septuagint in Hebrews*; Moffitt, 'The Interpretation of Scripture in the Epistle to the Hebrews', 77–97; Docherty, *The Use of the Old Testament in Hebrews: A Case Study in Early Jewish Bible Interpretation*; Moyise, *Old Testament in the New*, 149–67.

2 On this, see Hughes, *Hebrews and Hermeneutics*. Cf. also Lee, *Today When You Hear His Voice: Scripture, the Covenants and the People of God*.

3 Compton, *Psalm 110 and the Logic of Hebrews* has recently argued that Psalm 110 is the controlling theme of the epistle.

4 The structural analysis of Vanhoye, *La Structure Littéraire de 'L'Epitre Aux Hébreux'* is a primary representative of this approach.

5 For a comprehensive review of the use of the OT in this regards, and a defence of the resurrection as being central for Hebrews, see Moffitt, *Atonement and the Logic of Resurrection in the Epistle to the Hebrews*.

6 This was proposed by Caird, 'Exegetical Method of the Epistle to the Hebrews', but developed by France, 'Writer of Hebrews as a Biblical Expositor'.

7 Docherty, 'New Testament Scriptural Interpretation', 14–18. She argues: 'This emphasis on individual words from a citation is very

characteristic of early Jewish hermeneutics, in which every letter of scripture is regarded as true and significant' (16).

8 Hughes, *Hebrews and Hermeneutics*.

9 deSilva, *Perseverance in Gratitude: A Socio-Rhetorical Commentary on the Epistle 'to the Hebrews'*, 216.

10 Hooker, 'Christ, the "End" of the Cult', 209. This makes for an interesting parallel with Hays' suggestion, made in the previous chapter, that the righteous sufferer psalms were key texts understood within the *kata tas graphas* claim of 1 Corinthians 15.3.

11 Evans, 'Isaiah 53 in the Letters of Peter, Paul, Hebrews and John', 163, calls this an 'unmistakable allusion to the second half of Isaiah 53.12'.

12 Evans, 'Isaiah 53 in the Letters of Peter, Paul, Hebrews and John', 163.

13 Brown, *Death of the Messiah*, 227–33. Brown draws a number of parallels between the vocabulary of Hebrews 5.7 and that of Psalm 116, interestingly so when one considers how Paul uses Psalm 116 to relate Christ's suffering to his own experience.

14 The assessment of Cockerill, *The Epistle to the Hebrews*, 244, is therefore about right: 'Reference to Gethsemane is suggestive without being definitive.'

15 Attridge, *The Epistle to the Hebrews*, 148 is more sceptical of the purported Gethsemane relationship. He finds it difficult to see how Christ's plea to have the 'cup pass' from him can be said to be 'heard'.

16 See the examples in Aitken, *Jesus' Death in Early Christian Memory*, 145–7; she concludes: 'I would argue that there exists an early Christian hymn that draws on the psalms of the suffering faithful, whom God vindicates' (147).

17 Laws, 'Hebrews, Letter to the', 330. Allison, *Constructing Jesus*, 417, n. 10, avers that Hebrews 5.7–8 constructs a Gethsemane narrative halfway between Markan angst and Johannine confidence, which would fit well with a Lucan characterization (though the contested textual history of Luke 22.43–44 cautions against building too great a confidence here).

18 Richardson, 'The Passion: Reconsidering Hebrews 5.7–8', 51–67.

19 Laws, 'Hebrews', 330; for an alternative view see Allen, 'Why Bother Going Outside?: The Use of the Old Testament in Heb. 13:10–16', 239–52.

20 Allen, 'Why Bother Going Outside?', 239–52.

21 Buchanan, *To the Hebrews: Translation, Comment and Conclusions*, advocated, unpersuasively it must be said, that the whole of Hebrews was homily on Psalm 110. More recently, Compton, *Psalm 110*, has proposed that it is the core to the whole argument of the letter. See also Jordaan and Nel, 'From King-Priest to Priest-King: Psalm 110 and the Basic Structure of Hebrews'.

22 McKnight, 'Covenant and Spirit: The Origins of New Covenant Hermeneutic', 45.

23 Though it is more than that; cf. Allen, *Deuteronomy and Exhortation in Hebrews: An Exercise in Narrative Re-Presentation*: 'Hebrews' idea of covenant evokes a way of living that is not just a doctrinal explication of Christ's priestly sacrifice, but an all-embracing call to worship' (213).

24 Cf. Aitken, *Jesus' Death in Early Christian Memory*. Enactment of cultic or ritual performance was conceivably 'an important means by which to actualize the covenant' (139).

25 Aitken, *Jesus' Death in Early Christian Memory*, 139.

26 Peeler, *You Are My Son: The Family of God in the Epistle to the Hebrews*, 88.

27 Cockerill, *Epistle to the Hebrews*, 143.

28 So Johnson, *Hebrews: A Commentary*; Gheorgita, *Role of the Septuagint in Hebrews*; Hays, *Conversion of the Imagination*, 106.

29 Peeler, *You Are My Son*, 89, n. 84.

30 Steyn, 'Jesus Sayings in Hebrews', 435.

31 Johnson, *Hebrews*, 99.

32 Karrer, 'LXX Psalm 39.7–10 in Hebrews 10.5–7', 128.

33 Moffitt, 'Interpretation of Scripture', rightly points out that if Hebrews were creating a text form of Psalm 40.6–8 from scratch – that is, to suit its own purposes – then one might have expected some form of reference to *high* priesthood to be included.

34 Guthrie, *The Structure of Hebrews: A Text-Linguistic Analysis*.

8 The Old Testament in the 'Passion' of the Other New Testament Epistles

1 Nienhuis, *Not by Paul Alone: The Formation of the Catholic Epistle Collection and the Christian Canon*; Nienhuis and Wall, *Reading the Epistles of James, Peter, John, and Jude as Scripture: The Shaping and Shape of a Canonical Collection*.

2 The reference to the condemnation and murder of the righteous one (James 5.6) is ambiguous and, in the Jacobean context, unlikely to refer to Jesus.

3 See Foster, *The Significance of Exemplars for the Interpretation of the Letter of James*.

4 See Allen, *Historical Character of Jesus*.

5 Woan, 'The Psalms in 1 Peter', 228.

6 Woan, 'Psalms in 1 Peter', 229.

7 Bauckham, 'James, 1 and 2 Peter, Jude', 310, suggests that 'prophets' (1.10–11) be understood in broad scriptural terms, rather than just the prophetic corpus. Hence the psalmist of Psalm 118 (cf. 1 Peter 2.7) is incorporated by association into the designated grouping.

8 Evans, 'Isaiah 53 in the Letters of Peter, Paul, Hebrews and John', for example, suggests that 1.10–12 is an allusion to Isaiah 53, but the lexical association is fairly minimal. Evans' reasoning is based on the multiple references to Isaiah 53 in 1 Peter 2.21–25.

9 Barbarick, 'Milk to Grow On: The Example of Christ in 1 Peter', 234.

10 Jobes, *1 Peter*, 47.

11 Schutter, *Hermeneutic and Composition in 1 Peter*.

12 Horrell, *1 Peter*, 62.

13 Horrell, *1 Peter*.

14 Edwards, *Ransom Logion in Mark and Matthew*, 47–50.

15 Porter, *Sacred Tradition in the New Testament*, 137, n. 28. Porter notes the further association of both traditions in Justin Martyr (*Dial.* 111).

16 Jobes, *1 Peter*, 145.

17 Jobes, *1 Peter*, 146.

18 As with Romans 9.33, Peter seems to use a form of Isaiah 8.14 that follows the Masoretic rather than the LXX text form.

19 Moyise, 'Isaiah in 1 Peter', 183, suggests that 2.23a might draw on Christian tradition rather than Isaiah 53.7, but the contextual association between the two texts is hard to ignore and seems more than accidental.

20 Green, *Death of Jesus*, 317.

21 Davids, *The First Epistle of Peter*, 114, surmises that the 'Overseer' aspect of the 1 Peter 2.25 designation originates from the pagan understanding of a deity who looked after an individual's interests; the dual title of 2.25b thus combines both Jewish (OT) and pagan portrayal of divine concern.

22 Moyise, 'Isaiah in 1 Peter'.

23 See Watts, *Isaiah's New Exodus*.

24 Dalton, *Christ's Proclamation to the Spirits: A Study of 1 Peter 3:18—4:6*.

25 See further Allen, 'Genesis in James, 1 and 2 Peter and Jude', 147–65.

26 Horrell, 'Who Are 'the Dead' and When Was the Gospel Preached to Them? The Interpretation of 1 Pet. 4.6', 70–89.

27 Green, *1 Peter*, 55.

9   Conclusion

1 Brown, *Death of the Messiah*, 1045.

2 See Porter, *Sacred Tradition in the New Testament*, 127–52, for an extended discussion of the NT appropriation of the theme.

3 Cf. Moo, *Old Testament in the Gospel Passion Narratives*, 357: 'It is significant how few references are made to OT passages outside the four major background contexts which have been isolated.'

4 Hofius, 'Fourth Servant Song', 163–88.

5 Vermes, *Scripture and Tradition in Judaism: Haggadic Studies*, 193–227.

6 Green, *Death of Jesus*, 316.

7 See the discussion, for example, in Juel, *Messianic Exegesis*, 102–3. Also Hengel, *The Atonement: A Study of the Origins of the Doctrine in the New Testament*.

8 Borg and Crossan, *The Last Week*, 141.

9 Ahearne-Kroll, *Psalms of Lament*, 217.

10 One recent exception to the rule of thumb might be the role of the Isaianic Servant in Luke–Acts. In her recent volume, Beers, *Followers of Jesus as the 'Servant'*, argues that the Servant mantle is not just applied to Jesus but is also enacted or personified by Jesus' followers. If Beers is right, then there would be scriptural/Isaianic warrant for the disciples' suffering that would not necessarily be mediated by/through Jesus.

11 Cf. Hays, *Reading Backwards*, 93: 'the OT teaches us how to read the Gospels and . . . – at the same time – the Gospels teach us how to read the OT.'

12 Green and Baker, *Recovering the Scandal of the Cross*, 45.

Scriptural Index

Genesis
6.2–3 — 170
14 — 151
14.17–24 — 145
22 — 132, 145, 176
22.6 — 98
49.9 — 117

Exodus
3.6 — 90
3.14 — 42
10.21–23 — 51
12 — 217
12.5 — 164
12.14 — 79
12.22 — 109
12.25–27 — 79
12.46 — 109
21.32 — 60
23.20 — 27
24.6–8 — 163
24.8 — 79, 117, 125, 214
33.7–11 — 151
33.9–10 — 151

Leviticus
5.17–18 — 84
16 — 150
16.27 — 150
16.30 — 115
17.1–9 — 150

18.5 — 128
19.18 — 104, 160
21.10 — 107
25.9 — 115

Numbers
5.8 — 115
9.12 — 109
21.4–9 — 99
25.1 — 219
25.1–2 — 219
25.1–5 — 123
25.9 — 219

Deuteronomy
1.19–40 — 158
11.26–28 — 158
18.15–19 — 90
19.15 — 76
21.1–9 — 54, 64, 68
21.22–23 — 9, 60, 94, 128–9, 133, 168, 203, 214
27.26 — 128

Joshua
1.7 — 91
1.31 — 91

1 Samuel
24.1–22 — 107

2 Samuel
7.14 — 145
15.12 — 101
16.1–4 — 211

2 Kings
1.7–8 — 36

Esther
7.9–10 — 9, 60

Psalms
2 — 28, 43, 47, 176
2.7 — 28, 47, 74, 145, 152
2.10 — 77
6 — 97
6.3–4 — 97
8 — 147
16 — 23, 88–9, 179
16.8–11 — 88
16.10 — 89
22 — 4, 19, 20, 23–4, 28, 30, 33, 41, 44–50, 56–7, 64, 68, 74, 78, 83–6, 94, 108, 114, 149, 154–6, 159, 67–8,

	176, 180–1, 209, 215
22.1	4, 18–9, 32, 44, 46–7, 49, 51, 56, 77, 83, 85, 86, 107–8, 114, 142, 150, 154, 174, 177, 214
22.1–21	155
22.2	46
22.3	74
22.6	44–5, 56
22.6–7	45–6
22.6–8	45, 150
22.7–8	44
22.8	45, 57, 67, 74, 77, 84, 107
22.8–9	211
22.12–13	84, 167
22.13	168
22.14–18	46
22.15	107–8, 155
22.16	45, 84, 107
22.16–18	108, 167
22.17	107
22.18	44, 56, 74, 77, 83, 106–7, 112
22.21	84
22.21–31	46
22.22	153, 155, 174
22.22–23	58
22.22–31	210

22.24	49, 149
22.28	83
22.31	45, 74, 114
26.6	54, 64
31	45, 78, 85–6, 149, 167, 177, 215
31.1–3	85
31.4 LXX	50
31.5	16, 77, 83, 85–6, 107, 114, 139
31.6–8	85
31.11	85
31.14–15	85
31.16–18	85
31.21–22	85
31.23	149
34	78, 161–2, 164, 171, 177, 214
34.4	161
34.4–5	164
34.6	161
34.7	161
34.8	164
34.13–17	161
34.15	78
34.17	78, 161
34.19	78
34.20	109–10, 161
34.21	78
35	44, 105
35.4	105
35.11	105
35.16	105
35.19	105
38.10–11	207

38.11	32–3, 77, 213
40	4, 146–7, 156–7, 159, 172, 174
40.6	157
40.6–8	145, 156–7, 224
40.10	153
41	209
41.6	36
41.8	102
41.8–10	102
41.9	36–7, 79, 101–2
41.10	102
42	41–2, 44, 48, 64, 97, 149, 177, 209
42.5	56
42.6	41–2, 56, 174
42.11	41, 56, 174
43	41–2, 44, 48, 64, 97, 149, 209
43.5	41, 56, 174
69	33, 45, 64–5, 85, 107, 108, 116, 142, 148, 168, 176–7, 209, 217
69.1–18	47
69.3	108, 114
69.4	104
69.7	148
69.9	95, 105, 141, 143, 148, 177

69.9–10	148		159, 164,	45.23	133
69.19–20	148		179, 207,	50.4–9	50
69.19–36	47		224	50.6	50
69.21	45, 64–5,	118.5	29	52—53	131
	88, 105,	118.6	156	52.5	131
	109, 214	118.6–7	29	52.7	131
69.22–23	141	118.13–14	29	52.13	12, 90,
69.25	87–8	118.17–18	41		133–4,
69.28	116	118.18	29		147
89	29, 205	118.22	36, 74,	52.13—53.12	4,
89.20	20		91–2,		11, 79,
89.27	116, 205		136, 165		130, 142
89.36	205	118.22–23	28	52.14—53.2	133
89.37	116	118.25–26	29	52.15	131
89.50–51	29	118.26	74	53	4, 11–3,
95	158–9	132.11	88–89		30, 35,
95.1–7	47				37, 67,
95.7–11	47, 146	**Isaiah**			79–82,
109	87	5	123		92–4,
109.8	87–8	5.12	28		125, 127,
110	20, 43,	6.1–3	100		130–4,
	47, 94,	6.3	118		141, 143,
	146–7,	6.9–10	27		147–8,
	159, 172,	6.10	100, 110,		159, 163,
	223		168		165–70,
110.1	42–3, 76,	7.14	210		175–7,
	88–9,	8.14	135–7,		207,
	151, 174		165, 221,		214–5,
110.4	43, 145,		225		219–20,
	151–2	8.17–18	154		225
113–118	207	9.7	117	53.1	94, 100,
116	140, 142,	11.10	117		110, 131
	221, 223	25.8	126	53.3	208
116.3	140	28.11	122	53.4	13, 39,
116.4	140	28.16	135–6,		147, 166
116.8–11	140		165, 221	53.5	166
116.10	140	40—55	13, 27,	53.5–6	94
116.16	140		133–4,	53.6	39, 79,
118	22, 29–30,		169		125, 132,
	41, 43,	40.3	73		166
	47–8, 63,	40.4	73	53.7	34, 118,
	74, 107,	42.3	50		164, 166,
	136, 156,	43.3–4	27		225

53.7–8	92	31.31–34	79, 146, 214		112, 174–5, 208
53.8	92				
53.9	67, 166, 218	**Ezekiel**		9.9	62–3, 106, 110–1
53.10	37, 39, 79	34.1–31	168		
53.11	78, 118, 130–3	34.15	168	9.11	40
		37.13	66	9.16	40
53.11–12	18, 27, 84, 131			10.2	40
		Daniel		10.3	40
53.12	12–3, 35, 37, 67, 79, 80–2, 125, 130, 132–3, 147–8, 166–7, 173, 180, 214, 219, 223	2.34	213	11.4–17	40
		6	141	11.12	59, 68
		7	42, 116, 218	11.12–13	61
		7.9–10	43	11.14	61
		7.13	42–3, 76, 174	11.17	40
		7.13–14	30	12.10	110–1, 116, 181
		9.26	12	13	40
		12.1–3	66	13.7	4, 34, 37–41, 46, 51, 56, 59, 62, 77, 85, 97, 174, 208
		12.1–4	117		
54	169	**Hosea**			
54.2	169	6.2	31		
54.3	169	10.8	82–3		
54.5	169	13.14	126		
54.7	169			13.7–9	40
54.13	95	**Joel**		13.8	40
56	73	2.28–32	88	13.9	40
56.7	73			14.4–5	66
61	71	**Amos**		14.8	112
61.1–2	71, 73, 81	8.9–10	50		
64.4	134	8.10	51	**Malachi**	
65.17	134	**Jonah**		3.1	27
		4.8–9	42	3.1–2	27
Jeremiah				3.2	27
18.1–3	62, 211	**Habakkuk**		**Matthew**	
19.11	62, 211	1.5	94	1–2	52
32.6–15	62, 211	2.4	122, 128, 158	1.21–23	53
31	4, 125, 146–7, 152, 159			1.22–23	52, 210
		Zechariah		2.5–6	52
		9–14	38, 40, 62, 110,	2.13	63
31.31	37			2.13–16	55
				2.15	52

2.17–18	52, 62, 211	27.9–10	60–2, 179, 182
2.19–20	63	27.10	61–2
2.19–23	55	27.19	53, 58, 63
2.23	16, 52, 61	27.24	54, 64, 68
4.3	57	27.25	58
4.6	57	27.25–26	58
5–7	55	27.27–31	167
8.17	13	27.34	64–5
10	55	27.35	56, 106
13	55	27.39	56
18	55	27.40	57
19.24	67	27.43	57, 67, 84
20.28	3, 79	27.45	50
21.4–5	65	27.46	57, 77, 140, 180
21.4–7	181	27.46–47	67
21.4–9	211	27.47	57
21.5	62, 106	27.48	64–5, 109
21.6–7	63	27.49	57
21.9	29, 74	27.51	65
21.42	56, 91, 164	27.51–53	54, 65–6
24–25	55	27.52	58, 65
24.30	110	27.53	65
26.31	4, 56, 59, 62, 173	27.54	65, 78
26.32	59	27.57	67
26.38	56	27.57–60	66
26.17	97	27.57–61	66
26.54	53–4, 58, 72	27.62–66	53, 58
26.56	53–4, 58, 72	28.10	58
26.64	213	28.16–20	59
27.3	59		
27.3–10	58	**Mark**	
27.4	58, 64	1—10	1, 2
27.5	59	1.2	27, 213
27.6	58	1.2–3	26
27.7	62	1.3	163
27.9	53, 59, 63, 67	1.6	36
		1.11	28, 47

1.14–15	67
1.18	32
1.20	32
3.6	31
3.19	36
3.31–35	32
4.11–12	27
4.12	100, 163
4.17	39
6.1–6	32
6.3	39
6.34	38
7.6–7	163
8.22—10.52	31
8.31	23, 30–1, 36, 43, 163
8.34	183
9.7	47
9.12	36, 43, 208
9.12–13	33
9.13	37
9.31	23, 30–1, 36, 43, 132
10.28	32
10.33	43, 132
10.33–34	23, 30–1
10.45	3, 27, 30, 37, 43, 70, 79, 132, 138, 163, 207
11—16	1, 30
11.1	31
11.4–7	63
11.9–10	29, 74
11.15–20	27
11.17	73
11.18	31
12.1–11	28

Reference	Pages
12.9	29
12.10	36, 56, 91, 164
12.10–11	28, 50, 179
12.11	29
12.12	28
12.35–37	43
13.1–2	27
13.24	51
14—16	31
14.1	31
14.3–9	32
14.10–11	38
14.12	97
14.18	37
14.18–20	36
14.18–21	36, 38, 101
14.21	36–7, 43, 132
14.22–25	37
14.24	37, 40, 70, 79
14.26	31, 34, 113, 207
14.27	4, 28, 32, 34, 37–9, 41, 50, 59, 62, 77, 97, 173–4, 183
14.28	41, 59, 77
14.29	38
14.29–31	41
14.31	38
14.33–36	41
14.34	34, 41, 56
14.34–36	149
14.35	98
14.36	35, 212
14.41	43
14.43–49	28
14.45	36
14.47–48	32
14.49	5, 32–5, 37, 51, 53, 59, 72, 174, 176, 182
14.50	35, 97
14.50–52	38
14.51–52	32, 35
14.53–64	42
14.56	42
14.57–59	42
14.62	34, 42–4, 76, 174, 213
14.65	50
15	222
15.1–5	32
15.15	50
15.16–20	149, 167
15.17	50
15.17–20	45
15.19	50
15.20–22	150
15.23	45, 65
15.24	44, 56, 106
15.27	35, 45, 125
15.28	35
15.29	35, 45, 56
15.29–30	45, 211
15.29–31	44
15.29–32	111, 149–50
15.30	45, 57
15.30–31	84
15.31	45, 57
15.32	44–5, 125
15.33	50
15.34	4, 18, 19, 22, 28, 33–4, 41, 44–5, 47, 49, 77, 83, 86, 89, 97, 114, 140, 150, 174, 210
15.35–36	85
15.36	45, 64–5, 108–9
15.37	30, 45
15.37–38	76
15.38	65, 213
15.39	28, 49, 65, 78
15.40	32, 207, 213
15.41	32
15.43	67, 83
15.43–46	66
16	49
16.8	59
16.9–20	35

Luke

Reference	Pages
1.46–55	71
1.68–75	71
2.34–35	71
2.38	71
2.49	215
3.4	73, 213
3.5	73
4.4	75
4.5–7	75
4.8	75

4.12	75	22.32	77	23.39–43	78, 82, 214
4.13	74	22.35	80	23.43–44	213
4.16–30	71, 75	22.36	80	23.45	75, 213
4.17–19	72, 73, 81	22.36–38	13	23.46	16, 75, 77, 83, 85–6, 114, 139
4.18–19	71	22.37	13, 35, 67, 72–3, 75, 79–81, 173, 175, 180, 182, 217		
4.20–21	71			23.47	78
4.21	71			23.49	77
4.24	71			23.50–51	78
4.25–28	71	22.38	81	23.51	83
4.29	75	22.41–42	76	24	215
4.43	215	22.41–44	149	24.7	69
9.22	69, 215	22.42	85, 212, 223	24.18–21	10
9.43–44	75			24.25	70
10.1–12	80	22.43–44	81	24.25–27	5, 70–1, 90
10.21	85	22.49–50	81		
13.33	72, 215	22.50	77	24.26	69–70
13.33–34	83	22.51	76	24.27	17, 92, 176
13.34	74	22.52	81		
13.35	75	22.61	76	24.44	17, 182
17.24–25	75	22.63–65	75	24.44–46	5
17.25	215	22.66	79	24.44–47	70–1, 90
18.9	91	22.66–71	75–6, 98	24.46	70
18.31	71				
18.31–33	75	22.67	76	**John**	
19.5	215	22.67–68	76	1.1	95
19.28	29	22.69	90, 213	1.11	10
19.38	74	22.70–71	76	1.17	95
19.46	73	23.1–2	76	1.23	96
20.17	91, 164	23.4–12	76	1.29	109, 217
		23.12	76	1.35	97
20.17–18	74, 179	23.27–31	83	1.36	99, 109
22—23	79	23.30	82–3	2	217
22.1	22, 78	23.31	83	2.17	23, 95–6, 100, 105, 141
22.3	22, 78	23.34	74, 77, 83–6, 106, 167, 214		
22.7	215				
22.15	79, 97				
22.19	79	23.35	74, 77, 84	2.22	95
22.19–20	79	23.35–36	84	3.1–10	104
22.20	79	23.36	88, 109, 214	3.11–14	99
22.21	79				
22.22	79				
22.27	79				

3.14	99	12.38–41	100–1	19.26–27	97, 113
3.16	176	12.40	100	19.27	97
5.39	95, 100, 148	12.41	100, 148	19.28	10, 107, 112, 114
5.39–40	104	12.42	104	19.28–29	105, 108, 177, 179
5.40	100	13—17	22, 79, 99		
5.46	95, 100, 173	13.18	36, 101–2	19.28–30	113
6	101			19.29	97, 108–9
6.25–65	95	13.19	102		
6.31	96	13.26–27	101	19.30	108, 114, 217
6.39–40	102	13.30	101		
6.45	95, 102	14.26	103, 112	19.31–33	109, 149
6.54	101, 102	14.31	99		
		15	103	19.34	111–2
6.56–58	101	15.24	103	19.35	111–2
7.37	112	15.25	103–4	19.36	107, 109–10, 113, 161
7.37–39	112	16.2	104		
8.12	98	17	97, 216		
8.28	99	17.1	96		
9.5	98	17.12	101, 216	19.36–37	10, 101, 112
9.22	104			19.37	110–2, 116, 181
10.11	98	17.21	95		
10.30	95	18	99		
10.34	103	18.1	22, 99	20.9	23, 102
1.23–24	102	18.4	98	20.30–31	111
11.47–53	98	18.9	95, 216		
12.13	29, 74	18.11	98	**Acts**	
12.14–15	63	18.19–24	98	1.15–20	87
12.15	110	18.28	97	1.16	87
12.23	98	18.28—19.16	97	1.16–19	60
12.27	97	18.32	95, 99	1.18	60
12.27–36	97	19.14–16	109	1.19	60
12.32	10	19.16–18	150	1.20	18, 87
12.32–33	99	19.16–30	97	2.14–40	88
12.34	99, 205	19.16–37	105	2.23	88
		19.17	98	2.24	88–9
12.37	100	19.19	106	2.25	88
12.37–41	10	19.19–22	178	2.25–28	23, 88
12.38	100–1, 131	19.23–24	181	2.25–31	88
		19.24	10, 44, 106, 108–9, 113	2.25–32	179
12.38–40	18, 100, 110, 179			2.27	89–90, 140

2.29	89	13.41	94	10.4		121
2.29–32	180	15.6–29	17	10.11		136
2.30	88–9	15.16–17	17	10.15		131
2.31	89, 140	17.2	94	10.16		131
2.34–35	88–9	17.2–3	5	10.21		136
2.35	87	20.28	87,	11.8		136
3.1–10	90		211	11.9–10		87, 141,
3.12–26	90	28.23–24	94			181
3.13	90			12.12–21		141
3.14	90	**Romans**		12.14		141
3.17	84	1.2	4, 120,	12.15		141
3.18	5, 87,		176	12.21		141
	90–1	1.3–4	124	13.14		139
3.22–23	90	1.16–17	127, 136	15.3		87,
4.11	29, 91,	1.17	120			126, 134,
	162,	2.24	131			141–3, 148,
	164–5	3.19	217			153, 168,
4.25	91	3.21	121			172, 177,
4.25–26	176	3.21–26	14			181, 183,
4.27	91	3.24	14			222
4.30	91	3.25	124–5,	15.4		141
5.30	168		138	15.12		110, 114
5.31	87	4.7	219	15.21		131
7.59	16, 86,	4.25	125, 132,	16.26		4
	139		173, 175,			
7.60	84, 86		220	**1 Corinthians**		
8	215–6	5.8	18, 132	1—2		137, 179
8.26–39	92	5.19	132	1.17		128
8.28–35	93	6.6	125, 139	1.18		120, 133
8.32–33	13, 92,	8.3	138	1.18–31		9, 137
	175, 215	8.19–30	222	1.23		9, 128
8.33	93	8.32	132	2.2		8, 120,
8.34	92	9—11	125, 135,			128
8.35	92–3		137, 219	2.6–8		124
10.39	168	9.1–5	125	2.6–16		134
10.43	94	9.30	135	2.8		124, 135
13.22	20	9.30–33	135, 137	2.9		134–5,
13.27	84,	9.31	135			137, 141,
	87, 93	9.32	135			143, 172,
13.28	93	9.32–33	29,			179, 221
13.29	87, 93,		164–5	4.16–17		139
	168	9.33	135–7,	5.7		138, 175
13.33	74, 176		165, 179,	6.20		14
13.35	89		225	8.4–6		127

		Galatians		**1 Timothy**	
10.8	219	1.4	3, 132,	2.6	132
11.1	139		219–20	6.13	124
11.23	125	1.13–17	124		
11.23–26	7, 125	2.1	8	**2 Timothy**	
11.24	7, 133	2.19	125, 139	4.17	141
12.1–8	120	3.1	129, 143		
14.21	122, 217	3.10	120, 128	**Titus**	
15	129	3.10–14	9, 128	2.14	132
15.1	127	3.11	128		
15.3	2–4,	3.12	128	**Hebrews**	
	7, 9,	3.13	133	1.1–2	146
	33, 54,	3.13–14	128	1.2	156
	119–20,	6.14	139	1.1–4	147
	122, 126–30,	6.17	139	1.3	151
	132, 134,			1.5	145,
	138, 142–3,				154
	147, 172,	**Ephesians**		1.13–14	151
	176, 180,	2.20	29	2.8–18	155
	219, 223	4.9	170	2.9	154–5
15.3–4	2–3,			2.9–10	154
	5–7,	**Philippians**		2.11	154
	10, 23,	1.19	141	2.12	58, 153,
	31, 34,	2	134		155, 174,
	122–8,	2.5	139		177
	132, 176	2.5–11	93	2.12–13	153–4
15.3–5	211	2.6–11	6, 123,	2.13	154
15.3–8	124, 127		133–4,	2.14	155
15.4	23		173, 221	2.14–15	155
15.11	127	2.8	133, 139	2.17	155
15.15	219	2.9–11	133	2.18	156
15.33	15, 127	3.8–11	183	3.1–6	158
15.54–55	126	3.10	139	3.7	153
16.26	120			3.7–11	146
		Colossians		3.7–12	158
2 Corinthians		2.12–15	123	3.11	146
4.7–12	139–40	2.13–14	124	3.13	146
4.7–14	183			3.15–19	146
4.8–9	140	**1 Thessalonians**		3.16–19	158
4.9	140	1.6	139	4.1–2	158
4.10–11	140	2.14–15	129	4.1–11	146
4.13	140–1, 219	2.14–16	124	4.3	153
5.21	133	4.13–18	170	4.8–11	158
12.3–7	139	5	219	5.4	152
12.7	139	5.10	130		

5.5	152, 176	10.3	157	5.10–11	161
5.6	145, 152	10.4–10	4, 152,	5.11	160
5.7	149, 153,		157	5.17	160
	155, 223	10.5–6	156		
5.7–8	145,	10.5–7	153, 156,	1 Peter	
	149–50,		174	1.1	163,
	223	10.5–9	156		169
5.7–10	41	10.5–10	145	1.2	163
5.8	150	10.8–9	156	1.4	169
5.8–9	156	10.12	151	1.10–11	5, 224
5.9	150–1	10.15–18	4	1.10–12	162–3,
6.4–6	183	10.26–21	158		225
6.4–8	144,	10.27–31	144	1.11	162,
	158	10.36–38	183		165
6.6	150,	10.37–38	158	1.19	163–4,
	158	11.17–19	161		174
6.7	158	11.19	145	1.24–25	163
6.8	158	11.24–26	148	2	164
7–10	152	11.26	148	2.1–2	164
7.1–10.18	145	12.1–3	158	2.3	164
7.1–10	145,	12.2	149	2.3–8	29
	151	12.3	149	2.4	164–5
7.11–28	145	12.3–4	156	2.4–5	164
7.22	152	12.4	149	2.4–8	91, 164,
7.23–28	151	12.24	145		221
8.1	151	13.6	156	2.4–10	164
8.6	152	13.8	156	2.5	164–5
8.7	153	13.10	150	2.6	136–7,
8.6–13	145	13.10–16	150–1		163, 165
8.7–13	4	13.11	150	2.6–8	162,
8.8–12	146	13.12	151		164–5,
8.13	146, 153	13.12–13	148,		179
9.1–10	145		150,	2.7	162, 165,
9.5	138		156		224
9.6–14	145	13.12–15	156	2.8	136–7,
9.11–12	152	13.13	148,		163, 165
9.16	153		150, 183	2.9–10	164
9.18	145	13.20	146	2.11	163,
9.19–21	163				169
9.22	145	James		2.18–25	162,
9.23–28	145	2.8	160		165
9.28	147	2.21–24	16, 1761	2.21	162,
10.1–4	145,	2.21–26	160		167, 183
	156	5.6	224		

2.21–25	4, 13, 172, 183, 225	3.21	169	1.5	116, 205
2.22	166–7	4.1	168, 183	1.7	110, 116, 181
2.22–23	167	4.6	169–70	1.18	116
2.22–25	142, 162–5, 168–9, 175, 183	4.12–14	162	2.14	219
		4.16	162	2.20	219
		5.1	162, 168	3	116
2.23	164, 166–7, 225	5.8	167, 168	3.5	116
		5.13	162	4	117
				4 – 5	218
2.24	166–8	**1 John**		5	117
2.24–25	167	1.7	115	5.5	117
2.25	166, 168, 225	2.2	115	5.6	117, 175
		3.8	115	5.9	116–8
3.10–12	161	3.16	115	5.12	116–7
3.14	162–3	4.10	115	7.14	116
3.17	162			12.11	116
3.19	169–70	**Revelation**		14.5	218
3.20	169	1	116		
3.19–20	170	1.1	116		

238